TENTH ARMY COMMANDER

TENTH ARMY COMMANDER

The World War II Diary of Simon Bolivar Buckner Jr.

edited by

CHRISTOPHER L. KOLAKOWSKI

CASEMATE

Philadelphia & Oxford

Published in the United States of America and Great Britain in 2023 by
CASEMATE PUBLISHERS
1950 Lawrence Road, Havertown, PA 19083, USA
and
The Old Music Hall, 106–108 Cowley Road, Oxford OX4 1JE, UK

Hardback Edition: ISBN 978-1-63624-199-9
Digital Edition: ISBN 978-1-63624-200-2

A CIP record for this book is available from the British Library

Printed and bound in the United Kingdom by CPI Group (UK) Ltd, Croydon, CR0 4YY

Typeset in India by Lapiz Digital Services, Chennai.

For a complete list of Casemate titles, please contact:

CASEMATE PUBLISHERS (US)
Telephone (610) 853-9131
Fax (610) 853-9146
Email: casemate@casematepublishers.com
www.casematepublishers.com

CASEMATE PUBLISHERS (UK)
Telephone (0)1226 734350
Email: casemate-uk@casematepublishers.co.uk
www.casematepublishers.co.uk

Cover image: Lieutenant General Simon Bolivar Buckner Jr. *U.S. Army*

For Alice

"To render the greatest possible service to his government is the duty of every officer, and this should be his highest ambition."
—Simon Bolivar Buckner Jr.

Contents

Acknowledgements

In the climactic battles of the Pacific War, three U.S. Army officers commanded numbered field armies and played central roles in planning and conducting the campaigns. General Walter Krueger and Lieutenant General Robert Eichelberger led Sixth Army and Eighth Army, respectively, in the liberation of the Philippines, while Lieutenant General Simon B. Buckner Jr. commanded Tenth Army in the invasion of Okinawa. Buckner died in his battle, while Krueger and Eichelberger survived the war. Of those three, only Buckner has not had a full publication of his wartime writings.

I was aware of Okinawa and General Buckner, having read various accounts in years past. I also encountered Buckner's father while working at Perryville Battlefield and writing a book (my first ever book publication) on the 1862 Kentucky Campaign. I met General Buckner's grandson Chip (Simon Bolivar Buckner IV) at the 150th Anniversary commemoration of the battle in 2012. In 2018 the Phil Kearny Civil War Roundtable asked me to do a speech tracing the MacArthurs and Buckners, as both families had fathers in the Civil War and sons in World War II. It is a presentation I have given several times since. During my preparations for that talk, the story of Simon Bolivar Buckner Jr. gripped me. I found his diaries and writings, learned they had not been fully published, and realized this important voice had been muted for too long. This book is the result.

Writing a book like this is not a lone endeavor, and many people along the way have helped develop my understanding of these pivotal battles. First, thanks to Ruth Sheppard and the team at Casemate Publishers for their enthusiastic interest in this book and drive to make it the best it can be.

Special thanks also must go to William Claiborne "Bill" Buckner, General Buckner's youngest son. Bill's enthusiastic support for this project, and the information he provided about his father, has been invaluable.

Many people at various repositories helped with my research, in some cases providing the answers to questions I did not know I needed to ask. Thanks go to Jim Zobel of the MacArthur Memorial Archives, Brittany Strobel and Russ Horton at the Wisconsin Veterans Museum, David Holbrook of the Dwight D. Eisenhower Presidential Library, Kimberly Guise and her staff at the National World War II Museum, and Greg Statler and the staff of the Army Heritage and Education Center in Carlisle, Pennsylvania.

I'd also like to thank John Easterbrook, Ted Savas, Dave Powell, Sharon Tosi Lacey, Joe Truglio, Bryan Hockensmith, John McManus, Terry Rensel, Jim Triesler, Maggie Hartley, Walter Borneman, Art Boerner, Jim Kurtz, Chris Mackowski, Alisha Hamel, and Stuart Sanders, all of whom helped with encouragement, information, and perspective.

Special thanks to my parents, Peter and Jane Kolakowski, for their constant encouragement and support.

Very special thanks go to my wife Alice, who has been an unfailing source of support and encouragement in this project and all my writing endeavors.

Any and all errors are mine alone.

Editor's Introduction

Simon Bolivar Buckner Jr. was a major figure of the Pacific War, known for his command in Alaska from 1940 to 1944 and heading Tenth Army during the battle of Okinawa in the spring of 1945. Buckner became the senior U.S. officer killed by enemy fire in World War II when Japanese artillery cut him down on June 18, 1945, one month shy of his 59th birthday.

The shelling ended a remarkable life—that of the son of a Confederate Lieutenant General and Governor of Kentucky, the "Child of the Democracy" in the 1896 Presidential election campaign. Buckner received an education at Virginia Military Institute and West Point, with myriad service as a student and instructor at various Army posts and schools from 1917 to 1936, commanded in Alaska from 1940 to 1944, and ultimately led Tenth Army from July 1944 to his death. Two chapters of the history of World War II in the Pacific also lost key elements, as Buckner never got to write his planned memoir.

Despite this loss, there is much in General Buckner's diary and in the letters from his time as Tenth Army commander that can fill gaps and illuminate his temperament and thoughts. The Simon Bolivar Buckner that emerges in these pages is a strong, expressive, and decisive personality, with a skilled command of language. He is observant and curious about matters military and beyond, fascinated by what he encounters, and interested in recording his experiences and resulting impressions.

General Buckner's tenure as Tenth Army commander covered a key period of the Pacific War. From his arrival in Hawaii to take up his new post, he was involved in deciding some of the most important questions of strategy and command in the Pacific. Buckner's input on those matters helped determine what the final steps on the path to victory over Japan would be, and when they would occur. He also observed much about the people and places he encountered, offering important insights into the American high command as the Pacific War approached a climax.

Buckner led Tenth Army in the invasion of Okinawa on April 1, 1945. This was an event many months in the making, involving intricate planning and coordination of far-flung personnel and equipment. His diary documented his travels and activities throughout that process, demonstrating the energy he put into preparing, training, and leading his forces to Okinawa.

Lastly, the fighting on Okinawa was the largest sea-air-land engagement in history. General Buckner was one of the key figures in the battle, and the central land commander on the American side. His decisions during the fighting were sometimes controversial, and the debates about his leadership persist. A close reading of the diary reveals important clues to his thinking during the battle.

General Buckner's diary and letters during his time as Tenth Army commander have never been fully published together until now. They shed important light on how World War II in the Pacific was fought, and illuminate an underappreciated figure of that conflict.

A Note on the Text

General Buckner started keeping a diary in early 1944 as a record of the events he witnessed and the impressions he received. He planned to use the diary as part of the basis for his memoirs, but likely never intended it for publication as a raw text. Entries occurred nearly every day, usually at night before he went to sleep but sometimes the following morning, to recapitulate the events of each day. Buckner sometimes made quick notations before a day was over, especially regarding social engagements, that often appear as choppy or incomplete sentences.

Buckner's writings, broken up by time period for ease of reading, form Chapters 2 through 5 of this book. Chapter 1 provides background and biographical information on General Buckner up to 1944. Chapter 6 describes his death and its aftermath, including the conclusion of the fighting on Okinawa through to his final burial in Kentucky in 1949. Analysis of Buckner's tenure as Tenth Army commander is contained in Chapter 7.

As a transcriber and editor, I have strived to be as faithful to the original text as possible. Buckner wrote in a clear hand with few corrections; where strikethroughs or other alterations occur, I have left them in. I have corrected minor spelling errors and grammar (such as italicizing ship names), but have left General Buckner's sometimes idiosyncratic spelling of the people and locations he encountered. Where needed, I have noted the correct spelling in brackets or in a footnote. In a few entries, Buckner left blank spaces for various reasons, and those are reflected in empty brackets. I have inserted commentary in italics to help readers understand the context of various diary entries. Explanatory footnotes provide additional information on the people and places referenced.

Language used in the diary and other primary sources is true to the original, and may be offensive to modern readers. Place names are given as they were in 1944 and 1945. Japanese names are rendered surname first.

CHAPTER I

Simon Bolivar Buckner Jr.'s Life to 1944

Simon Bolivar Buckner Jr. took his first breath on Sunday, July 18, 1886, in the library of Glen Lily, his family's home in Munfordville, Kentucky. His parents christened him after his father, Simon Bolivar Buckner, who had waited a long time for a son to carry on the Buckner lineage. He was known as Bolivar to differentiate him from his father.

From the beginning, this boy's life would have an unusual aspect. At the time of Bolivar's birth, his father was 63 and his mother, Delia Claiborne Buckner, was 29. The family was accomplished in Kentucky and beyond. The elder Simon Bolivar Buckner was born in Munfordville on April 1, 1823, the son of Aylett and Elizabeth Buckner, the former a veteran of the War of 1812 and local businessman. Aylett named his son after Simon Bolivar, who had just successfully thrown off Spanish colonial rule in South America.[1]

The Buckners lived in Munfordville until 1838, when they moved into western Kentucky so Aylett could expand his iron-making business. In 1840 Buckner Sr. took an appointment to the U.S. Military Academy at West Point, graduating in 1844. He became an infantry officer in the 2nd U.S. Infantry Regiment before returning to West Point as an instructor. He rejoined his regiment during the Mexican War, seeing active service including Winfield Scott's famous campaign to Mexico City in 1847. After occupation duty, Buckner Sr. returned to West Point to instruct before serving in a series of posts in the West and in New York City. At the latter place, he helped an old West Point friend, Ulysses S. Grant, cover some bills and stay financially solvent.

In 1850 Buckner Sr. married Mary Jane Kingsbury, a member of a prominent Connecticut family. The Kingsburys owned some land in Chicago, and in 1855 Buckner Sr. left the U.S. Army to help manage the family holdings in Illinois. He remained active in the Illinois militia, serving as the state's adjutant general for a short time in 1857. Yet the Buckners wanted to return southward; in late 1857 they relocated to Louisville, where on March 7, 1858, their daughter Lily was born. Buckner became active in Kentucky militia and political affairs.

The Civil War's outbreak in 1861 found Kentucky caught between the Union and Confederacy. Governor Beriah Magoffin appointed Buckner Sr. adjutant general and commander of the State Guard, charged with protecting the state against any incursion as it tried to stay neutral in the conflict. As it became clear that neutrality was untenable, Buckner Sr. and his State Guard units split between North and South. For his part, Buckner Sr. turned down a general's appointment in the U.S. Army, opting for one in the Confederate Army. As for his reasons behind this decision, Buckner Sr. cited the actions of the U.S. government: "When citizens were arbitrarily arrested, without warrant, and imprisoned in remote fortresses, without trial or charges on the will of one man," he said in 1908, "I considered it the right of every citizen to resist by force of arms, these lawless encroachments upon the rights of freemen. I therefore cast my lot with those who opposed these arbitrary assaults upon individual rights."

Having made his choice, Buckner Sr. assumed a prominent command in southern Kentucky. In early 1862 he and his troops were among the besieged garrison at Fort Donelson in Tennessee, where after a failed breakout the decision was made to surrender to the forces of General Grant outside. The two senior officers, John Floyd and Gideon Pillow, found excuses to escape, and thus Buckner Sr. was the man who handed over 16,000 Confederates on February 16, 1862. It was the first major Confederate land surrender of the war, and the first of three armies Grant would capture during the conflict.

After several months as a prisoner of war in the North, he was exchanged in time to command a division in General Braxton Bragg's invasion of Kentucky, which culminated in the battle of Perryville and resulting Confederate retreat. During the campaign, Buckner distinguished himself by negotiating the surrender of the Federal garrison in his hometown of Munfordville, spearheading recruitment of Kentuckians into the Confederate Army, and commanding a division at Perryville. Nonetheless, the expedition failed, and Kentucky remained in Union hands for the rest of the war.[2]

Buckner Sr. spent the balance of the Civil War in regional commands in East Tennessee and as second-in-command of Confederate forces in the Trans-Mississippi Theater. In the former capacity, he rejoined Bragg's army and led a corps at the battle of Chickamauga in September 1863. In the latter, he oversaw the last major Confederate land surrender in late May 1865.[3]

Lieutenant General Simon Bolivar Buckner Sr. was paroled in New Orleans on June 9, 1865. He could not return to Kentucky for three years, so he settled in New Orleans and wrote for a local newspaper. In late 1868 he received a pardon as part of President Andrew Johnson's general amnesty of Confederate leaders. Buckner Sr. became editor of the *Louisville Courier* and a prominent Democratic voice in Kentucky politics.

For the Buckner family, the decade after the war's end was years of struggle. Buckner sought to reclaim property both in Kentucky and Illinois, including the Chicago land that he had put into Mary Jane's name in 1861. The Chicago Fire of 1871 damaged his holdings in that city, while subsequent economic downturns affected his investments and insurance businesses. Mary Jane Buckner died of tuberculosis in 1874, leaving just Simon and 16-year-old Lily. They moved to the family estate outside Munfordville, which Buckner Sr. renamed Glen Lily; a widowed sister joined them from 1877 until her death in 1883. That same year, Lily married Morris Belknap of Louisville and moved there.

Buckner Sr. was not alone for long. Shortly after his daughter's wedding, Buckner Sr. met Delia Claiborne of Richmond, and they married in 1885. On their honeymoon, they visited Grant in New York shortly before the latter's death on July 23, 1885; Buckner Sr. stayed in New York and served as a pallbearer at Grant's funeral. Almost exactly a year later, Simon Bolivar Buckner Jr. was born.

In August 1887, a little over a year after Bolivar's birth, Buckner Sr. was elected governor of Kentucky. The family moved with him to

Frankfort, the state capital, which meant that Buckner Jr. lived his early and toddler years in the Governor's Mansion while his father ran the state from 1887 to 1891. Buckner Sr. expanded education and infrastructure, while also starting a review of the state's constitution. He faced unrest in eastern Kentucky and a statewide financial crisis, not helped by the state treasurer disappearing with $250,000 in state money. Nevertheless, as his term ended, the *Louisville Courier* called Buckner Sr. "a Governor who is one of the ablest and most popular in the history of the state."

Not being able to run for re-election due to term limits, Buckner Sr. returned to Glen Lily with his family. The former governor was a sought-after figure in Kentucky and national politics. In 1895 he was proposed for election to the U.S. Senate, but nothing came of it. Fate delivered a larger role for him a year later.

The presidential election of 1896 found the United States at a crossroads; it was divided politically and socially. The nation was struggling to recover from the depression known as the Panic of 1893, which exacerbated economic inequalities and tensions between urban and rural areas. Conflicts over monetary policy, prohibition of alcohol, race, and national vision split the nation and its two main parties. In the end, the Republican and Democratic candidates, William McKinley and William Jennings Bryan respectively, would be joined by candidates from five other parties in one of the most fractured presidential elections in history.

This divide affected the Democratic Party, which nominated Bryan at its regular convention in Chicago. Bryan's anti-establishment platform and fiery rhetoric alarmed many Democrats, who split off into the Gold Democrat party and arranged a convention of their own in Indianapolis. Buckner Sr. attended as part of the Kentucky delegation, taking his wife and 10-year-old son with him. On September 3 the Gold Democrats selected as their candidates retired U.S. Major General John M. Palmer for President and former Confederate Lieutenant General Simon B. Buckner Sr. for Vice President. Both candidates were chosen to great acclaim, while a reporter noted that Buckner's name was greeted with "shouts and hats thrown into the air ... making about the greatest demonstration of the convention."[4]

The Buckner family made a major impression among the convention delegates. Reporters described Buckner Sr. as "witty, a good story teller, extremely dignified, and a man of wide experience and broad sympathies." A reporter had noted Delia's "royal reputation for hospitality and brilliance" not long before, and it was on full display in Indianapolis. The same could be said for Bolivar, who by age 10 had grown into "a genuine boy who loves dirt, jam, barefeet, and dogs." Before adjourning, the convention named Simon Bolivar Buckner Jr. "The Child of the Democracy," a unique honor. Bolivar's reaction at the time is not recorded, but he later tried to keep the title quiet. "A good way to see General Buckner flush," noted a reporter in 1943, "or become embarrassed is to remind him of that [distinction] today."[5]

Despite an energetic campaign, the Palmer-Buckner ticket finished third behind Bryan and the victor McKinley, who became the 25th President of the United States. The Buckners retired to Munfordville to run the estate and travel. They often went on trips to the East Coast, but sometimes further afield. When possible, Buckner Sr. brought his son along to broaden his horizons. On a trip to Europe in 1900, the family visited many battlefields, climbed the Eiffel Tower, and watched Kaiser Wilhelm II review troops. "That young fellow," Buckner Sr. told his son, "will get his country into very serious trouble some day."

Buckner Sr. remained connected to state and national politics. He supported the War with Spain in 1898, and opposed Bryan in the 1900 presidential election as McKinley won a second term. These stands made an impression among McKinley and his allies in Washington, including Theodore Roosevelt, an old acquaintance who was McKinley's running mate in 1900. Roosevelt succeeded to the presidency upon McKinley's assassination in 1901, and remembered his ally in Kentucky.

Simon Bolivar Buckner Jr. turned 14 in 1900. When not traveling, he lived an active and inquisitive life around the estate. "I went barefooted," he later recalled, "hunted, trapped, fished, swam, canoed, raised chickens, fought roosters, rode five miles daily for the mail, trained dogs, did odd farm jobs, learned not to eat green persimmons, and occasionally walked eight mules to Munfordville to broaden my horizon by seeing the train come in, learning the fine points of horse trading, or listening to learned legal and political discussion on county court day." The boy wanted to follow in his father's footsteps, and military service seemed a natural fit for someone of his intellect and interests. In 1902, Buckner

Jr. went to the Virginia Military Institute (VMI), a route considered good preparation for potential appointment to West Point. He spent two years there as a cadet.[6]

In the spring of 1904, Buckner Sr. and Delia were in Washington and accepted an invitation to visit Theodore Roosevelt at the White House. The invitation was as much personal as professional. In addition to the mutual regard Roosevelt and Buckner had for each other, Roosevelt was up for reelection in November 1904 and needed to cultivate his allies. The group had a pleasant chat, and toward the end Roosevelt asked if there was anything he could do for his guests. Buckner mentioned a family tradition of military service, and asked for Bolivar's appointment to West Point as a cadet. "By George," exclaimed Roosevelt, "it shall be done!" Accordingly, on June 16, 1904, one month and two days shy of his 18th birthday, Simon Bolivar Buckner Jr. reported to the U.S. Military Academy to begin his course of study.[7]

West Point, at the time, was one of the finest engineering and leadership schools in the United States, and an essential provider of officers for the United States Army. Recent graduates included Douglas MacArthur and Ulysses S. Grant III in 1903, and Joseph W. Stilwell in 1904. Victory over Spain made the United States a major global power, and the Army faced new missions in far-flung places, especially in Asia. Major structural reforms and modernization programs were underway to adjust the Army to these new obligations. When Bolivar arrived, West Point was transitioning into a new century to provide officers capable of leading this modern force in future conflicts. These changes occurred mostly in the classroom and curriculum; the cadet conditions remained much the same as when Buckner Sr. attended, with an emphasis on drill, discipline, and honor. Living standards in the barracks were spartan, with the day governed by a strict schedule from reveille to lights out.

Buckner Jr. spent much of the next four decades associated with West Point and its Corps of Cadets, which retained much the same organization as from his father's era. Cadets joined as plebes, and went through an intense form of basic military training known as Beast Barracks. Then classes began, interspersed with drilling and military instruction. Athletics and campus clubs provided additional extracurricular outlets. Cadets were regularly ranked according to their performance in academic and military subjects, and had to maintain standards to stay with the class. They also were assigned demerits and punishments for such things as sloppy uniforms or rooms, failure to correctly recall memorized text, smoking, drunkenness, lateness, speaking out of turn, and the like; two hundred demerits in the class year resulted in dismissal. Successful fourth-class plebes became third-class yearlings, then second-class cows, and finally first-classmen. Upon graduation, class ranking determined the order in which cadets chose their first assignments as commissioned officers in the United States Army.

When Buckner Jr. arrived, the Corps of Cadets was divided into a regiment of six companies. Cadet lieutenants and captains commanded each company, with younger cadets acting as corporals and sergeants. Exemplary first-class cadets formed a regimental staff under the cadet first captain. These leadership assignments were determined by class, with yearlings getting the lowest-ranking and working upward. Regular U.S. Army officers, known as tactical officers or tacs, oversaw the cadet leaders and the corps' military training. A commandant of cadets, the second-ranking officer at the Academy and equivalent to a civilian dean of students, directed all cadets and tacs. The West Point superintendent, a serving general officer, commanded the entire Academy.[8]

Buckner survived Beast Barracks and soon took to cadet life. Like his fellow plebe George S. Patton, he found VMI's rigors were good preparation for, and in some ways harder than, West Point's discipline. Unlike Patton, there is no record Buckner ever admitted that opinion to his fellow cadets. Patton also had to repeat his fourth year for failing mathematics, whereas Buckner passed all subjects on time.[9]

Bolivar proved a solid if not brilliant student, ranking in the middle of his class all four years. A popular cadet known as "Simon" and "Buck," he was a cadet corporal as a yearling, a cadet quartermaster sergeant as a cow, and ultimately a cadet lieutenant. He also played football and lacrosse, and excelled at boxing and wrestling. The 1908 yearbook called him "a man who can be recognized in the distance by his beaming countenance, for Simon has an inexhaustible supply of smiles … Buck is the possessor of a wonderful vocabulary, and has been known, when 'up against it' in the section room, to repeat again and again a single fact, each time in different words, while his instructor listens with unconcealed admiration." A classmate called him "the bright spot of every party he attended."[10]

Through all this, the voices of his proud parents provided important perspective. In regular correspondence and conversations during visits and leaves during Christmas and summer, Bolivar received counsel and encouragement. "I was most agreeably impressed with a remark which you made in one of your recent letters to your mother," wrote Buckner Sr. in 1905, "to the effect that you were discharging with fidelity the duties which came to you and allowing the consequences to take care of themselves. There is no higher standard of excellence for a soldier or a citizen." This theme came up again in conversation: "Do your duty in whatever field it may lie," said Buckner Sr., "and never forget that you are a gentleman."[11]

Buckner Sr. also lived vicariously through his son. "I recognized the gorgeous autumn tints which you described so well in a previous letter," he wrote to Bolivar in November 1906, "for I had myself often revelled in their glories—perhaps from the very points from which they excited your admiration." Another time Buckner Sr. recalled a hike to the nearby Revolutionary War-era Fort Montgomery, which Bolivar had visited. In a literal sense, the son was following in his father's footsteps.[12]

On February 14, 1908, the class of 1908 graduated and the cadets took the oath as U.S. Army officers. Buckner Jr. ranked 58th of the 108 members of his class, and commissioned as an infantry officer in the 9th U.S. Infantry Regiment.[13]

As part of his 90-day post-graduation leave, Bolivar visited the construction site of the Panama Canal. He hiked through the jungles, and later tried to publish an account of his travels. In May he joined his regiment at Fort Sam Houston, Texas, outside San Antonio. Buckner Sr. came to visit, and father and son spent time touring former battlefields of the Mexican War.[14]

Buckner Jr.'s equestrian skills made an impression in the regiment. Soon after arriving, Buckner found a horse in the regimental stable that was so unruly that nobody had attempted to ride it for a year. Finding a free 45 minutes, Buckner had the horse saddled and mounted it as an attendant held the horse. The animal bucked and reared, finally twisting to the ground as Buckner rolled off. He promptly remounted and endured another bout of bucking without falling off. "When he got through," Bolivar wrote his father, "I fed him sugar and cakes. Next day I tried him, and he got comparatively tame. I fed him again, and now he follows me around like a dog. I can ride him anywhere. He is not afraid of a street car, a locomotive, an automobile, or anything."[15]

In 1910 the 9th Infantry rotated to duty in the Philippines and was posted to Cebu, in the central part of the archipelago. Duty was leisurely in that hot climate, and servants for hire were easily to hand. It was unlike anywhere Buckner Jr. had seen, and he eagerly explored his new surroundings. Bolivar kept up an active correspondence with his parents, sharing his impressions privately and occasionally for publication. His father encouraged him to read and sent books, most notably Edward Gibbon's *Decline And Fall of the Roman Empire*. "Your letters are a source of infinite pleasure to your mother and me," wrote Buckner Sr. "I was much interested in your description of the Phillipino [sic] character. It shows you to be a close observer. Let me caution you, however, not to reason from particular to general. We doubtless find many rogues and liars in the World; but it does not necessarily follow that all men should be classed in that category." Bolivar compiled a manuscript titled *Tales of the Philippines*, but could not find an interested publisher.[16]

On the third anniversary of his graduation from West Point, Bolivar found himself on a transport ship from Cebu to Manila. He had decided what he wanted to do with his life. He wrote to his mother:

> The date reminds me that just three years ago Secty. of War [William H.] Taft handed me my diploma from West Point. At that time my idea of the Army was little more than a surmise. One of the thoughts which entered my mind at this time was the fact that as promotion was not according to merit, there was little in the military service to encourage an officer to excel in his profession. Three years, however, have proven to me beyond all doubt that such is not the case. It is true that an officer can not by his own efforts raise his rank, but it is equally true that he can raise his standing. Strict attention to duties will unquestionably raise an officer to a place in his regiment which no amount of rank can give him. In civil life, success is inseparably linked with money, but in military life there is a much higher aim. To render the greatest possible service to his government is the duty of every officer, and this should be his highest ambition. The civilian works chiefly for himself and is considered successful according to what he has done for himself. The incentive which we have in our work is expressed in the motto of our Alma Mater, "Duty, Honor, Country", and it is far more satisfactory

to have this before us than to feel that we are working purely from motives of self-interest. It is thus that I have learned to love the Army, and I grow more attached to it every day.[17]

This philosophy would guide him for the rest of his life.

In 1912 the 9th Infantry transferred to Fort Thomas, located in northern Kentucky south of Cincinnati. The proximity to Munfordville meant Bolivar was able to see his parents more often and make up for his long absence in the Philippines. Buckner Sr. turned 90 on April 1, 1913. A few days later, the Ohio River and its tributaries flooded, endangering many towns. Bolivar and some sergeants went to Hamilton, Ohio, "to represent the Federal Government, and assist in whatever way we could to straighten the town out, restore order and sanitation, and deliver supplies in whatever way we saw fit," he told his mother. The team later moved to Paducah, Kentucky and Cairo, Illinois. Fortunately, the worst had passed. "My orders are to act upon my own initiative, purchase and distribute supplies where necessary, charter boats or make any needed expenditures, and keep the proper authorities in touch with the situation, making a thorough report of whatever measures I have adopted, and such recommendations as I care to make. You can easily see what an interesting position I am in, and what a valuable experience it has been."[18]

A few months later, Buckner Jr. managed to arrange a detail to Gettysburg National Military Park to support the 50th Anniversary commemoration of the U.S. victory on July 1–3, 1863. Seeing old Union and Confederate veterans together made a strong impression:

> At the "Bloody Angle" the survivors of Pickett's Charge shook hands with those who fifty years ago had met them in a bloody struggle. Each was proud to be in a country which had produced the other. Each was glad to call the other his friend.
>
> The Gettysburg semi-centennial has not been the celebration of a victory of war. It has been the celebration of a victory of peace.[19]

His excitement about this assignment raised an eyebrow with Delia, who was from the Confederacy's former capital, had Confederate ancestors, and was married to the highest-ranking Confederate still living. Bolivar explained in a letter that he relished the professional challenges of supporting a camp of 55,000 veterans. He also recognized that "being associated with officers who will in a very few years be at the top in the Army, and having an opportunity to meet many of those who are now prominent in National politics, is always of advantage professionally." He reassured Delia that "I love the South, and all that it stands for. I love its people, its traditions, its gentility, but I do not feel that loyalty to the South compels me to hate the North. As the son of one who fought for what he knew was right, I do not feel patriotic to promote sectional bitterness; but you can rest assured, Mother, that my loyalty to the South is unshaken, and that I have not forsaken the principles with which I was reared."[20]

During this time Buckner Sr. was noticeably weakening, although his mind remained clear. As 1914 dawned, uremic poisoning set in. Bolivar hurried to his father's side at Glen Lily. On January 6, 1914, Buckner Sr. slipped into a coma. Two days later, he died. On January 10 Simon Bolivar Buckner Sr. was buried in Frankfort's cemetery in a plot near the grave of Daniel Boone and overlooking Kentucky's State Capitol.[21]

After a short leave to help his mother get affairs in order, Bolivar returned to his regiment, which soon transferred to Texas. He was promoted to first lieutenant in August 1914 and went to Washington as assistant superintendent of public buildings and grounds. In 1915 he went back to the Philippines as part of the 27th Infantry Regiment.[22]

Along the way, Buckner found love. In Washington he met Adele Blanc, a vivacious and intelligent daughter of a New Orleans physician who had gone to college in Louisville. One of Bolivar's cousins called her "almost a beauty" and "very intellectual … a prize." Bolivar and Adele struck up a correspondence that continued when he transferred to Manila. In 1916 he was due for home leave and indicated as much to Adele, expressing serious intentions toward her. She telegraphed him her acceptance and said to come. He sailed from Manila in September and arrived in early October. On December 30, 1916, Bolivar and Adele married in Louisville. Their honeymoon was spent in the Philippines.[23]

U.S. entry into World War I occurred on April 6, 1917. The next day, Bolivar sent a letter to Theodore Roosevelt. "The fact of our having declared war yesterday against Germany is very naturally followed by the thought that you will again be on the firing line at the head of a volunteer force," Bolivar wrote. "I still recall with gratitude that I received my appointment to the Military Academy from you, and hope that it will now be my privilege to serve under your command against the enemy." But it was not to be, as Roosevelt soon informed him. "You were down on my list," came the reply, "but the president [Woodrow Wilson] will not send me."[24] After several more months of effort, Buckner, newly promoted to captain, received a transfer to the Aviation Section of the Signal Corps at Kelly Field, Texas with the wartime rank of major. It appeared he'd get his chance to fight the Germans in the air.

Fate kept Buckner in the United States during World War I. He went through flight training and soloed in a Jenny biplane, but his eyesight was ruled too deficient for full flight status. An angry Buckner, a good shot and skilled hunter who had taken private flying lessons in the Philippines, raged at the medical board. "Gentlemen," he exclaimed, "I have been flying for two years!"[25] The protestation had no effect; instead of going overseas, he would stay in the United States. Bolivar drilled aviation recruits and ran Kelly Field's ground school from November 1917 to August 1918, followed by duty in Washington on the Air Service General Staff. He was in Washington when the Armistice occurred on November 11, 1918.

Buckner's disappointment at not getting overseas was tempered by becoming a father. On November 18, 1918, Adele bore a son in Louisville, who they named Simon Bolivar Buckner III. Father met son as he transferred between posts, assisting with demobilization at Camp Beauregard and recruiting in Denver. Two more children followed in four-year intervals: Mary on August 22, 1922; and William Claiborne (known as Claiborne and later Bill) on June 29, 1926.[26]

In May 1919 Buckner was ordered to West Point as a tac. The need for officers in France had resulted in rapid graduation of cadets in 1917 and 1918, some after as little as two years of instruction. The traditional structure of the corps had been wrecked, and incoming plebes had few upperclassmen to lead and mentor them. Worse, the class that graduated in November 1918 was immediately recalled to the Academy to finish the school year as "student officers," with predictable discontent in the ranks; they graduated again just as Buckner arrived. Other officers were recalled as cadets and could graduate in three years if they chose. The

West Point classes of 1919 and 1920 both spent less than two years at the Academy, while the 17 members of the class of 1921 (by far the smallest in over a century) all graduated after three years.[27]

The upshot of all this was that West Point was in complete disarray. General Peyton C. March, the U.S. Army chief of staff, chose a group of smart officers and skilled instructors to put the Academy on a solid footing and modernize it. They would be led by Superintendent Brigadier General Douglas MacArthur. Among the officers selected were a young Omar Bradley as a math instructor, Matthew B. Ridgway as athletics director, and Simon Bolivar Buckner Jr. as a tac. Buckner stayed at his alma mater for four years, from May 1919 to September 1923.[28]

MacArthur arrived at West Point determined to incorporate the experiences of the war just ended. Chief among these included preparing officers to lead a large citizen army instead of a small professional force. MacArthur loosened rules on cadets and encouraged more interaction with society, including trips to New York City. He emphasized athletics and broader study of the liberal arts, despite some opposition from his instructors. MacArthur also formalized a cadet honor code and a system of enforcement among the cadets. His term ended a year early, and some of his reforms were rolled back, but his mark remained indelible.[29]

Because of the thin upper-class ranks, the tacs needed to be more involved with direct cadet supervision than previously. The three seniormost tacs—Majors Buckner, Edwin Butcher, and Charles H. Bonesteel—formed the "Three B's Board," which handled cadet discipline normally meted out by cadet officers. In this way, the board established standards and re-created the structure of the corps of cadets. Many cadets regarded their rulings and dictates as harsh and capricious. Notably, Buckner always based his decisions on rules and standards. "A cadet could always tell beforehand exactly what punishment he would get from Buckner," noted a reporter. "If the rules suggested five demerits for a particular infraction, that was what Buckner would mete out; no more, no less."[30]

Buckner combined this discipline with physical performances. He earned great respect by attending a wrestling class and defeating two cadet champions. He avidly hiked and trapped in the hills surrounding the

Academy. On marches, he often led his companies up hills, sometimes carrying extra rifles and packs from cadets who were struggling.[31]

When Buckner and his colleagues ended their tours at West Point, they could be justifiably proud of the institution they had rebuilt. They also stamped a new generation of leaders. Some of the most prominent graduates from Buckner's years were Lyman Lemnitzer, Earl "Red" Blaik, Thomas D. White, and Henry I. Hodes in 1920; Maxwell Taylor and Cortlandt V. R. Schuyler in 1922; and Frank Dorn, Thomas S. Timberman, and Hoyt S. Vandenberg in 1923. Three other names from those classes would come back into Buckner's career later: Lawrence Schick (1920), Lawrence Castner (1923) and Elwyn "Eddie" Post (1923).[32]

Buckner left West Point as a major of infantry. He went to Fort Benning and the Advanced Infantry Course at the Infantry School, followed by attendance at the Command and General Staff School for a year, where his work was so impressive that he stayed for three more years as instructor until 1928. While a student, Buckner also became friendly with a fellow student and Marine aviator named Roy S. Geiger; the men agreed to keep in touch. Then it was on to the Army War College, first as student for a year then as executive officer from 1929 to 1932.[33]

Buckner's writing and speaking abilities, plus natural intelligence, had made him a success at these schools. In 1932 he was selected to return to West Point to lead the Corps of Cadets as a lieutenant colonel, beating out George Patton and several others in the process. In the small interwar U.S. Army, Buckner had won a great prize.[34]

Buckner's glow of professional success was tempered by his mother's death. Some years before, she had sold Glen Lily and moved to Louisville. In the beginning of 1932 she had a serious fall and pneumonia set in. On March 3, she passed away in Louisville, aged 74. The next day she was buried next to her husband in Frankfort. That summer Bolivar reported for his new assignment.[35]

Buckner served at West Point as assistant commandant for the class of 1933's final year, as understudy to Commandant Robert C. Richardson Jr. After the 1933 graduation, Buckner succeeded Richardson as Commandant for the classes of 1934, 1935, and 1936. The class of 1936 saw his leadership for all four years of its time at the Academy, and its graduates included some of the most influential officers of the Cold War and Vietnam periods: Bruce Palmer, William Westmoreland, Creighton Abrams, John H. Michaelis, and William P. Yarborough.[36]

The class of 1936 also included Benjamin O. Davis Jr., a black man appointed from Illinois. His father, Benjamin O. Davis Sr., was then the only black commissioned officer on duty in the segregated U.S. Army. Davis Jr. sought to be only the fourth black man, and first since 1889, to graduate from West Point. He also wanted to join the Army Air Corps. His presence caused quite a stir amongst the Corps of Cadets, and after Beast Barracks he was subjected to the silent treatment from his fellow cadets. This included living alone and exclusion from social activities. "Apparently, certain upperclass cadets had determined I was getting along too well at the Academy to suit them," Davis recalled. "I was to be silenced solely because cadets did not want blacks at West Point. Their only purpose was to freeze me out. What they did not realize was that I was stubborn enough to put up with their treatment to reach the goal I had come to attain." Davis endured, graduating 35th in the Class of 1936.[37]

Commandants Richardson and Buckner were both aware of what was going on, and periodically checked in on Davis to see how he was faring. Richardson had ordered that Davis be "treated like a white man," which Davis found condescending. But both Richardson and Buckner held to the long-standing tradition that roommates and messmates were voluntarily chosen among the cadets, and thus they could not intervene. This left Davis to his ostracism, which lasted throughout his time at West Point. "My feelings about this type of treatment," Davis later stated, "oscillated between embarrassment, anger, hate, and pity. Pity was the emotion that sustained me."[38]

Davis's treatment added to what all cadets found a demanding experience, retaining the rigors of previous generations. Commandant Buckner made a strong impression among his charges. William Westmoreland described the 47-year-old Buckner as "a muscular man with a big frame, bulging thighs, and a barrel chest," in his memoirs. "He was proud of a reputation as an outdoorsman and of the father for whom he was named ... No matter how cold the weather—and it can be bitter chill along the Hudson River—he never wore an overcoat." Davis remembered Buckner as "a tough old field soldier." One former classmate noted that Buckner's "rule is remembered for constructive progressiveness, with a share of severity tempered with hard, sound sense, and justice. His regime, as commandant thus highlighted and typified, marks him as an outstanding leader among those to fill that important office."[39]

Buckner believed in physical conditioning and periodically led the cadets on maneuvers in nearby Camp Popolopen, which included long marches and tactical scenarios. These marches were intended for toughening up cadets. Their reactions to this program varied. "After fighting the mud and mosquitoes for five days as a field soldier," recalled Davis, "I wanted more than ever to fly airplanes."[40]

In late summer 1933, a five-day field exercise occurred during several days of pouring rain and resultant mud. Buckner lived out of a pup tent like his men, and did not change the training program. Some cadets had brought extra blankets and clothing; Buckner sent excess gear back, telling the cadets that they were soft if they could not get by with one blanket and one poncho. "He got a Bronx cheer for that statement," noted Davis.[41]

Buckner encouraged his viewpoints on the cadets in other ways. Finding perfumed shaving lotion among many cadet tents, he henceforth declared that only witch hazel would be allowed for aftershave scent. "I say to you, gentlemen," Buckner told the corps, "if you have to smell, smell like a man." He also demanded high standards, once forcefully correcting Westmoreland for his poor reading of the Declaration of Independence at a ceremony on the Fourth of July. To many, Buckner did not seem quite human. "Rumor had it among the cadets," recalled Westmoreland, "that although there was a Mrs. Buckner, he slept alone on a cadet cot with a hard mattress and only a sheet as cover."[42]

Buckner had a warm and gracious side, but he reserved it for his family and his peers. A convivial host, he and Adele entertained officers in the commandant's quarters next to the superintendent's house, in a central part of the post. The Buckners also played important roles in the socializing around each June's graduation. Usually, the secretary of war and other dignitaries would attend to speak and hand out diplomas; General MacArthur, U.S. Army Chief of Staff, spoke in 1933, while

General of the Armies John J. Pershing spoke in 1936. Some graduates would return for the occasion. When these luminaries were in town, it fell to the commandant and the superintendent to provide suitable entertainment.[43]

The 1935 graduation was especially demanding, as President Franklin D. Roosevelt was scheduled to be the speaker. In addition to the considerable entourage he would bring, MacArthur would attend, as would many other senior officers. The superintendent, Major General William D. Connor, was a teetotaler, and arranged for Buckner to make mint juleps for the occasion using an old family recipe. "A hot Graduation Day was correctly anticipated," remembered Claiborne, then aged 8. "Huge blocks of ice were delivered to the quarters, an enlisted detail crushed the ice, and juleps were prepared and served to the thirsty guests. The juleps were well received by all, particularly the President. My father later divulged that a waiter approached him at the reception and said, 'Sir, Colonel, the President wants another drink, but I don't think he oughta!' General MacArthur prudently declined a second julep, saying, according to family legend, 'No, thank you. I think I will stop now while I still know who is President.'"

Later, Connor asked for the mint julep recipe. The reply revealed more about Buckner than the drink. "Your letter requesting my formula for mixing mint juleps leaves me in the same position in which Captain Barber found himself when asked how he was able to carve the image of an elephant from a block of wood. He replied that it was a simple process consisting merely of whittling off the part that didn't look like an elephant," Buckner wrote.

> The preparation of the quintessence of gentlemanly beverages can be described only in like terms. A mint julep is not the product of a FORMULA. It is a CEREMONY and must be performed by a gentleman possessing a true sense of the artistic, a deep reverence for the ingredients and a proper appreciation of the occasion. It is a rite that must not be entrusted to a novice, a statistician, nor a Yankee. It is a heritage of the old South, an emblem of hospitality and a vehicle in which noble minds can travel together upon the flower-strewn paths of happy and congenial thought.

After a basic explanation of the process, Buckner closed by saying, "Being overcome by thirst, I can write no further."[44]

Toward the end of his tenure as commandant, Buckner recruited Omar Bradley to return to West Point as a tac. The two got reacquainted, sharing stories and comparing notes. Buckner assigned Bradley to construct a skeet shooting range and associated cadet training curriculum. Bradley enjoyed working for Buckner, and later recalled one of Buckner's many sayings: "Judgment comes from experience, and experience comes from making bad judgments."[45]

The class of 1936's graduation ended Buckner's tenure at West Point. It also capped 17 years involved with the Army's schools as student, teacher, and administrator. From now on, he would have duty with troops and put his teachings into practice. Buckner also developed a professional association with Elwyn "Eddie" Post, who would serve as aide, friend, and chief staff officer for the next eight years.[46]

Buckner next moved through a succession of troop commands to get him reacquainted with the field forces. First, he was executive officer of the 23rd Infantry at Fort Sam Houston, followed by a promotion to colonel and command of the 66th Infantry (Light Tanks) at Fort George G. Meade, Maryland, from March of 1937 until a reorganization in September 1938 rendered the regimental headquarters surplus. He next commanded the 22nd Infantry at Fort McClellan in Alabama until November 1939, followed by appointment as chief of staff to the 6th Infantry Division at Fort Lewis, Washington.[47]

This simple list of assignments should be considered alongside the war clouds assembling over Europe and Asia in the years 1937–40. Buckner was clearly a rising star in an Army starting to understand it would likely need to fight another major war soon. The time with the 66th also acquainted Buckner with armored warfare, a new tactical concept still under development. The regiment went on several long road marches, and Buckner learned how to maneuver a mechanized unit. Combined with his earlier air experience, he was becoming a well-rounded officer in modern warfare.[48]

Anyone wishing to see where warfare was going need only have attended the parade in Gettysburg on July 2, 1938, which was part of the commemoration of the battle's 75th anniversary. Buckner led a battalion of the 66th's tanks in the procession through downtown Gettysburg, directly behind Colonel Jonathan M. Wainwright's horse-mounted 3rd Cavalry Regiment.[49]

During Buckner's time at Fort Lewis, the international situation considerably darkened. Nazi Germany invaded Poland on September 1, 1939, overrunning it by early October. The Soviet Union and Finland fought a war over the winter of 1939–40, while Japan continued her offensives into China, which had started in 1937. In April 1940 the Germans invaded Denmark and Norway. Then in May and June 1940, France fell to a lightning six-week German campaign, with the British forces barely escaping at Dunkirk.

France's collapse shocked the world, and compelled the United States to reassess the state of its defenses. Suddenly, defense of America's outposts became a very pressing matter. Of critical importance in the Pacific were the territories of Alaska and Hawaii, both seen as vital bases for operations and support to U.S. garrisons in Guam and the Philippines.

General George C. Marshall, who became U.S. Army chief of staff the day Germany invaded Poland, sought an officer to organize the defense of Alaska. Administratively, the Alaska defenses fell under the Ninth Corps Area and Fourth Army, headquartered at the Presidio of San Francisco. Marshall turned to Lieutenant General John L. DeWitt, Fourth Army's commander, for a nominee. DeWitt recommended Buckner, and Marshall concurred. On July 9, 1940, Buckner received his formal appointment as commander of the new Alaska Defense Force. The job also came with a promotion to Brigadier General effective September 1, 1940, making Buckner one of the first of his class to make general officer rank.[50]

Buckner faced a daunting task. Alaska was known as the Last Frontier with some justification, as it was the northernmost territory of the United States. Purchased from Russia in 1867, in 1912 Alaska had been formally organized with a territorial government. The discovery of gold had spurred economic development to a degree, but in 1940 it was still sparsely populated with only 72,524 people.

Geographically, Alaska was vast and important. Its land area totaled 20% of the size of the continental United States, and measured 900 miles long by 800 miles wide. The Aleutian Islands ran westward over one thousand miles from Kodiak to Attu, just 700 miles from the Japanese base at Paramushiro in the Kuriles. Rugged mountain ranges compartmentalized much of the territory, with elevations ranging from sea level to over 20,000 feet atop Mount McKinley (Denali), north of Anchorage. The territory's varied terrain included tundra, permafrost, forests, muddy muskeg, and glaciers. The most important settlements were Anchorage, Fairbanks, Seward, and the capital of Juneau. Seward was the main port of entry, with Anchorage 126 miles to the north, and Fairbanks a further 358 miles beyond.[51]

Alaska was "the aerial crossroads of the world," as one reporter described it. "He who holds Alaska owns the world," declared General Billy Mitchell in 1935. Looking at a globe, there is some justification to the claims, as many major air routes ran over or near Alaska. Fairbanks was 1,550 miles

Alaska and the North Pacific. *U.S. Air Force*

by air to Seattle, 2,135 to San Francisco, 2,800 to Chicago, and just under 4,000 to London and New York. The Soviet Union was only 57 miles across the Bering Strait from Wales on Alaska's west coast. Tokyo stood 1,700 miles from the western Aleutians. Vancouver was 775 miles from Juneau, and 1,330 miles from Anchorage.[52]

For all this, the territory was poorly defended. "A handful of enemy parachutists could capture Alaska overnight," stated newly-appointed Governor Ernest Gruening in 1940. The only military installation in Alaska was Chilkoot Barracks, located in the southeastern part of the territory near the Canadian border. Its garrison numbered 400 troops, armed only with infantry weapons; the lone artillery piece, a decommissioned Russian cannon, was a monument. Shortly after assuming office in December 1939, Gruening visited Chilkoot and came away less than impressed. The post "had about as much relevance to modern warfare as one of those frontier Indian-fighting posts from the days of Custer and Sitting Bull," he recalled. "It had no road or air connection with the outside world. Its only transportation was provided by a 51-year-old harbor tug … If war had come, we'd have had to sue for peace and ask for a wind-check."[53]

It was Simon Bolivar Buckner's job to ready Alaska for defense. "He started with virtually nothing," recalled a reporter in 1943, "and did a ten-year job in about eighteen months." A classmate called his task "that of a pioneer." Fortunately, Buckner was not completely on his own. Reinforcements were on the way in the form of the 4th Infantry Regiment and some support units. Marshall's staff had been planning for Alaskan defense, and resources were coming for airfield and base construction. These were useful starts, but the vast territory needed considerably more troops, planes, and bases to ensure an adequate defense.[54]

Buckner set about touring his new area of responsibility, and quickly discovered two major challenges that would affect his plans and operations. The first was the primitive infrastructure in Alaska. Much of the territory lacked electricity or reliable telephone or radio communications. Roads were mostly localized and of varying quality. Two railroads operated: one a narrow-gauge in the territory's east, and the government-owned Alaska Railroad, an all-weather, standard-gauge line connecting Seward and Fairbanks via Anchorage.[55]

On top of this, there was no overland communication with Canada and the continental United States. "Until November 1942, when the Alaska Highway was opened for traffic," noted the U.S. Army history of the war in Alaska, "the only direct connection between the continental United States and Alaska was by sea or air. To all intents and purposes Alaska was an island, not a peninsula. Almost all food and supplies for the military garrisons as well as for the civilian population had to be imported by sea, a situation not changed by the opening of the highway."[56]

The other great challenge was the weather. Alaska was a region of extremes, from Arctic conditions in the north to a climate in the south comparable to Minnesota or even West Virginia. Fairbanks' temperatures ranged from 90 degrees Fahrenheit in the summer to −60 below zero in winter. The sun never set during summer months, while winter days contained just a few hours of sunlight. In addition, several air currents combined with a recurring low to create winds and storms over the territory, especially along the southern coast. In the Aleutians, wind and fog combined to make the islands treeless, with fully clear weather available on only a handful of days per year.[57]

Buckner realized that Alaska's main threat was probably not a major ground invasion, but a string of localized landings to secure bases along the Aleutians and south coast. The U.S. Navy had already mapped out a series of installations to guard against threats from Japan. In September 1940, Buckner advocated for building a series of airbases, supported by ground troops, to both defend the territory and project U.S. air power south and west of Alaska. The goal was to detect and counter enemy approaches, and support Navy operations. Buckner soon cultivated the support of General DeWitt, Governor Gruening, and Captain Ralph C. Parker, who had been appointed to oversee the Navy's base construction, and these plans were approved. Over the next year, installations sprung up all over Alaska.[58]

The construction process was not always easy or comfortable. Barracks were not ready when the first troops arrived in Anchorage, so the 4th Infantry lived the winter of 1940–41 under canvas in heated tents. Buckner lived with them, and seemed to relish the experience. "He would stride across the frozen, sometimes snow covered ground," recalled an observer, "breathing great drafts of air with relish, as if it were a balmy spring

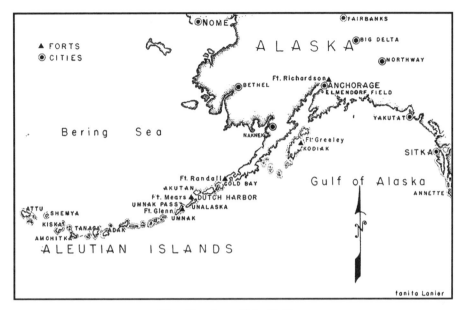

The Aleutians. *U.S. Air Force*

morning in his native Kentucky." Buckner soon became known as "The Silver Stallion of Alaska," a nickname he enjoyed. "He looks exactly as if he were specially cast for his present role," commented a reporter. "He is like that rugged land: huge, uninhabited, hard."[59]

Buckner and his men moved to Fort Richardson, outside Anchorage, when it opened in early 1941. Adele, Mary, and Claiborne joined him there, as Simon III was in college. The family quickly discovered how much Buckner enjoyed Alaska's opportunities for hunting and outdoor life. Bolivar and Adele also became a hit in the territory's social life, where engagements often advanced both personal and professional agendas. Buckner's friendly ways and font of stories enlivened many an evening and helped build relationships. Colonel Post and his wife Virginia would often go along, and find a way to steer the conversation in just the right way for Buckner to make a point or spin a tale. In fact, Buckner found Alaska and its people so agreeable that he started talking about retiring there once his Army career ended.[60]

Not everyone enjoyed the general's company, especially some younger people. A demonstration of this occurred one night when the Buckners were hosting a party at their home. The bell rang, and Buckner answered the door to find two attractive young ladies outside. He invited them in, but they demurred. "We wish we could," one said, "but we have to go to that damned General Buckner's party. Where is his house?"

Buckner's expression and tone did not change. "You'd better come in," he replied. "From what I hear about him, you'll need something to bolster you up first."[61]

As 1941 progressed, Buckner continued to work with great energy. There were bureaucratic delays in getting materials, and Buckner cultivated the key relationships he needed to get things done. Aware that General DeWitt was the essential conduit for supplies and plans, Buckner kept in regular touch with him about progress, requirements, and recommendations. Buckner and Parker established a warm relationship and worked closely to develop their bases. Many chosen sites required both Army and Navy installations to be sited near each other, if not directly adjacent; this was especially true of places like Sitka, Kodiak, and Dutch Harbor along the Aleutians' eastern end. It helped that Parker was a straightforward person focused on results, as was Buckner.[62]

This amity could not prevent interservice rivalries from occasionally interfering. The Army and Navy high commands in Washington argued over where one service's jurisdiction ended and the other began, the effects of which required mitigation between Parker and Buckner. There were also different perspectives about the Aleutians, many of which were poorly charted yet had the potential to become future battlefields. Parker loaned a ship to Buckner for a personal reconnaissance of the chain, but the captain and crew proved reluctant to sail too close to the stormy and foggy islands. "The Naval officers have an instinctive dread of Aleutian waters," reported Buckner to DeWitt, "feeling that they were inhabited by a ferocious monster that was always breathing fogs and coughing up williwaws that would blow the unfortunate mariner onto unchartered rocks and forever destroy his chances of becoming an admiral." Ironically, an impressed Parker gave Buckner a commission as "Brevet Brigadier Admiral" in tribute to his support of the Navy's efforts.[63]

Buckner continued to fiercely advocate for his requirements, especially for planes. "If we hit them [the Japanese] while they are at sea and weak, we can destroy them," he told DeWitt. "There are two ways of dealing with a rattlesnake. One is to sit still and wait for it to strike. The other is to bash in its head and put it out of business. That is what I favor." Buckner told Marshall, "Under present conditions, I would rather have an additional heavy bombardment squadron than a division of ground troops."[64]

DeWitt backed Buckner in these requests. He also helped demonstrate their necessity where he could. On July 4, 1941, the Fourth Army's area of responsibility, including Alaska, went on a practice alert. The troops in California and Panama got the word immediately and responded accordingly. Some parts of Alaska didn't get the word for four days, and even then it was delivered by plane or dogsled. Buckner's command went up the priority list for communication equipment.[65]

Buckner also fought to cut the red tape. In answer to a question from Marshall, Buckner complained about Washington bureaucrats dictating construction plans without understanding the unique requirements of Alaska. "The most effective measure of assistance which you can render us in our building program," he told Marshall, "is a greater degree of decentralization. In many cases it takes a great deal longer to get a construction measure approved after the appropriations are made than it does to do the actual building. Our Area Engineer here put it very aptly when he said that quick-drying cement did him very little good in speeding up construction unless some quick-drying ink was used on the approval of his plans."[66] Marshall approved this request in late 1941.

Meanwhile, work continued apace. Soldiers and civilian contractors built roads and installations on a scale unprecedented in Alaska, in all kinds of weather. The runways at Fairbanks' Ladd Field alone included more concrete than in all the roads in the territory. Forts, barracks, airfields, and ports all came into existence within months. Army engineers also rebuilt part of the Alaska Railroad, tunneled a new railroad to Whittier, and built highways connecting Anchorage to Fairbanks and several ports along the southern coast. Buckner also created two shell companies to funnel non-military government funds into base development in the Aleutians, including later-approved airbases at Umnak and Cold Bay.[67]

Buckner and his staff were fortunate to have Captain (later Colonel) Benjamin B. Talley, an excellent engineer, at their disposal. He fully agreed with Buckner's desire to get things done with minimum red tape.

"Talley was convinced that the United States would soon be at war," recalled his wife Virginia. He pushed his work crews accordingly. "Much of the steel in the arch hangars at Elmendorf was put up at temperatures colder than fifteen degrees below zero, and the workers erected steels at Fairbanks until the temperature reached twenty-five degrees below zero. Carpenter work stopped only when the wood froze and a nail couldn't be driven into it ... the concrete was warmed with steam boilers after it was poured."[68]

"Build the nests," Buckner told the engineers, "and I'll bring the birds." But Alaska was the last territory to get Army planes, and precious few at that. The 18th Pursuit Squadron and 36th and 73rd Bombardment Squadrons arrived in early 1941 and formed a composite air group under Lieutenant Colonel Everett Davis. Davis and the 36th's plain-spoken commander, Lieutenant Colonel William O. Eareckson, set up a training program to get the aviators familiar with flying and maintaining aircraft in Alaska's harsh climes.[69]

All of this defensive preparation came against the increasing likelihood of war with Japan. In September 1940 Japan had allied with Germany and Italy. Northern French Indochina fell under Japan's dominion in late 1940, which raised alarms in Washington and London. Germany invaded the Soviet Union on June 22, 1941, and their rapid progress stoked fears of a Soviet collapse. On July 26, 1941, Japan took control of the rest of French Indochina. This expansion prompted sanctions and a hurried U.S. buildup of garrisons in the Philippines, Guam, Wake Island, Hawaii, and Panama, along with Alaska.[70]

In recognition of its growing status, the Alaska Defense Force became the Alaska Defense Command in early 1941. There was some discussion of making Buckner and his forces independent of DeWitt, but they remained under Fourth Army and Western Defense Command until 1943. Buckner became a major general on August 4, 1941. By December 1941, Alaska's garrison included 22,000 personnel, mostly ground troops in infantry, antiaircraft, artillery, and engineer units, plus a company of tanks. The air forces numbered 2,000 aviation personnel with 12 obsolescent B-18 bombers and 20 P-36 fighters. Given Alaska's size, this was not adequate—and Buckner knew it. "We're not even the second team up here," said Buckner, "we're a sand lot club."[71]

As international tensions rose, on November 27, 1941, Washington issued a "war warning" message to all commanders in the Pacific. On December 1, 1941, Buckner placed Alaska Command on alert.[72]

Six days later, on the morning of December 7, 1941, a radio operator at station KFAR in Fairbanks heard a faint radio report describing a Japanese attack at Pearl Harbor, Hawaii. The radio station immediately telephoned Fort Richardson, and soon word spread. Buckner coolly activated his contingency plans to secure all key locations and institute a blackout, while Eareckson's planes flew patrols out into the North Pacific. Governor Gruening conferred with Buckner on civil defense measures as rumors of imminent attack swept the territory. Alaska was at war, ready or not, but overall had responded well to the first shock. That night Gruening wrote in his diary, "This action [at Pearl Harbor], however damaging to our defense, is probably worth all the battleships, planes and personnel that we have lost in welding the country."[73]

The next day Buckner sent a message to General Henry H. Arnold, commander of the U.S. Army Air Forces. "At dawn this morning," he said, "I watched our entire Alaskan Air Force take to the air so as not to be caught on the field." To DeWitt he wrote, "We were fortunate not to have been included in the official calls paid by the Japanese yesterday."[74]

Buckner's point was not lost on Washington, which soon dispatched more planes, communication equipment, and support troops. In addition, the Navy augmented its PBY Catalina force to over two dozen aircraft, organized into Patrol Wing 4 under Captain Leslie E. Gehres. In February 1942 the Alaskan Army Air Force units became Eleventh Air Force under Brigadier General William O. Butler. By June 3, 1942, Eleventh Air Force contained 156 aircraft, including 6 B-17 bombers, 21 B-26 bombers, and over 75 first-line fighters.[75]

As these reinforcements came in, Buckner ordered dependents out of Alaska. "If we get hit," he said, "I want my men thinking of their posts, not their families." Buckner timed the departure deadline for the end of 1941 to give his people an opportunity to spend Christmas with their families one more time. This directive included the Buckner family, who went to San Francisco and kept up a warm correspondence with Bolivar over the next years.[76]

The needs of wartime took hold of Alaska in other ways. Blackouts set in along the coast, while regular air patrols flew into the murky North Pacific. Several reports of Japanese ships turned out to be false, although one time a PBY bombed a whale thinking it was a Japanese submarine. Buckner's chief of intelligence, Lieutenant Colonel Lawrence V. Castner, also created the all-volunteer Alaska Scouts, a group of backwoodsmen and natives who could perform reconnaissance as needed.[77]

Rumors of espionage swept the territory. Castner set about investigating pro-Axis spies in Alaska, finding some German-Americans sending information to Nazi spymasters in Tokyo. He broke up the spy operation and had the men arrested.

Accusations of disloyalty also embroiled Alaska's 230 Japanese-descent residents, many of whom were U.S. citizens. Several faced arrest and short confinement immediately after the war's start, and at least one committed suicide. On February 19, 1942, President Franklin Roosevelt ordered the evacuation of Japanese-Americans from states along the U.S. West Coast, an order that on March 6 was extended to Alaska. Buckner complied without public comment, although Gruening and DeWitt both expressed reservations. Of those evacuated, some ended up in the U.S. Army as translators or as part of the famous 100th Battalion and 442nd Regimental Combat Team. Less than half returned after the war.[78]

Meanwhile, the war seemed to have forgotten Alaska. Japanese forces struck south and southeast from Japan against many Allied strongholds. Guam, Wake Island, and Hong Kong all fell in December, while MacArthur's forces in the Philippines retreated to Bataan. Malaya and Singapore surrendered on February 15, 1942, in the largest surrender and greatest defeat in the British Army's history. Further attacks secured the Dutch East Indies, the Gilberts, the northern Solomons, and parts of New Guinea. Japanese forces also invaded Burma and marched to the Indian border, cutting the famous Burma Road. At the same time, a Japanese fleet raided British bases in India and Ceylon. Bataan capitulated on April 9, followed by the rest of the Philippines a month later.[79]

Amongst this litany of Allied defeats, the United States looked for a way to strike back at Japan. The result was the Doolittle Raid, a daring strike by 16 B-25s flown from USS *Hornet* on April 18, 1942. In broad daylight, the raiders bombed Tokyo, Yokohama, Nagoya, and Osaka before flying westward. One plane was interned in Vladivostok, while the remainder crashed in China as fuel expired. This was the first American airstrike on Japan's home islands in the war.[80]

Japan's leaders were shocked. "One has the embarrassing feeling of having been caught napping just when one was feeling confident and in charge of things," wrote Admiral Yamamoto Isoroku, commander of the Japanese Combined Fleet, to a colleague. "It's a disgrace that the skies over the imperial capital should have been defiled without a single enemy plane shot down."[81]

The Doolittle Raid ended debates among Japan's senior strategists, who had been torn between launching offensive operations in the South Pacific, Indian Ocean, or Central Pacific. To eliminate any possibility of further attacks on the home islands, the Central Pacific flank needed to be secured. The Japanese decided to strike eastward in a two-pronged effort. Operation *MI*, under Yamamoto's personal direction, would secure Midway Island and destroy the U.S. Pacific Fleet in a decisive battle. At the same time, Operation *AL* aimed to neutralize Dutch Harbor and secure bases at Adak, Attu, and Kiska in the western Aleutians. The overall commander of *AL* was Vice Admiral Hosogaya Boshiro of Fifth Fleet, while the Dutch Harbor strike was assigned to Rear Admiral Kakuta Kakuji's 2nd Mobile Strike Fleet (*Dai-ni Kido Butai*). Both *AL* and *MI* would occur in the first week of June 1942.[82]

American codebreakers in Hawaii were able to read much of these plans. They also understood that the Japanese overestimated the American naval strength in the North Pacific, while underestimating the Eleventh Air Force's assets. The Pacific Fleet commander, Admiral Chester Nimitz, decided to accept battle in both places. He sent the bulk of his fleet, including its three aircraft carriers, to Midway against Yamamoto. He also dispatched the North Pacific Force (also known as Task Force 8) to Alaska with cruisers *Indianapolis, Louisville, Nashville, St. Louis,* and *Honolulu,* plus several destroyers and submarines.[83]

For command of the North Pacific Force, Nimitz chose Rear Admiral Robert A. Theobald, a veteran officer of great intelligence and intense mannerisms. Theobald had been in command of the Pacific Fleet's destroyers during the surprise attack at Pearl Harbor, and the experience left a deep impression on him. Nimitz ordered Theobald to defend

Alaska, cooperate with Buckner and Butler, and damage the Japanese fleet whenever possible.[84]

On May 27, Theobald met with Buckner, Butler, and Gehres at Kodiak. The meeting started on a sour note, as Theobald made a point of using naval terminology when asking that maps be put up on an office wall. This off-putting stance antagonized the Army officers, which boded ill for interservice cooperation. Theobald then explained his strategy, which was to defend Dutch Harbor and points east. Buckner challenged some of Theobald's assumptions, but the admiral stuck to his plans. Significantly, Theobald discounted the codebreaking reports and suspected a trap; as he told his subordinates two days later, "The continued repetition of the messages by radio transmission leads to the inevitable conclusion that the Japanese desire certain information to reach us in the event that we are breaking their codes."[85] He then went to sea aboard *Nashville*, which observed radio silence, and would play no role in the events of early June.

Kakuta's planes raided Dutch Harbor on June 3 and 4, causing some damage. U.S. planes attacked his fleet without result, as fog hindered the air operations of both sides. The Japanese got a nasty shock on June 4, when their strike force was jumped by P-40s from Umnak on their way back to the carriers; the Japanese had not known Umnak's airbase existed. That development, plus the destruction of four carriers off Midway and the defeat of Operation *MI*, caused Kakuta to retire. However, Japanese troops successfully landed on Attu and Kiska—the first foreign power to land on U.S. territory in North America since the War of 1812.[86]

American reconnaissance planes discovered the Japanese on June 15, and the news created consternation in Washington. Reinforcements were earmarked for Alaska to drive out the invaders. Gehres and Butler dispatched regular air strikes against Kiska, which had the better harbor and base possibilities, throughout the summer. The weather as much as anything hampered the aircrews' efforts, attritting planes far faster than Japanese fire and limiting damage inflicted on the enemy. Some planes never found Kiska, while the 700-mile distance from Umnak was exhausting to all pilots.[87]

It soon became clear that bases closer to Kiska were needed. In August Castner and his Alaska Scouts reconnoitered Adak and Amchitka, respectively 200 miles and 60 miles east of Kiska. They determined both islands were feasible for U.S. bases, while reporting evidence that the Japanese had also been scouting them as possible base locations. American forces landed at Adak in early September and established a garrison of 3,000 men. Talley's engineers drained a lagoon for an airstrip that could support heavy bombers, and soon Eareckson had his men making daily runs to Kiska when weather permitted. In early 1943 Amchitka became an outpost base, which placed American forces within 60 miles of Kiska.[88]

To augment the bombing, Theobald put to sea twice to bombard Kiska with his cruisers. Both times his efforts were thwarted by fog. It was so especially thick on the second mission that several ships collided with one another, forcing Theobald to abort. Nimitz ordered Theobald to stay ashore, so Rear Admiral William W. Smith commanded the third mission to Kiska. This time the weather was relatively clear, and Smith executed a successful bombardment of Kiska on August 7.[89]

American leaders felt that Attu and Kiska needed to be suppressed until such time as a reconquest campaign could start. In addition to the risk to Alaska, the Japanese occupation of Kiska and Attu posed a latent threat to the Alaska-Siberia (ALSIB) Lend-Lease route to the Soviet Union. Throughout the war, ALSIB ferried 8,000 aircraft to the Soviet Union for use against the Germans. The planes flew via the Northwest Staging Route to Fairbanks, where they were winterized and handed over to the Soviet Air Force. Soviet pilots then flew them via Nome and St. Lawrence Island into the Soviet Union. Soviet merchant ships also picked up cargo along Alaska's southern coast. These efforts were just getting going in the summer of 1942, and a Japanese offensive against them could not be ruled out. Buckner deployed troops to points along Alaska's west coast and increased air patrols in the Bering Strait.[90]

As operations in Alaska expanded, it was clear that the territory needed land connection with the continental United States. Starting in 1942, 10,000 engineers under Brigadier General William M. Hoge carved out a road running 1,700 miles from a railhead at Dawson Creek, British Columbia, to the Richardson Highway in Delta Junction, Alaska. The road, named the Alaska Highway, opened to traffic on November 21, 1942.[91]

Fully one-third of the Alaska Highway's work crews, and a high percentage of the Alaska Defense Command's logistics troops, were black soldiers in segregated units. Buckner let it be known they were not welcome. "I appreciate your consideration of my views concerning negro troops in Alaska," he wrote a colleague in 1942. "The thing which I have opposed principally has been their establishment as port troops for the unloading of transports at our docks. The very high wages offered to unskilled labor here would attract a large number of them and cause them to remain and settle after the war, with the natural result that they would interbreed with the Indians and Eskimos and produce an astonishingly objectionable race of mongrels which would be a problem here from now on. We have enough racial problems here and elsewhere already." As for road crews, they would be acceptable "if they are kept far enough away from the settlements and kept busy."[92]

Even in the segregated U.S. Army of the times, these views were extreme. Buckner's beliefs on segregation deteriorated his relations with Governor Gruening, and led the latter to issue proclamations outlawing racial discrimination in bars and recreational facilities. There is evidence that Buckner moderated his stance as black engineer and port units arrived and performed exemplary service. "Given the stridency with which Buckner expressed his antipathy toward blacks," commented a historian of the war in Alaska, "I find it particularly remarkable that his Alaska Defense Command and its successor, the Alaskan Department, managed, as the war progressed, to provide an atmosphere comparatively conducive to the success of its African-American soldiers."[93] How much of this change can be attributed to Buckner, and how much to Gruening, is an open question.

Between December 1941 and June 1942, the Alaska garrison doubled to 45,000 men, and 13 months later it would contain over 144,000 men. Accommodating this expansion stressed Buckner's facilities and administration. In addition, Alaska was not considered an overseas combat post, which affected pay rates, promotion and medal eligibility, and a host of other related matters. To top it off, War Department censorship also ensured nobody in the United States knew much about the war in Alaska. The combined pressures created morale problems.[94]

Buckner did what he could to help. He commandeered the lodges at Mount McKinley National Park as a rest haven, and arranged for amenities to be constructed as quickly as possible at bases. "General Buckner has been behind every detail of this operation," noted Lieutenant Colonel John Karlton, "He said if we undertook the plan, he wanted it done right." Buckner also personally tested cold-weather gear and sought the best options for his troops. He argued for residential hunting licenses for soldiers who had been in Alaska long enough to qualify. Such measures helped to a degree. By late 1943, Karlton was able to announce that "Your Commanding General, Lieutenant General Simon Bolivar Buckner Jr., is always on our side."[95]

As a whole, in the summer and early fall of 1942 the Army and Army Air Force seemed to be doing the most to be carrying on the war in Alaska. These active operations contrasted sharply with Theobald's apparent naval inactivity. Already unpopular with Army leaders, Theobald did not conceal his frustration about the limitations of operating in Alaskan waters, which did little to repair relationships.

Buckner spilled his contempt into the open during a gathering of Alaska's senior military officers, when he read a poem he'd composed from Theobald's perspective:

> In far Alaska's icy spray,
>   I stand beside my binnacle
> And scan the waters through the fog
>   for fear some rocky pinnacle
> Projecting from unfathomed depths
>   may break my hull asunder
> And place my name upon the list of those
>   who made a blunder.
>
> The Bering Sea is not for me
>   nor for my Fleet Headquarters.
> In mortal dread I look ahead in wild
>   Aleutian water
> Where hidden reefs and williwaws and
>   terrifying critters
> Unnerve me quite with woeful fright and give me
>   fits and jitters.

An enraged Theobald walked out, and filed a protest to General Marshall in Washington.[96]

This break between the senior Army and Navy leaders in Alaska nearly cost Buckner his job. Marshall considered relieving Buckner, but held back because of Buckner's overall success in Alaska. However, Admiral Ernest J. King, Marshall's counterpart, had been considering Theobald's relief for some time because of lackluster performance. One of the two had to go, and Buckner had gotten results while Theobald had not. Rear Admiral Thomas Kinkaid relieved Theobald in December 1942.[97]

Buckner and Kinkaid hit it off immediately. A selling point was that Kinkaid had just come from the Solomons, had successfully fought against the Japanese, and wanted to evict them from the Aleutians. Both men co-located their headquarters at Adak, and made a point of eating and socializing together. They quickly determined that everything east of Kodiak was Buckner's primary responsibility, while Kinkaid took the lead on operations to the west. Frequently messages to Nimitz or Marshall from one would mention that the other concurred.[98]

The authorities in Washington decided to prioritize clearing the Aleutians in 1943. The campaign would start with Attu's capture in May, followed by an invasion of Kiska in August. In preparation, Kinkaid stepped up an air and sea blockade of Attu, successfully interdicting Japanese efforts to reinforce and resupply Attu's garrison of 2,900 men. Hosogaya tried to fight through with a convoy, but an American task force thwarted him on March 26 in the battle of the Komandorski Islands.[99]

Meanwhile final planning and preparation for the invasion of Attu, codenamed Operation *Landcrab*, went ahead. The plan involved securing Chichagof Harbor on Attu's northeast tip, while other forces captured nearby islands for future base development. The 15,000 men of Major General Albert E. Brown's 7th Infantry Division would land on Attu in two groups, a detachment on Attu's north coast and the bulk of the division along the southeast coast at Massacre Bay. These forces would then advance inland to meet each other and sweep northeast to eliminate the last Japanese resistance. Castner's Alaska Scouts would assist these operations as scouts and guides. Rear Admiral Francis W. Rockwell commanded the amphibious force that would put Brown's troops ashore. Kinkaid would direct the overall operation, with Buckner accompanying. DeWitt was at Adak as an observer. On May 4, 1943, the day the Attu invasion force sailed, Buckner received his third star as a lieutenant general.[100]

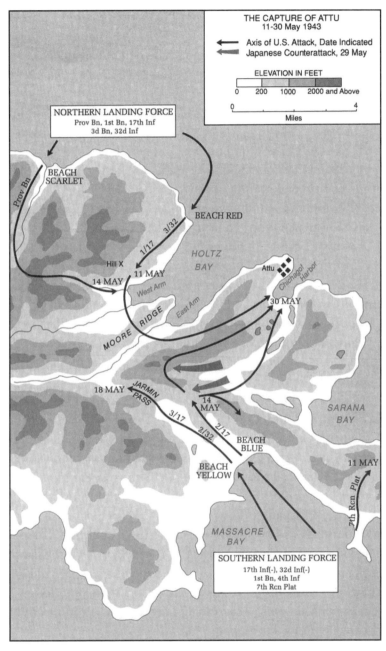

The capture of Attu, May 1943. *U.S. Army*

A week later, after delaying several days due to foul weather, the Americans came ashore on May 11, 1943. The Japanese commander, Colonel Yamazaki Yasuyo, chose to mount his defense inland. Nonetheless, the American advance slowed due to logistic issues and muddy conditions in Attu's muskeg.

General Brown quickly realized he needed more troops and supplies, as the battle would take longer than the expected three days. His requests surprised Kinkaid, and communication breakdowns prevented a full exchange of information. Kinkaid consulted Buckner and DeWitt, both of whom recommended Brown be replaced. On May 16 Brown was relieved of command. At Buckner's suggestion, Major General Eugene M. Landrum, the man who had led the Adak invasion, took command.[101]

The fighting at Attu continued for another thirteen days, as the 7th Infantry Division made slow progress. Buckner visited the front often to observe Landrum's forces in action. The elements proved as much an enemy as the weather; over 1,800 Americans reported sick against 1,700 killed and wounded to enemy action during the entire battle. On May 29 Yamazaki mounted a final, futile, charge and afterward committed suicide with many of his men. Landrum's forces took only 28 prisoners at the end of the battle. Proportionate to the forces engaged, only the 1945 battle of Iwo Jima had a higher casualty rate in the Pacific War.[102]

Attu's fall turned attention to Kiska. A Canadian–American force of 34,000 men was assembled for the invasion, scheduled for August 15, 1943. Kiska was expected to be a hard battle, as there were over 5,000 Japanese defenders on the island. But the Japanese high command decided not to sacrifice Kiska's garrison. In a nighttime evacuation in late July, all 5,183 Japanese troops on Kiska escaped to Japan.[103]

The Americans appeared not to notice, and continued their bombardment of the island by air and sea. One naval task force also shot at radar signatures on July 26, in what was dubbed the battle of the Pips. On August 15 the troops went ashore as planned, but found Kiska deserted. Except for some unfortunate friendly-fire incidents, the island was captured without bloodshed.[104]

Despite the anticlimactic ending, the Aleutians campaign was a significant Allied victory. "The loyal courage, vigorous energy and determined fortitude of our armed forces in Alaska—on land, in the air and on the water—have turned back the tide of Japanese invasion, ejected the enemy from our shores and made a fortress of our last frontier," Buckner announced to his command in October. "But this is only the beginning. We have opened the road to Tokyo; the shortest, most direct and most devastating to our enemies. May we soon travel that road to victory."[105]

This optimism appeared justified, as Eleventh Air Force launched its first raid on Paramushiro on September 11, 1943. But as the winter approached, it became clear that other Allied priorities would intercede and prevent further advances. The War Department postponed any invasion of the Kuriles until at least 1945. The Aleutian forces were dispersed to other battlefronts around the world, and Eleventh Air Force was reduced to a skeleton size. Buckner lost over 30,000 troops withdrawn in the last months of 1943, with more cuts planned in 1944. Significantly, Alaska became an independent command known as the Alaskan Department. But this administrative change could not disguise that the war was moving on from the Aleutians.[106]

As 1944 dawned, the Alaskan Department and its commander remained determined to do what was possible to help the Allied cause.

CHAPTER 2

Alaska: January–May 1944

1944

Saturday, January 1
Egg nog—Chichester
Egg nog—Downs
Dinner at Zido—Colonel Ohlson

Sunday, January 2
6:30 PM supper with Howards.

Monday, January 3
Left Anchorage and spent night in Fairbanks. Temp −10 degrees. Command Colonel Keeler

Tuesday, January 4
Went to Galena. Temp −36 degrees on ground and +22 degrees at 4,000 feet. Planning on running around camp like chickens. Happy garrison and commander.

Wednesday, January 5
Tried to land at Saint Lawrence but crosswind prevented. Flew around King Island. Boys and dogs on ice. Saw walrus. Flew between Diomedes. Many open boats South of Bering Str. Solid pack ice above. Ice piled up around stranded Crown city at Shagets.

Our Nome Garrison better friends with Russians than A.T.S.[i] and after rather non-cooperative all around (see Gaffney)

---

i   Army Transport Service.

Dinner with Grant Jackson

Thursday, January 6

Returned Anchorage via Bethel and McGrath. Former to be reduced to 50 men. Commander—McGrath[i]

(No entries for Friday, January 7 to Tuesday, January 11)

Wednesday, January 12

Left in my plane for Juneau. With pilot Lord, Cols. Robinson and Newkirk along. Also Joan Barton (Beck) from USO troop who had been left in Anchorage hospital with a cold. Blinding snowstorm made us spend night at incomplete Gustavus field.

Thursday, January 13

Engine trouble. Got plane started after seven hours' work. Reached Juneau before supper and boarded *Clarke* (except Cone who stayed with plane) to meet me later at Annette Island.

On *Clarke* were: Ingrid Bergman (Mrs Peter Lindstrom) Hollywood studios, Culver City, California. Neil Hamilton 1518 Condon Ave, Los Angeles 25, California. Joan Barton (Bock) 1245 N Vine Hollywood 38, California. Manville Andre (Adams) 1224 N Lincoln, Burbank California. Nancy Barnes (Kinsall) 495 S Roxbury, Beverly Hills, California. Cocktails, supper, Bubble Room and returned to boat. Sailed during night for Excursion Inlet.

Friday, January 14

Arrived Excursion Inlet at sunup. Coral frank mountains, moon, porpoises all around, about 100, snow on trees. Drove all over post with Col ... Could be used as stocked base but is no longer needed as a barge terminal. Marine ways will take 200 ft. boat. Well-tooled safe. Negro troops to be sent back to U.S.

Sailed for Sitka after dark. "Phosphorescent gulls."

Saturday, January 15

Arrived Sitka before lunch. Had Post Commander ... Shooff, Naval Commander ... and Marine Commander for lunch. Toured post and

---

i   Bethel and McGrath Army Air Bases in Alaska. The last note appears to be a reminder to himself about McGrath's commander.

had supper at army mess followed by drinks at [ ] house and dance in honor of 9 departing nurses. During afternoon visited Russian Church, museum and totem park. Sailed for Ketchikan after midnight.

Sunday, January 16
On board.

Monday, January 17
Arrived Ketchikan. Brunch with Ginsler. Looked into travel control. Cumbersome and some racketeering by notary and clerical personnel. Quonsets to be erected for personnel now in fish warehouses (fire trap). MPs guard city institutions. Not working with Annette MPs. Need to keep civilian crews of small boats away. Get drunk. Need rounding up if there.

Left during night for Annette Island.

Tuesday, January 18
Arrived Annette after daylight. Rain. Cone there with plane. Don Adler in command. Port inspected and in good shape.

Had party after show until after midnight on board. Left boat reluctantly and spent night in B.O.Q.

Wednesday, January 19
Flew to Juneau, inspected port and took off for Cordova. Could not land but continued to Elmendorf, breaking through clouds in heavy snowstorm.

Thursday, January 20, D-1[i]

Friday, January 21, D-1

Saturday, January 22, D-1

7—Dinner Dunkle

Sunday, January 23, D-1

(No entry for Monday, January 24)

---

i   These notations indicate that Buckner took game while hunting.

Tuesday, January 25, D-1

(No entry for Wednesday, January 26, or Thursday, January 27)

Friday, January 28, D-1

(No entry for Saturday, January 29)

Sunday, January 30, D-1

Monday, January 31

(Total D-9)

Tuesday, February 1, D-1

(No entry for Wednesday, February 2)

Thursday, February 3
Flew to Cordova in A.T.7. Major ... wants cold storage plant for all-year fishing. Post Commander helps fishing boats with his repair unit. This I approved if Govt. interests are kept paramount.

3 ft. of snow, bright sun, clear sky, trees loaded with snow. Coyotes eat at dump. Log chapel made by troops very picturesque. C.O. solicitous about dental survey and evacuation of emergency sick (City Hospital closed and no post surgeon).

Flew to Seward. Gorgeous day. Went to country home of [ ] Douglas.

Friday, February 4
Weather too bad to fly back to Anchorage. Post S-2 went to field to inspect plane in truck and backed into it and knocked off aileron. New one sent for by train. Arrived that night.

Party at Bill Baker's in town (School Supt) lasted all night. Drank to Cardinal Puff.[i]

On February 5, the Eleventh Air Force bombed the Kurile Islands for the first time since September 11, 1943. It was the first of a series of intermittent raids from the Aleutians that would last for the rest of the war.

---

i   Cardinal Puff is a drinking game that involves ritualistic draining of a complete glass of beer to the last drop.

Saturday, February 5

Took train for Anchorage. Snow near tunnel above top of cars. About 10″ deep on the level.

Attended USO 3d Anniversary banquet. (Speech.) Gov there—electioneering for Bob Bartlett as delegate to replace Dimond.[i]

Sunday, February 6

D-1.

Monday, February 7

Flew to Adak in Lodestar with Cone, gassing at Heiden and Cold Bay. C.O. at latter shows initiative in providing recreation site for troops.

Found Post[ii] in Hospital with kidney stones but improving.

(No entries for Tuesday, February 8 to Friday, February 11)

Saturday, February 12

Flew to Amchitka and spent night with C.G. Linden.[iii] Showed me his slides—splendid. He is also carving ivory. Many relics discovered on island.

Needs roller bearings for D-8 cats, and Hospital needs four dental technicians. Euclid tires also short. Good sick record new Hospital and officers club about complete. Good training methods.

Flew back to Adak, circled Andrew Lagoon in snowstorm unable to land and returned to Amchitka and landed in 60-mile gale.

Sunday, February 13

Spent day inspecting. Saw sea otter, about six dump at east end of island.

Command shows snap and good discipline. Met senior officers and talked to HQ mess officers at supper. Gen Linden has taken to ivory carving. He also has some splendid Aleutian color slides.

Monday, February 14

Flew back to Adak just above water. Very low ceiling.

---

i   Anthony J. Dimond served as Alaska's delegate to Congress from 1933 to 1945. Bartlett was Dimond's successor, serving as delegate until Alaska became the 59th state in 1959. After statehood, Bartlett was one of Alaska's first two U.S. Senators.

ii Brigadier General Elwyn D. "Eddie" Post, Buckner's chief of staff in Alaska and during his command of Tenth Army.

iii Brigadier General Henning Linden.

Attended party at Admiral Fletcher's[i] in honor of officers returning from bombardment of Paramushiro.

(No entries for Tuesday, February 15 to Sunday, February 20)

Monday, February 21

Flew with Post in Lodestar to Dutch Harbor, landed in sunshine and spent night with Longino.[ii] Latter and his aide not conversant with game regulations. Also seemed surprised at direct reports between his staff and mine. Living in the past.

Navy Club and BOQ looks like N.Y. Club; A. and N. relations[iii] seem very harmonious. Longino's house has beautiful view of Unalaska back to town.

Worked to go to Chernovski but fogged in there and Umnak.

Tuesday, February 22

Weather still clear. Flew to Kodiak and had lunch at mess with Robinson.[iv] Inspected post, met senior officers at HQ and took off for Richardson. Ground fog over field prevented landing. Tried to lower but could scarcely see RR track without hitting telephone posts. Flew back to Homer and landed on icy field. Had moose steak supper with [ ] Putnam, his <u>divorced</u> wife, six children and Cone, Post and civilian pilot. An efficient and well behaved household.

Wednesday, February 23

Drive around looking over farms with Putnam. Might buy one.

Flew to Richardson and landed about 3:00 PM. Attended 177th Engineer Anniversary dinner (Speech), Col. Williams, Commanding, and field various calls with Post until about 3:00 AM.

Thursday, February 24, D-1

(No entries for Friday, February 25, and Saturday, February 26)

---

i   Vice Admiral Frank Jack Fletcher, commanding North Pacific Area (NORPAC).
ii   Brigadier General Olin H. Longino, commanding Fort Mears, the Army post at Dutch Harbor.
iii Army and Navy relations.
iv Brigadier General Donald B. Robinson, the post commander.

Sunday, February 27

5:00–7:00 PM+ Entertained the following with eats and drinks:
Gen Downs,[i] Gen Whittaker,[ii] Col Carlton.
Capt Featherstone—with Canadian hockey team.
LT Badger—with Canadian hockey team
Olivia de Havilland—movie star.
Mary Taylor—Pacific skating champion.
Priscilla Newton
Jean McKenzie
Jane Harven
Virginia Dyer [the last four] "Doughgirls" troupe of USO Camp Shows

Monday, February 28

Attended ski-jumping contest at 2:00 PM and skating exhibition at post 7:30 PM. Had a group in for an anti-pneumonia shot afterwards. Showed slides.

Tuesday, February 29

Canadian research group reported in. Col John T. Wilson, Dr. Donald Crowe and Major Herbert F. Wood. The first two from General Murchie's[iii] staff and the last from Gen Pearkes.[iv] They want to see results of our winter tests at Amchitka and later go to interior and Aleutians.

Presented trophies to winners of all events at end of boxing finals.

Crowd booed boxing referee and Downs called off heavyweight match until crowd had left.

Supper at service club with Canadians.

(No entry for Wednesday, March 1)

---

i   Brigadier General Sylvester D. Downs, commander of Fort Richardson.
ii   Brigadier General Frank L. Whittaker, deputy commander of the Alaskan Department.
iii Lieutenant General John C. Murchie, Canadian Army, assigned to the General Staff in Ottawa.
iv   Major General George R. Pearkes, Canadian Army, commanding Canada's Pacific Command.

Thursday, March 2
Dinner at Mumfords—6:30 PM.

(No entry for Friday, March 3)

Saturday, March 4
8:00 PM Dunklin birthday party (not dinner).
Played games afterwards and got some interesting pictures with my
F1.5 lens.

Sunday, March 5
Dinner Atwoods 5:30? 6:00 7:00 PM.

(No entry for Monday, March 6, or Tuesday, March 7)

Wednesday, March 8
Skiied at Ship Creek run

(No entry for Thursday, March 9, or Friday, March 10)

Saturday, March 11
Skied at Ship Creek run.
Got word to meet Admiral Nimitz[i] in San Francisco March 14.

On March 12 the U.S. Joint Chiefs of Staff issued a new directive for the Pacific War. The Alaska Department would be reorganized and prepared to support offensives westward from Hawaii and northwest from Australia. Airfield construction would continue at Adak, Shemya, and Amchitka, in preparation for possible use as bases for B-29 attacks on the Kuriles and northern Japan. Buckner's headquarters would also plan for a possible invasion of northern Japan from Alaska to be executed in 1945.

Sunday, March 12
Flew to S. F. in Lodestar with Post and Cowart.[ii] Left 8:15 AM,
stopped at Yakutat and Vancouver for gas ¾ hour each and reached S. F.
in 12 ½ hours.
Kept Mary and Claiborne up until 1:00 AM.

---

i   Admiral Chester Nimitz, commander in chief of Pacific Ocean Areas (CINCPOA).
ii   Major Byron Cowart, General Buckner's personal aide.

Monday, March 13

Adele and Viera Matthews got in from Victorville.

Dinner with Posts at Club Zido.

Tuesday, March 14

Conferred with Admiral Nimitz and Admiral Bagley[i] (Western Sea Frontier). Former left for Honolulu next day.

Decided to have further conference with staff officers. Sent for my Sig O [Signal Officer], Kaufman and Rep from COMNORPAC. Captain Redman, Lieutenant Commander Blazedell of CINCPAC staff and Lieutenant Commander Holtzappel of Joint Security Command to arrive March 21.

Had Posts to dinner at Cliff house.

Wednesday, March 15

Post left for Carmel

Photographed in Park.

Thursday, March 16

Visited Chinatown—took pictures with concealed Leica (they turned out well).

(No entry for Friday, March 17 to Monday, March 20)

Tuesday, March 21

Blazedell arrived. Also Post with Virginia and Chris Orsinger. Captain Redman delayed 24 hours.

Lt. Comdr Sergeant arrived from Adak.

Wednesday, March 22

Dinner at Yacht Club with Sherwood Halls. He wanted to know about Maj. Lintner whom he expected to propose to his daughter when he got his divorce.

Thursday, March 23

Had Conference. To meet again March 25.

Had Posts, Chris Orsinger, Cowart, Capt Redman and his friend Miss Crowe in for C.T. followed by dinner at Yacht Club.

---

i   Vice Admiral David W. Bagley.

Friday, March 24
Photographed in the park with Adele.

Saturday, March 25
Final conference—highly satisfactory. Ended 4:00 PM.

Sunday, March 26
Took off at 8:25 AM. Hamilton Fld. Stopped at Boeing Fld, Seattle and saw Nold,[i] Chubbuck and B-29. (Stopped painting planes recently. 700 lbs of paint on B-17's and 10 MPH less.)
Stopped at Annette for gas.
AV. [arrived] Anchorage in 14 hours.
Printed pictures before retiring.

Monday, March 27
Lots of mail to answer.
Called in town after attending Bond Sale banquet and making speech at request of War Dept representative Maj (Snuffy) Smith.

Tuesday, March 28
D-1

(No entry for Wednesday, March 29, or Thursday, March 30)

Friday, March 31, *took 5 (D-1)
Skied back of air base.

Saturday, April 1
Atwoods 7:00 PM dinner—Bob's birthday and wedding anniversary.
Downs and I took Miss Dunkel via [ ]
Had Ofr. boottaps and "theatricals" after dinner.

Sunday, April 2
Skated and skied.

Monday, April 3
Went skiing in PM.
Capt. Parker—LT (nurse) Hood wedding 8:30 PM—a very happy affair.

---

i   Major General George G. Nold, chief engineer of the Alaska Department and later Tenth Army.

Saw Olivia de Havilland there.
Called later on Douglases from Seward and later at Wolkowskis
Left "Ceramic" picture at Mumfords

(No entry for Tuesday, April 4)

Wednesday, April 5
Goat dinner with Farley (he is an expert cook).

Thursday, April 6
Dinner with Bud Thompson—called off—Ignico[i] couldn't go.
So call Bud Thompson Tues or Weds.

Friday, April 7
Jewish Passover. Community Hall 7:15 PM. Called on to speak. Told them that Jews had better be in front line shooting Germans for if we lost war there would be a complete extermination of the Jews. Forok [Farouk] was a rank amateur at persecution.[ii]

Saturday, April 8
Cowart's.
Olivia de Havilland with her pilots and the SSO dropped in for an hour or so. Showed slides and had a couple of whiffles. She thinks the slides should be reproduced in *Life*. She flies back Monday to Los Angeles.
Read "Back to Methuselah" and indexed color slides until 2:30 AM.

Sunday, April 9
Cowarts wedding—Chapel 4:00 PM—Rec [reception] at Qrs 65A.[iii]
Toasted them at reception. Got them off in separate cars headed in different directions.
Attended Easter services at theatre. Called in PM on Cuddys, Gracie, Odons, Mumfords, Mickie, Ella Coker (Party going on) and Billie Dunkle. The first three were out.

---

i   Brigadier General Robert V. Ignico, deputy commander of Eleventh Air Force.
ii King Farouk of Egypt.
iii Major Cowart married Bernice Elizabeth Siebert at Fort Richardson's post chapel.

Monday, April 10

Flew to McKinley Park Hotel for anniversary of Recreation Center. Left 2:00 PM. Had inspection, dinner, ceremonies and entertainment program.

Was taken from airfield to hotel in dog sled and nearly photographed to death.

Tuesday, April 11

Went skiing in the morning and had lunch at the ski run. Took some movies and returned and had a walk and photographed dogs (stills). Returned to Richardson after supper by plane.

Wednesday, April 12

Dinner with Bud Thompson—bring Ignico. Ignico couldn't come.

Dined at Lido blue room followed by ping pong and slides of my house and dancing at officer's club.

Other guests were Mrs and Miss Redfield. The former's husband runs the aviation school in town.

Thursday, April 13, D-1

Dinner with Mrs Howard—bring someone.

Brought Schick[i] and showed my slides.

Friday, April 14

Home-cooked supper at Dunkles.

She showed her movies, which were bad.

Saturday, April 15

Printed pictures until 2:00 AM. Very pretty northern lights 2:00 AM.

Sunday, April 16, D-1

Called in town.

Mrs. Howard said she would file on Kachemak Bay homesite for her daughter and release to me when I return after the war.

---

i   Colonel Lawrence E. Schick, Buckner's deputy chief of staff for the Alaska Department and later Tenth Army.

Monday, April 17

Conference with Ignico and Johnson[i] Re B-29 facilities.

Cocktails at my house for staff 5:30 PM. Decorated Castner (L of M)[ii] at dinner. 47 officers came for Manhattans. (3 qts of vermouth and 3 of Bourbon gave each about 2 ½ glasses)

Went to Nolds after dinner.

Tuesday, April 18, D-1

Saw Mrs. Howard about staking homestead and coal claim on Kachemak Bay. She will have papers ready Sunday. I will have to submit request every six months asking to postpone work due to war. Howards and Miss Haley to stake adjoining claims.

Dropped by Dunkles on way home.

Wednesday, April 19

Left for Kodiak 3:15 PM by plane and arrived 4:45 PM. Lived with Schick in house on Lake Louise next to C.G's. Gulls all flying in circles screaming in preparation for mating.

Had drink at Robinson's before dinner and he had same with me later. Went to Sgts Club to see dance.

Mrs Johnson, Torgeson and Dawson sponsoring dance.

Thursday, April 20

Inspected post and went to ski lodge—still skiing. Miss Griswold of Red Cross there. Trains Kodiak with Johnsons.

Formal dinner at mess.

Dr. Johnson's cabin the best I have seen in Alaska. Splendid log work, windows and fireplace.

Earlier went to inspect Cheneak [Chiniak] and Spruce Point. Rainy and gusty.

Friday, April 21

Went to Long Island for firing. Chance afternoon for seacoast practice. Not very accurate.

---

i   Major General Davenport Johnson, commanding Eleventh Air Force.

ii Buckner awarded Colonel Lawrence V. Castner with the Legion of Merit for "exceptionally meritorious conduct in the performance of outstanding services to the Government of the United States" while leading the Alaska Scouts.

Had dinner with Capt. McDay,[i] of Navy and took Miss Meister of Red Cross to dance at club.

Saturday, April 22
10:00 AM. Flew back to Anchorage via sawmill on Afognak and Homer.

Attended 714th Ry Bn[ii] anniversary dance after 9:00 PM. Went with Downs and party. Caldwells also there.

Sunday, April 23, D–1
Dinner 7:00 PM—Mrs Howard (Bring Castner) Castner couldn't come. Brought Harding. Got papers for homestead. Mrs Howard will try to cancel mineral claims on property as of no commercial value.

Monday, April 24
Left by plane for Adak 7:15 AM. Gassed at Cold Bay and arrived 2:30 PM (Adak Time). Approved Shemya project after conference with Nold and Whittaker who then started back to Anchorage.

Tuesday, April 25
Approved Hospl site for Adak with some alterations including bombing protection.

Went to supper at Finger Bay with Adm Whiting. Present also were girls of U.S.O. Doughgirls Troupe: Miss Jean McKenzie, Miss Jane Harven and Miss Priscilla Newton. Post and I took them home and there saw Miss Virginia Dyer who had a cold and couldn't come.

Wednesday, April 26
Flew to Attu, leaving 7:30 AM. and arriving at 10:00 AM. Inspected post and drove through new storage tunnel with Dunkleberg.[iii] Contractor expects to finish rock work by July. Snow just melting off of stores.

At 2:30 PM flew to Shemya. Just starting to haul rock to start break-water. Short of rock hauling eqpt. Nickell expects to unload 100,000 tons next month. 52,000 tons still at Attu to be brought over.

---

i   Captain William M. McDade, the air station commander.
ii 714th Railway Battalion.
iii Brigadier General William E. Dunkelberg, commanding Camp Earle on Attu.

Saw middle of *Scotia* on rocks, bow and stern both washed off.[i]

Insufficient scattering of planes at Attu and Shemya to meet night bombing. Only B25s to take off.

Returned to Adak Lv 5:30 PM Av. 8:00 PM.[ii]

(No entry for Thursday, April 27, or Friday, April 28)

Saturday, April 29

Took Lt. Cummings over to my new house to get his views regarding interior decoration.

Attended Adm Fletcher's birthday party followed by ping pong and movies. Also put him (Cummings) in charge of decorating new officers' mess.

Sunday, April 30, 1st 5-D

(No other entry)

Monday, May 1

Attended opening of Doughgirls show. Post had paper roses sent up at finale.

Went to Adm Fletcher's for hot buttered rums afterward.

Tuesday, May 2

Left Adak 2:25 PM in plane, flew over and photographed smoking crater of Great Sitkan. At 4:30 PM saw about 1500 sea lions and tens of thousands of moose at Bogoslof I. Landed at Dutch Harbor at 5:00 PM and stayed with Col. Parmalee, post commander. Inspected searchlight positions and saw searchlight drill after supper until 11:30 PM.

The *Clarke* got in before dark with Smith, Schmidt, Skinner, and Farley all somewhat rocked and frazzled.

I drank coffee for supper and slept only two hours.

Wednesday, May 3

Up at 5:00 AM. Inspected C.A.C.[iii] installations all day. Weather, rain, snow and fog prevented artillery firing. Played ping pong with Lt

---

i   The steam freighter *Scotia* wrecked December 23, 1943, in Shemya's Alcan Cove.

ii   These note the departure and arrival times.

iii Coast Artillery Corps.

Col Olson at club for an hour and when to reception and dance after supper. Met Wingfields of Unalaska at party—she from Junction City, Kan. Knows Patton[i], Goldy King[ii] & old Riley[iii] crowd.

Boarded *Clarke* and retired 1:30 AM.

Thursday, May 4

Clarke sailed at 6:00 AM & arrived at Chernovski 12:30 PM. Inspected post with Col Johnson. Everything seemed to click, particularly A.A.A.[iv] Good dummy positions.

Johnson wants tug and use of oil tanks on beach. Wooden tanks leak oil. O'Brien started over to see us but we sent him back. Sailed 2:00 PM & Av. Bogoslof 5:00 PM. Went ashore. 500 sea lions swam out, roced, jumped out of water & watched us. About 15,000 on island. Biggest at end of spit. Rocks covered with mosses. No people or eggs. Grass already getting green. Some mosses oil-soaked. Full oil drums on beach, also crate from "Toloa." Took pictures & returned to ship. Sailing at 8:00 PM for Atka. No lions returned shore after after [sic] taking to water.

Friday, May 5

Av Atka 7:00 PM after rough trip. Harbor smooth with N. wind. Deck of *Clarke* very leaky.

My plane had arrived from Dutch Hbr. Inspected post with Capt Kane (?) who commanded & found conditions good.

Spent night on *Clarke*.

Saturday, May 6

Started in plane for Anchorage at 8:25 AM, leaving others to go on to Adak in *Clarke*. Took 7 soldiers along on plane. Gassed at Naknak and AV Anchorage 3:45 PM.

Attended 903d Sig Co's annual cabaret in Anchorage. Called afterwards and later developed pictures.

---

i Lieutenant General George S. Patton.
ii Brigadier General Edward L. King, commandant of the Command and General Staff School when Buckner and Patton attended.
iii General Buckner was never stationed at Fort Riley, Kansas. It is likely he meant Fort Leavenworth, Kansas, where the Command and General Staff School is located.
iv Antiaircraft artillery.

Sunday, May 7, D-1

Developed & printed pictures.

USO show gave cabaret program at men during dinner. Very good.

Monday, May 8

Flight had 8 pups but somewhat undersized & weak. 2 died.

Called in town after dinner.

Tuesday, May 9

Flew to Homer in AT-7 at 8:30 AM. Cowart also. Took Joe[i] & bred Kitcher's bitch to him. Cut tails of Putnam's 2 pups. Little bitch pups. Very lively & a growler.

Saw nurse Martha (widow of Rasmus P) Nielsen about land. Will see her son Stanley for final dickering. (Good land sells for $30 to $35.) Left Joe.

Flew to Kenai & inspected air warning property left there. Some pilfering among plumbing. Deputy Marshal wants Yakutat hut for P.O. His name is Grover C. Triber. Local Trader: Hartley. Returned to Anchorage & found 2 more pups dead and 2 almost so. Stayed up all night with hot water bottles and fed pups with medicine dropper. They improved slightly.

Wednesday, May 10, D-1

Had 14 people to cocktails at my house & dinner in Eagle room later. Canadian Lt Col Francis and Herbert Hilscher there. Also Atwoods, Odoms, Momfords, Downs, Miss Dunkle, & Miss Walkowski.

Worked with pups some more. One still very weak & one improving.

Thursday, May 11

Saw Maj Forrest Re: mountain school at Mean. Idea look promising.

Flew to Homer 10:30 AM. Bought 40 acres from Mrs. Nielsen: "Northeast quarter of the southeast quarter of Section 1, Township 6, south of Range 13, West of the Seward meridian, Alaska." Paid $1,200.00.

Brough Joe back & box of crabs from Putnam. Latter wants a jeep as soon as they are released.

---

i   General Buckner's dog.

Friday, May 12, D-1
Had supper with Lt Col Knutson at his qrs. With 6 or 8 others. Delicious steaks broiled by Ashton.

Saturday, May 13
Another pup died.
Developed & enlarged pictures.
Went to movies.

Sunday, May 14
Enlarged pictures.

(No entry for Monday, May 15)

Tuesday, May 16, D-1
Decorated Medill & Peterson with L of M 11:30 AM.
Called on old Dr Romig who has just returned. He is interested in the agricultural development of the Kenai. Wants photographs. He thinks Alaska will eventually be three states: SE, S & SW and North. The north much later than the others.

Wednesday, May 17
McKinnon dropped in Re rehabilitation of Aleuts.

(No entry for Thursday, May 18, or Friday, May 19)

Saturday, May 20
Called in town. Munfords & Odoms returned with me for nightcap. Want me to go on fishing trip to Kenai next Sat.

Sunday, May 21 D-1
Heard from Dougherty at St. Lawrence Is, inclosing Weird Order of Ooseck Wielders for me to sign & send to Gov for Sig.
Ice reported good for landing at Gamball.[i] Plan to go Wed.

Monday, May 22
Had a dozen people in after supper to see a 16mm movie preview and a little refreshment. Expected to start on St. Lawrence Is walrus

---

i   Gambell is a town and airstrip on western St. Lawrence Island. It is only 36 miles across the Bering Strait to the Russian coast.

hunt next day but got radiogram that Warren Taylor of Kodiak was suing me for evacuating a soldier's wife, Mrs Fry. Looks like politics, he is running for office.

Tuesday, May 23

Ice reported good for landing at Gamball and plenty of walrus. Am attempting to defer court hearing and bring trial to Anchorage where my files are available. J.A.G.[i] notified and requested to have Atty. Gen. furnish counsel.

Court action deferred. No support from War Dept who sent message from JAG questioning legality of involuntary evacuation in compliance with War Dept Orders. Sent radio to ChofS[ii] smoking them out on this subject.

Wednesday, May 24

Flew to Nome, had lunch there and then flew over to Gamball. Saw large herds of walrus 60 mi east of St Lawrence Is on ice—about 250 altogether. Stayed with school teacher & factotum Frank Dougherty & met Miss "Buster" Keaton an Indian Bureau nurse and remarkable woman of the Arctic. Met by dog team and out on lake. At 5:30 PM, went out with Eskimo crew in skin boat with outboard motor in well hunting walrus. Saw none but crew shot numerous marres and crusted onklets which abounded. Boat owned by Harold Koonooker.

Thursday, May 25

At 9 AM went out in Montokolis' wooden whaleboat about 15 mi to ice accompanied by Cowart Edmunds and crew of Montokoli, Frank Sippines, Walunga, Moses Soongarook and Willard Kanganook. Shot 2 cow walrus in water, one with calf which was harpooned. I shot one in the head with my .375 and killed it with one shot. The other took about 10 shots beginning with one in the back. I photographed. Also shot a seal which sank. Natives called my .375 "Very strong gun." Walrus were hauled up on ice flow and butchered in about ½ hour each. Calf is valued for thong leather. Skin of old walrus is ¾ in thick. Raincoats

---

i   Judge Advocate General.
ii   This is a reference to General George Marshall, U.S. Army chief of staff.

are made of the intestines. Returned to Gamball 7:30 PM and found about a dozen walruses (large) and six or eight calves had been brought in. Watched natives carve ivory and visited skin hut encased frame house with 12 Eskimos living in it, 2 oil lamps, electric lights, a radio. Turned about 100 degrees.

Friday, May 26

8:30 AM went out again with same boat and crew to ice about 20 mi. Saw 2 walrus asleep on ice. Both were shot at about 40 yds. One rolled into water and sank. Both were bulls. Later we shot a cow in the water and caught its calf. Got back at 7:30 PM. Had walrus liver for supper, not unlike beef liver. Walrus meat very black. Natives sew meat up in slabs of skin and let it "mellow" in the ground in cellars often lined with whale ribs and cover the opening with a whale scapula. Saw some whalebone toboggans. Natives free of venereal diseases but badly inbred and tubercular. All had colds. Average life 12 yrs.

Wolves = Aivok
Seal = Nukauk
Bearded seal = Muckluk.

Saturday, May 27

Watched ivory carving etc in village and started to take off in plane at 10:15 but wheels stuck & plane bellied down. 20 dog teams and about 65 Eskimos turned out to help but could not move it. Radioed to Nome for 2 jacks which came in an AT-7. Left Edmunds who got plane out that night. Engines will have to be changed. Returned to Nome, arriving at 6:30 PM. Attended banquet and dance at officer's club opening. Sat next to Col Kornilof, new Russian Comdr. He said Russia will join us against Japan when Germany is whipped. 40 girls flown to party from Fairbanks. Danced until about 2:30 AM. Jones wants interpreter to report to him & not to Hackford. Machin suggested this.

Sunday, May 28

Went around post with Hackford in morning and flew to Anchorage at 11:30 PM, in AT-7 arriving about 4 hours later. Had dinner with Howards.

Monday, May 29, D-1

Recd somewhat insulting radio from Gov[i] and "War Council" regarding Fry case. Sent Riegal to Kodiak to look into Mrs Fry's residential status.

Called in town in evening.

Joe returned form Eskamine by Supt: Herbert Tomlinson.

Tuesday, May 30

6:30–7:45 went to Munford's. Trudy's birthday and grand march at Alpha Gamma Chapter of Beta Sigma Phidance with Mrs. Sidney Lawrence. Later at 1:30 AM had party at hotel until about 3:00 AM. Atwoods also were along.

Tom Comps wants me to locate one of Nell's descendants for him at Fort Knox.

Wednesday, May 31, 1st D-6

Old man Tolson from Loving dropped in. Wants to borrow a D-4[ii] to fix road. Rear Adm Sherman[iii] called on the way to the Aleutians. He commands naval air forces on west coast.

Had fish fry at Lake Shore Club at lunch time with Dr Roning & Board of Directors.

Took off for Seward 5:00 PM. Landed 5:30 PM. Spoke at dedication of U.S.O. Bldg and later migrated to houses of various Seward citizens.

---

i   Alaska Territorial Governor Ernest Gruening.

ii   A D-4 bulldozer.

iii Rear Admiral Forrest Sherman.

CHAPTER 3

New Appointments and Assignments: June–December 1944

June 1944 started much the same as previous months, but within five days General Buckner's life changed dramatically when he received orders to leave Alaska and take command of the new Tenth Army, to be based on Honolulu. Before going to Hawaii, Buckner reported to Washington for consultations, followed by a short leave in San Francisco.

Thursday, June 1

Inspected activities with Post Comdr Dows.

Slipway now better manned

During the night truck had dented end of plane wing (2d time at Seward)

Flew back to Richardson 11:30–12:00, bringing Dows.

Another insulting and petty radiogram from "His Excellency." Replied by letter without display of temper.

Friday, June 2

Find that Gov is implicated in Fry case and has sent Geo Folts to Kodiak to assist in case against me. Also Mrs. Fry did not know she was in the case until she saw it in the newspaper. Taylor got her to sign some papers she hadn't read. She is much embarrassed.

Dinner at Idle Hour with Mumfords and [ ].

Saturday, June 3

(No entry)

Sunday, June 4 D-1
11:00 AM Breakfast at Atwoods
Grumrides were there, also Mutydorf and the Cuddys.

Monday, June 5 D-1
Secret orders arrived Re my movements. Called at Dunkles'.
Post arrived after midnight. Invasion starts in France.[i]

Tuesday, June 6
7:00 PM Helschar's wedding anniversary beginning at Atwoods'. Had
Hoover's Old Jordan (20–30 yrs old).[ii] Wound up at Idle Hour for dinner.
Packed up & cleared desk.
Transported mumford lilac and currant bushes to nursery.

Wednesday, June 7
Post got in. Continued packing. Called on Dunkles & Mumfords.

Thursday, June 8
Assembled Staff at 9:30 AM & expressed appreciation of their work
but said I might be back and wasn't saying good-bye.
Left Anchorage in Loadstar with Post at 1:45 PM. Capt Edmunds, 2
Lt Anderson, pilots
Av Watson Lake 6:30 PM, local time.
Lv   "   "   7:10   "   "   "
Av. Edmonton 1:10 AM Fri.

Friday, June 9
Av Edmonton 1:10 AM. Met by newspaper man (NY Hearst
Papers) ... who offered and joined in refreshments. Lv. Edmonton
8:10 AM, local time.
Av Fargo 2:10 PM
Lv Fargo 3:10 PM
Av Muskegon 7:45 PM. No gas there.
Raining. Spent night in Occidental Hotel.

---

i   Buckner is referring to Operation *Overlord*, the invasion of Normandy on June 6,
     1944. Because of the time difference, it was the evening of June 5 when Buckner
     got the news.
ii   A type of Kentucky bourbon.

Saturday, June 10

Lv Muskegon 8:45 AM. Gassed Romulus 10–10:45 AM.

Saw DeArcy and Howland. Also Breckinridge.

Av Washington [ ], met by Russ[i] and went straight to Pentagon Bldg.
Saw Gen Hull[ii] about assignment & started on selection of new staff.

Stopped at A&N. Club.[iii]

Called on Nancy, O'Briens & Win.

Called others on telephone.

Sunday, June 11, J-2[iv]

Spent morning getting staff lined up.

Saw Helen Peabody at Walter Reed in afternoon. Took 5:00 PM train
for Baltimore. Had juleps and supper in rose garden with Betty Jones.
Joined by Davises then went over to Pagans'. Returned about 10:45 PM.
Train so crowded I had to stand in vestibule.

Monday June 12

Saw Gen DeWitt[v] re: staff members.

Worked on staff assignments with Johnson & Tyler.

Brown A.E. wants me to see McNarney[vi] Re getting him back into
good graces of W.D. after his relief from 7th Div at Attu.

Saw Asst. Secy. War McCloy[vii] at his request. Interested in Aleutian
morale, and thinks better quarters will improve it. I told him that a
consistent furlough and rotation policy was the only answer.

Tuesday, June 13

Saw McNarney re Brown & got Nold transferred without demotion.[viii]
Sent for by Und Secy War Patterson. He talked a good deal about

---

i   Brigadier General Carl A. Russell of the War Department Operations Division.

ii   Major General John E. Hull, chief of the War Department Operations Division.

iii   The Army and Navy Club in Washington.

iv   The meaning of this notation is unclear.

v   Lieutenant General John L. DeWitt. Since late 1943 General DeWitt had been in
command of the Army & Navy Staff College.

vi   Major General Albert E. Brown and Lieutenant General Joseph T. McNarney,
deputy chief of staff of the Army.

vii   Assistant Secretary of War John J. McCloy.

viii   Buckner's conversation helped Brown, who in late 1944 was sent to Europe. He
commanded the 5th Infantry Division in the late stages of the war against Nazi
Germany.

Kermit Roosevelt.[i] Also saw Duke Edwards in his office. Had dinner with Gen DeWitt. Afterwards called on Kate Hughes. (Post and Walter Wilsons at dinner)

Saw Tom Kent and his bride.

Wednesday, June 14

Lv Washington in my plane 7:05 AM

Gassed Lambert Fld. 10:25 AM–11:25 AM. Unusually good Red Cross canteen there. British naval training station.

Gassed Cheyenne 2:45–4:00 PM. Waited for weather.

Gassed at Reno 7:30–8:45 PM. Tel. Adele "Wish you were here."

Gassed Monterey 11:20 PM–12:45 AM (3 hoses). Saw Va. & Pat Post, left Eddie and picked up Claiborne[ii] who had followed a 3-day Ft Ord maneuver.

Thursday, June 15

Left Monterey 12:45 AM.

Arrived Hamilton Field 2:30 AM.

Drove to San Francisco & found Adele still up at 4:00 AM. awaiting my arrival.

Went to Presidio in morning and had lunch at St Francis with Adele and the Jack Elliotts.

Discussed Alaskan affairs & staff with Bathchurch who will be new CofS.

Talked with Mary & Claiborne most of evening. They still know nothing of my orders. Mary anxious to go to Alaska with Red Cross.

Friday, June 16, –1[iii]

Conference with Emmons[iv] and got his concurrence in taking staff members from Alaska. Notified Alaskan Dept. and War Dept.

---

i   Undersecretary of War Robert P. Patterson. Kermit Roosevelt was son of Theodore Roosevelt, the 26th President of the United States. On June 4, 1943, while a U.S. Army major and acting as an intelligence officer at Fort Richardson in Alaska, Kermit Roosevelt committed suicide. He was buried in the Fort Richardson National Cemetery. Kermit Roosevelt was a Patterson family friend.

ii William Claiborne Buckner, General Buckner's second son.

iii The meaning of this notation is unclear.

iv Lieutenant General Delos C. Emmons, who succeeded Buckner in command of the Alaskan Department on June 21, 1944.

Drove to Park with Adele & Claiborne. Spent evening at home. Adele showed some pictures.

Cowart arrived in afternoon with his wife.

Talked to Alaska with Harding & Whittaker. Find that Mrs. Fry has withdrawn court case—all Taylor's doings. She didn't want to start it.

Saturday, June 17

Talked to Cowart & Emmons at Presidio. Had Cowarts to lunch at St Francis. Ran into Mrs Clyde Ellis downtown, also Mrs [ ]

Told children about orders

Called on Sandersons.

Sunday, June 18, –1[i]

Dictated letters most of morning. Had the Eric Reynolds in to dinner after which she showed bird movies—the best I have ever seen.

Monday, June 19

Arranged for re-investments at bank.

Started Claiborne off for West Point with some advice my father gave me: "Do your duty in whatever field it may lie and never forget that you are a gentleman."

Went to movie with Adele.

Tuesday, June 20

Saw Mr Kelly again at bank, completing investment arrangements.

Left Va. Post & Adele at hotel and went to P.A.A. Clipper dock on Treasure Island. At office on dock 4:45–6:00. Left dock 6:00 & taxied. Took off 5:25.

General Buckner was now on his way to Hawaii and his new assignment. Upon arrival, he entered a complicated command arrangement. Admiral Chester Nimitz had overall command as Commander in Chief of Pacific Ocean Areas (abbreviated POA, with Nimitz known as CINCPOA), a massive zone covering the Pacific Ocean except for the region between Australia and the Philippines, which fell under General Douglas MacArthur as the Southwest Pacific Area (SWPA). POA was subdivided into a North Pacific Area, Central Pacific Area, and South Pacific Area. Nimitz had his headquarters at Pearl Harbor, Hawaii, where he oversaw all areas and directly commanded the Central Pacific.

---

i   The meaning of this notation is unclear.

Under Nimitz were deputies for his air, land, and sea forces, headquartered on various installations around Oahu. Air units came under Lieutenant General Millard F. Harmon, an Army Air Forces officer who had distinguished himself during the campaigns in the Solomon Islands. The fleet was commanded in alternate operations by Admirals Raymond Spruance and William F. Halsey, under the names Fifth Fleet and Third Fleet, respectively.

Ground forces under Nimitz had a more divided authority. Lieutenant General Robert C. Richardson, Jr., Buckner's predecessor as Commandant of Cadets at West Point, administratively controlled all Army units under Nimitz as commander of U.S. Army Forces Pacific Ocean Areas. The terms of his appointment gave Richardson primary responsibility for training and preparation, but not battle command. A parallel command existed for Marine Corps units under Lieutenant General Holland M. Smith as commander of V Amphibious Corps, and Smith had helped plan and execute several operations already in that role.

Up to this point in the war, most of POA's ground battles had been limited in scope, often involving a division or less. Nimitz had committed Army troops alongside Marine units under Holland Smith's overall supervision. As operations in the Central Pacific grew in size and scope, and more U.S. Army personnel arrived to serve under Nimitz, corps were created to provide the needed tactical direction. By mid-1944 it became clear that a field army headquarters was needed to oversee even larger forthcoming battles—especially Operation Causeway, *a planned assault on Formosa and the China coast by Major General John Hodge's XXIV Corps from the U.S. Army and Major General Roy Geiger's III Amphibious Corps from the Marines. To command the* Causeway *attack (which Buckner calls "my project" in the diary), General Marshall in Washington set up Tenth Army and assigned General Buckner to its command. As Tenth Army commander, Buckner answered to Richardson for administration, training, and supply, and to Nimitz for when and where to fight.*

When Buckner arrived, the Central Pacific Area had just opened Operation Forager, *the invasion of the Mariana Islands, its largest offensive to date. On June 15 Holland Smith's Army-Marine Corps force landed on Saipan, with follow-on landings at Guam and Tinian scheduled to come. The Japanese fleet offered battle, and Spruance's Fifth Fleet defeated the Japanese in the battle of the Philippine Sea on June 19 and 20.*

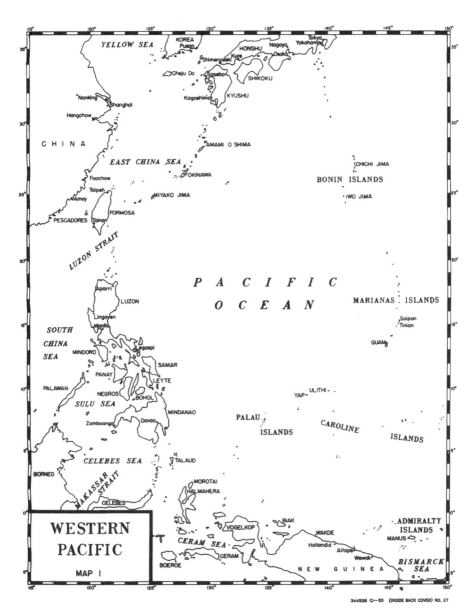

The Western Pacific, showing areas of battle from summer 1944 through to the war's end in August 1945. *U.S. Marine Corps*

Wednesday, June 21

Landed Honolulu 7:40 AM—local time. Met by Richardson & went to his house.

Attended conference at his office 11:30 AM with Harmon, M.F., Maj Gen Breen, his Service Comdr, Col Keleher.[i]

2:45 called on Adm. Nimitz with Harmon & Post. His CofS, McMorris, Adm Towers, Adm. Sherman also present.[ii]

Discussed turnover of property & troops to MacArthur in S. Pacific. Incomplete reports of fight near Saipan came in.

3:30 PM Called on Adm Ghormley, 14th Naval Dist[iii]

4:30 Arrived at Schofield Bks to discuss new quarters & office space with Post Comdr Col Sandman & Post Exec Col DuPree.

Went to war movies after supper and discussed Pacific Theater organization with Richardson until about 11:30 PM.

Weather breezy & pleasant. Don't mind heat at all.

Thursday, June 22

9:00 AM—Attended morning news summary conference at Adm Nimitz Hq.[iv] Saw Adm. Halsey who remembered serving with me at War College. Also Adm Shafroth,[v] Capt Parker, Gen Smith (USMC Leavenworth, trap shooting)[vi] and many others. Adm Nimitz in optimistic

---

i   Major General Millard F. Harmon, commanding U.S. Air Forces Pacific Ocean Areas; Major General Robert G. Breene, commanding Harmon's service and administrative troops; and Colonel John Keliher, deputy chief of staff to U.S. Army Forces Pacific Ocean Areas.

ii   Admirals Charles H. "Soc" McMorris, John Towers, and Forrest P. Sherman. They were respectively chief of staff, deputy commander, and deputy chief of staff to Nimitz.

iii   Admiral Robert L. Ghormley, best known for his role in command of the Guadalacanal campaign's early stages. As commander of 14th Naval District he oversaw all naval installations on the Hawaiian Islands, Midway, Wake (then in Japanese control), Kure, and Johnston.

iv   Admiral Nimitz had these conferences daily, and Buckner made a point of attending them.

v   Rear Admiral John F. Shafroth, Jr., inspector general for the Pacific Ocean Areas.

vi   Major General Julian C. Smith, commanding Expeditionary Troops, Third Fleet. He had been at Fort Leavenworth with Buckner.

mood over Saipan fight said he would hate to be in the present fix of the Jap naval Comdr.

Moved out to Schofield after lunch.

Went swimming before supper at Haliewa [Haleiwa].

Friday, June 23

Attended 9:00 AM Navy meeting & 11:30 meeting at Richardson's Hq. Had lunch at Moana with Post. Swam at Haliewa. McCunniff[i] dropped in after supper. Says Gen Krueger[ii] retarded his promotion.

Attended 11:30 conference at Richardson's Hq.

Saturday, June 24

Morning naval news conference, 9:00 AM with more Saipan news.

Looked over G-2 material at Fielders'.

Swam before dinner at Haliewa where we ran into Col Logie[iii] who we joined in a beer and steak dinner there.

Sunday, June 25

Usual routine. Called with Post on Monsarratts in evening who gave us each a jar of pickled pineapples.

Royal poincianas (Flame or Fire Trees) African tulips and shower (pink, yellow & rainbow) trees are in bloom.

Monday, June 26

Gen Hodge dropped into office & asked us to attend Saipan movies at 3:30 PM. Swam later.

Attended party at his house 6:15 PM followed by dinner at club. Sat next to Adm. Halsey.

---

i   Brigadier General Dennis E. McCunniff, commanding the Combat Training Command, Pacific Ocean Areas. He had succeeded Buckner as commandant of cadets at West Point.

ii General Walter Krueger, commanding Sixth Army and Alamo Force in the Southwest Pacific Area.

iii Colonel Marc J. Logie, commanding the 32nd Infantry Regiment of the 7th Infantry Division. Logie had led the regiment in the invasions of Attu and Kwajalein.

Tuesday, June 27

Lunch with Adm. Nimitz at his house 12:30 PM. Sat next to Adm who said Gov. Gruening was the most unpleasant looking, acting and talking man he had ever seen. The Adm. sounded like a real Alaskan.

Swam again at Haliewa.

Wednesday, June 28

Usual routine.

7:00 PM. Heard Yehudi Menuhin's violin concert. His accompanist, [ ] was equally good. The soldier audience was enthusiastically appreciative of his classical selections.

Thursday, June 29

Dinner at 7:00 PM at Pavillion Ft. DeRussy with Keleher & Herd. The most beautifully appointed party I have ever seen. Danced in moonlight. Took Sis Lyman home. Also met Mrs Dillingham & Mrs Davis of Honolulu and Mrs Keleher (Navy). At sunset a rainbow spanned Diamond Head.

Friday, June 30, ToT 6 (J2–D2)

8:30 AM—visit jungle school with McCunniff. Got thoroughly wet and then dried off again.

Dinner 6:00 PM, Gen Bruce[i] Ft Hase. Post & Yount there also—the latter an hour late.

Saturday, July 1

Maj Daniels, formerly in my CCC district called at my office. Also B.G. Thomas A.C.[ii]

I called in evening on Adm Nimitz, Richardson & Sis Lyman—all out.

Sunday, July 2

At morning naval conference saw Sutherland Gen MacArthur's CofS. He is now a Lt. Gen.[iii] (Probably here to see Adm. Nimitz Re my project).

---

i   Major General Andrew D. Bruce, commanding 77th Infantry Division.
ii Brigadier General Charles A. Thomas, assigned to XXI Bomber Command.
iii Lieutenant General Richard K. Sutherland.

Went to Kaina Point to fish in surf but after seeing 7 Japs fish ½ hour without a bite, returned to Haliewa for a swim.

Monday, July 3
(No entry)

Tuesday, July 4
Attend 12:05 speech by Adm Nimitz at Navy Yard Administration Bldg followed by 12:30 PM luncheon with Adm Furlong, his Qrs (Comdt Pearl Harbor Navy Yard).[i]

Saw aquacade in afternoon, went swimming and went to professional slap-stick wrestling in evening.

Wednesday, July 5
9:00 AM. Got formal letter of instructions from Richardson with numeral designation. Hq & Hq Co only assigned to unit. Orders to prepare plans with Adm Nimitz & Joint Staff.

Ordered to be Pres of Ralph Smith inquiry board—a delicate assignment affecting Army-Navy relations.

July 5, 1944, was an important day for General Buckner, as it was the day of the formal creation of Tenth Army. Richardson also handed Buckner a difficult assignment as president of a board of inquiry into the relief of the 27th Infantry Division's commander, U.S. Army Major General Ralph Smith, by Holland Smith on June 24 during the fighting on Saipan. Holland Smith was notoriously prejudiced against Army troops, and made no secret of his feelings. Ralph Smith's relief generated heated controversy in the Pacific, and threatened to rupture interservice relations at a critical point in Central Pacific operations.

General Buckner chaired Richardson's board of inquiry, which was called the Buckner Board. The board also included General Hodge, Brigadier Generals Henry B. Holmes and Roy E. Blount, and Lieutenant Colonel Charles Selby. The men investigated whether Holland Smith had acted within his authority, and whether Ralph Smith's relief was justified. Buckner recognized that his board's deliberations and conclusions would have an important effect on the controversy, interservice relations in the Pacific, and possibly his career. The board met between July 7 and July 26, 1944.

---

i   Rear Admiral William R. Furlong.

Thursday, July 6
Bill Grinder & B.G. Easley[i] called in evening.

Friday, July 7
Dinner with Dr. Frank.[ii] 5:30 PM 1805 Poki St., opp. Prehono School. Saw his guns & trophies. Broiled steak & dined in gardens.

Among guests met: [left blank]

Eugene Burns, A.P. correspondent in for lunch. Said British in Burma won't fight but extravagant with our lend lease. Take press credit for our fighting. Says Mountbatten[iii] has no authority. Command system mixed up.

Had Smith Board preliminary meeting. Gen Blount going to Saipan for original orders, journals etc.

Saturday, July 8
(No entry)

Sunday, July 9
Dinner with McCunniff at club preceded by drinks at his house beginning 6:00 PM.

Monday, July 10
(No entry)

Tuesday, July 11
(No entry)

Wednesday, July 12
Attended Bob Hope's show in the stadium. 10,000 soldiers were there, many of whom had come as early as 2:30 for a 7:30 show, bringing sandwiches with them, so as to get a good seat. After the show, Hope & his party came to our house for a couple of hours. Party consisted of: Bob Hope, Jerry Colonna, Tony Romero, Frances Longford and a dancer, "Pat" Thomas.

---

i   Brigadier General Claudius M. Easley, assistant division commander of the 96th Infantry Division.

ii   Dr. Clarence E. Frank, who lived at that address with his wife Laura.

iii   Admiral Lord Louis Mountbatten, supreme commander of Southeast Asia Command.

Thursday, July 13

7:30 PM. Supper with Gen Blount, his Qrs. Sand Is. (Postponed due to his Saipan trip.)

5:30 Supper with Col Shea, 101-A Wyler Ave, Hon. Roasted steak in the garden.

Friday, July 14

Adm. King[i] was at morning naval conference.

Tried out my new fish spear at Haliewa and got one small fish.

Called on Dr Frank in evening. He wants me to hunt with him on the Parker Ranch about three weeks hence.

Saturday, July 15

(No entry)

Sunday, July 16

Speared another fish at Haliewa.

Had supper with Monseratts. Met Mrs Sanders (Navy Dr). Also met [ ]

Monday, July 17

Staff members (head of each section) arrived by boat from Seattle. 500 Italian prisoners came by same boat. They had to be driven aboard with sticks.

Smith Board met in afternoon. Blount full of indignation and just back from Saipan with Richardson. He thinks Smith relief is a naval plot to discredit the Army, fight the Pacific War with the Marines and make Howland Smith a full general.

While visiting Saipan, Richardson reviewed and handed out decorations to Army troops, to the consternation of Admiral Spruance of Fifth Fleet and Vice Admiral Richmond Kelly Turner, in command of Forager's amphibious forces. Richardson also argued with them about the recent battle and Holland Smith's conduct.

Tuesday, July 18

Made greeting and general policy talk to staff members in morning. Smith Board met in afternoon after which Richardson had Hodge (of

---

i   Admiral Ernest J. King, chief of naval operations and commander-in-chief, U.S. Fleet.

the board) and myself to dinner & showed Saipan movies afterwards. Richardson several times intimated that the Navy & Marines were ganging up against the Army and expressed, with great delicacy, the same sentiments that Blount had expressed yesterday. It seems not unlikely that Richardson invited us to indoctrinate us along these lines.

Clicked off another birthday without incident.[i]

Wednesday, July 19
Board met again. Holmes wants to go into Marine tactics and get into the discussion that the papers have started which would be most ill-advised. Would merely accentuate differences and stir up more ill feeling.

Thursday, July 20
5:30 Dinner at Blounts Qrs, Sand Island.

Friday, July 21
Attend opening ceremony of Kapaloma Basin, Pier 39, Honolulu Harbor 2:30 PM.

1:00 PM—Luncheon with Adm Nimitz for Adm King.

Dinner at Richardson's Qrs in honor of Adm King at 6:30 (Zoot suits)

Saturday, July 22
Went to [ ] Chinese restaurant with some of the staff for a steak supper.

Sunday, July 23
Spent 2 ½ hours in midday sun at Haliewa. Got very red all over but not very sore.

Mint julep party with Judge Yates 5:00 followed by dinner. Post, Cowart & Chambliss came along. Among guests were:
Mr & Mrs Fraser—noted Leica photographer
"   "   "   Makin—Travel man. Also Exporters
"   "   "   Cullen
Mr Anthony
Mrs Smith
Mrs Smith

---

i   General Buckner turned 58.

Mrs O'Brien—wife of Judge.

Gov & Mrs Stainback.[i]

Monday, July 24

Went through new submarine and attended ceremony where Adm Nimitz presented medals to distinguished sub-crew members. Among them [ ] Cutter, (All American football & intercollegiate boxing heavyweight Champ) got 3 Navy Crosses for sinking 18 Jap ships.[ii]

Tuesday, July 25

Had "dry run" for Presidents visit. Lunch at club with Hodge.

6:30 PM. Dinner with Mrs Walter Dillinghams at her house on Diamond Head. Bring Archie Arnold.[iii] Start at his house in my car 5:15. Met: Farringtons, Mr Fagan? (in charge of lepers).

Wednesday, July 26

Wound up Smith Board. Members finally swung to my point of view.

The Buckner Board reviewed relevant documents and heard testimony from Ralph Smith and other Army officers involved. The board ultimately found that Holland Smith was within his authority to relieve Ralph Smith, but "was not fully informed regarding conditions in the zone of the 27th Infantry Division," and consequently Ralph Smith's relief "was not justified by the facts." Holland Smith and Turner both criticized the board for only consulting Army sources. When the Buckner Board report reached Washington, it circulated among General Marshall's staff before being quietly shelved in November. Public debate continued in the press and in postwar publications.

Immediately following the Buckner Board's conclusion, General Buckner became involved in events surrounding President Franklin D. Roosevelt's visit to Pearl Harbor. Roosevelt had just been nominated for a fourth term, and came to Hawaii to meet with General MacArthur and Admiral Nimitz to discuss Pacific War strategy—specifically, the merits of attacking the Philippines or Formosa. Roosevelt also visited installations and toured parts of Oahu.

---

i   Governor Ingram Stainback and his wife Cecile. He was Hawaii's territorial governor from August 24, 1942, to May 8, 1951.

ii   Commander Slade D. Cutter, commanding USS *Seahorse*.

iii   Major General Archibald V. Arnold, commanding 7th Infantry Division.

Thursday, July 27

The President came ashore. Roads were lined with troops. All general officers had lunch with Pres. at Schofield club. I sat to left of Adm. Nimitz & Pres on his right. Norman Davis to my left. Pa Watson[i] sick and couldn't come. Gen MacArthur sat on Pres' right.

Attended review of Archie Arnold's 7th Div afterwards. It was good.

Swam at Haliewa later and had Cowart, Nold and Harris for dinner at old Haliewa Hotel—now a U.S.O. Club.

Friday, July 28

5–7 PM—Party at Chauncey B. Wightmans to meet Mr. Ernest Greene. [Unintelligible erased text]

Saturday, July 29

12:45 PM—Lunch with Adm Nimitz for President. Sat on President's right, our host on his left. Adm Halsey, Richardson, Adm Leahy[ii] & others opposite. Pres talked cheerfully & made everyone feel relaxed & at home. Pa Watson was there but looked seedy. Pres looked well but his hand shook a little when he raised his cocktail glass.

Swam at Haliewa and had supper there. About 10:00 Post came home with some of staff, Miss Edney & Mrs Denson and had a stentorian ping pong game. Miss Edney had been in Europe a year or so and spoke with a foreign accent.

Sunday, July 30

Speared a squid at Haliewa.

Had steak on beach with Col Logi.

Monday, July 31

(No entry)

Tuesday, August 1

Spent Day 7:00AM–2:30 PM observing Col Logis [ ] Inf on field problems.

Followed Lt. Col. Finn's Bn.

---

i   Major General Edwin "Pa" Watson, military aide and appointments secretary for President Roosevelt.

ii Admiral William D. Leahy, chief of staff to the commander in chief, and senior military officer in the Roosevelt Administration.

Wednesday, August 2

10:00 A.M.—War dog show & lunch at Jungle Training Center. Saw silent scout dogs. Lunched at home of [ ] Castle near the Pali.

Thursday, August 3

(No entry)

Friday, August 4

5–7 PM. Party by Mr Chauncey Wightman to meet Mr Ernest Green

8:45 AM. Started going to Adm Nimitz' special conferences of restricted information daily at 8:45.

Harmon (Millard) called to ask if I wanted to fly to S Pacific with him for a week, Sun or Mon.

Saturday, August 5

Harmon came out and conferred about air support of my operation. We are in agreement that more is needed.

Sunday, August 6

(No entry)

Buckner and Harmon left for a visit to the newly-conquered Marianas. After Saipan was secured on July 9, the 2nd and 4th Marine Divisions captured Tinian between July 21 and August 1. Meanwhile, Geiger's corps with 3rd Marine and 77th Infantry Divisions liberated Guam between July 24 and August 10. The aftermath of battle was still present, but already development of the Marianas as an airbase to bomb Japan had begun.

Monday, August 7

Left Honolulu with Harmon's converted B-24 at 6:20 AM. with him, his aide Capt [ ], BG Thomas (AC) Col Davy CE.[i] They were reconnoitering for VLR fields.[ii]

Arrived Kwajalein 11 hrs 40 min later, 3:30 PM local time. Stayed with (B.G.) C.H. Tenney.[iii] Looked over island before supper & went swimming. Evidence of severe bombardment. All construction levelled

---

i   Corps of Engineers.

ii   Very Long Range bombers—shorthand for the B-29s. The Marianas would become the major B-29 base, launching its first B-29 mission against Japan in November 1944.

iii Brigadier General Clasen Henry Tenney, the island commander.

and vegetation destroyed. Japs used coral in cements, which was very soft but reinforced heavily with steel. No two pill boxes alike and fire not mutually supporting. (BG) Holmes arrived.[i]

Had supper with 5 girls of SSO Troupe showing "Personal Appearance" and attended their show afterwards. Met (BG) Ross of the 27th Div.[ii] Also (MG) Willis Hale Comdg combat land based aviation in Pac Area, headed for Saipan.[iii]

Seems Elmer Davis of the OWI[iv] came in about 1:30 AM and occupied the bunk next to mine.

Having crossed the 180th Meridian, we jump forward one day.

Tuesday, August 8 (Wednesday, August 9)[v]

Took off at 7:45 AM. Finished reading "A Short History of the Chinese People" (Goodrich) and "A Naturalist at Large" (David Fairchild Barber) on plane. Arrived Saipan 3:00 PM local time (8 hrs and 45 minutes later). Drove around island in a jeep for a couple of hours. Evidence of heavy fighting everywhere. Sugar mills, machine shops, storehouses, distillery and entire towns of Garapan and Tanapac [Tanapag] completely destroyed by naval fire. Also every farm building destroyed by Arty.[vi] Much of this could have been saved for our own use. Evidences of wanton destruction. Small boys love to break glass. Cattle, goats, chickens, and pigs running at large. No horses. Two-wheeled bull carts with shafts used for transportation. Sugar, tapioca, bananas & bread fruit principal crops. Saw some large doves, a kingfisher, a white heron, and some shore birds.

Jarman, Colliday, HM Smith, Adm Spruance, (VA) Turner[vii] met me at airfield. Stayed in one of few Jap houses left standing. VAdm Turner joined us for a drink and supper with Jarman.

---

i   Brigadier General Henry B. Holmes, Hawaiian Department chief of staff.
ii   Brigadier General Ogden J. Ross, assistant division commander of the 27th Infantry Division.
iii Major General Willis H. Hale, commanding general, Seventh Air Force.
iv   Office of War Information.
v   Buckner has crossed the International Date Line, and noted the local date next to the pre-printed dates in his diary.
vi   Artillery.
vii Major General Sanderford Jarman, island commander; Brigadier General Edgar B. Colladay, commanding Western Pacific Base Command; Lieutenant General Holland M. Smith; Admiral Raymond Spruance; Vice Admiral Richmond K. Turner.

Wednesday, August 9 (Thursday, August 10)

Visited refugee camp. About 15,000 Japs, Coreans[i] and Chamorros[ii] segregated by race. The last named looked better than the others. The Okinawa Japs were the most animal-like. Some were just coming in and being processed. They looked dazed, emaciated and frightened. The Japs had told the civilians that the women would all be raped and the men torn apart with jeeps. Some had cut their children's tongues out and killed their children. The Jap children were having sitting up exercises and their Jap leader wanted them to salute me. The boys gave a military salute while the girls bowed in unison. The hospital was pathetic, particularly the orphan ward. —I followed the course of the battlefield with (MG) Greiner, 27th Div[iii] and inspected his units in the rain. Saw patrols working and Japs being brought in. About 100 a day were being killed or captured. 6,000 had been killed since "organized resistance ceased." Many were still in caves.

Col Shellmeyer with 1st contingent of B-29 service units arrived just before supper.[iv]

Word came that Adm Spruance and VAdm Turner were to escort my expedition.

Saw Spanish nuns & priest in refugee camp.

Thursday, August 10 (Friday, August 11)

9:00 AM. Flew over to Tinian with Harmon and inspected battlefield with (MG) Schmidt[v] USMC who had commanded the 2d & 4th Marine Divs. The island is more open and better in all respects than Saipan except that it lacks a harbor.

About 11,000 Jap and Corean refugees were in camp—no Chamorros on the island. About 200 Jap soldiers were found in the refugee camp pretending to be civilians. The Coreans reported most of them.

---

i   Koreans. From 1910 to 1945 Korea was a dominion of Japan.

ii   The indigenous people of the Marianas.

iii   Major General George Griner, commanding the 27th Infantry Division.

iv   This is the 804th Engineer Battalion, Aviation. Within three months, runways and hardstands were ready for B-29 operations.

v   Major General Harry Schmidt, who commanded 4th Marine Division on Saipan and V Amphibious Corps for the capture of Tinian.

Visited an elaborate Japanese shrine (with a radar on it) on the highest point of the island. Saw some white birds along the cliffs about pigeon size but too far away to identify. Flame trees and hibiscus in bloom.

Prehistoric stone columns in pairs, each surmounted by hemispheres, were in a park in the demolished town. Some 35 ft high.

3:45 PM returned to Saipan and called on VAdm Turner on his ship where I met VAdm Hoover.[i] Turner referred to Army divisions or Natl Gd Divisions and extolled the Marines in amphibious warfare. I referred casually to the European expeditions (without Marines) after which his attitude improved. He asked me to recommend a good Brig Gen for his Asst CofS.

Friday, August 11 (Saturday, August 12)

After breakfast flew to Guam with same crowd plus Holmes. Landed on old Jap field & went to Hq of new island Comdr, Maj Gen Larsen USMC.[ii] Got a jeep and drove about 25 or 30 mi through blinding dust to CP of 77th Div (MG) Bruce. Chamorros were at large on the island some in trucks & jeeps returning to their ruined homes. Agana was completely destroyed by naval fire. I can see no reason for destroying our own towns when they are not being used by the enemy on defense.

Bruce had his CP well dug in with a bulldozer. His Div. apparently set the pace for the attack and is still fighting isolated groups holed up in caves & hiding in the jungle. He likes the Marines and gets along well with them & their Comdr, Gen Geiger. He told me of finding 46 recently decapitated bodies of Chamorros with their hands tied. He also spoke of Tweed, the white radio operator who had remained in hiding ever since the Japs came and had swum out to meet our expedition. He said his Div needed more patrolling and jungle crossing.

Left for Saipan 4:40 & arrived 6:00 PM. At supper there were further indications of Army-Navy discord. Jarman spoke of Richardson as having

---

i   Vice Admiral John H. Hoover, commander, Central Pacific Forward Areas. His responsibility was to organize American forward bases and oversee air operations, both in support of further Central Pacific offensives.

ii Major General Henry L. Larsen, governor of Guam from August 1944 to May 1946.

rows with H. Smith & Adm Turner. The latter had accused R. of coming into the area without orders or authority (He came to decorate some of his officers).

Jarman thinks Adm Hoover wants publicity at Army expense, that Turner picks rows with the Army and that H. Smith is a vindictive idiot. Greiner says that Smith is a liar not to be believed on oath. Turner says that FJ Fletcher is a SOB—too bad.

Saturday, August 12 (Sunday, August 13)

Accompanied Jarman in a jeep looking over his projects. He expects to be able to berth 9 Liberty ships simultaneously soon. Met Capt Gordon? (former Del. from Hawaii) and Houston? Civil Govt. representative. Rain poured down. Everywhere I was impressed with wanton destruction of useful property. Entire rim of island & Tinian had foxholes & MG. positions with no fortifications behind them except prepared caves. Property was well dispersed. Moving AA guns, searchlights 26" British Armstrong guns had just arrived and the Japs were apparently working feverishly to get them in place. Some of the bunkers for supplies were at least 3yrs old but the shore defenses (foxholes) were apparently new. None of the sand bags had yet rotted.

Note: Send some liquor to Jarman, Colliday and Tenney.

Sunday, August 13 (Monday, August 14)

At 7:15 watched a B-24 group take off to attack the Bonins. We took off at 7:30 AM. Passed over Eniwetok about 1:30 PM and saw an immense fleet of naval fighting ships of all kinds in the atoll.

Read "Garden Islands of the Great East" David Fairchild. Arrived Kwajalein 3:45 (local 4:45 PM.) Heard that 110 Navy fighters had been destroyed by fire at Eniwetok when a P.B.Y.[i] landed among them and the bombs went off.

Met by Tenney (in straw hat) & stayed with him. Soldiers on island have made wind mill washing machines with plank sails, a pipe crank, a dasher and an oil drum. Scores are to be seen fluttering in the constant breeze.

---

i   A PBY Catalina floatplane.

Went to the movies after supper.

At Saipan dug up some bulbs with flowers resembling blue crocus with green contours.

Monday, August 14 (Tuesday, August 15)

Took a walk along the beach before breakfast. Found a live sea urchin with purple spines the size of lead pencils. It had a mouth with 5 jaws each with one tooth. Also found numerous shells inhabited by hermit crabs. If removed from their shells, the crabs appeared most embarrassed by their nakedness and would hastily screw their tails back into their own or other shells if given opportunity.

Met [ ] Dillingham, nephew of Walter D of Honolulu. Col Saffrons of the Oahu jungle school arrived on his way to Guam to study cave warfare. We toured around in a jeep looking over pill boxes and other Jap fortifications which were numerous but ill arranged. Saffrons said that some sailors had tried to dig up a ripe Jap admiral and two captains for souvenirs, but Tenney had stopped them and had them ordered off the island. Took off 7:00 PM.

Tuesday, August 15

Read "The Duke" (Wellington) by [ ] during the night. Flew at about 9,500 ft. Fairly cool. Arrived Honolulu 8:15 (local 10:45 AM) Had to leave my bulbs with plant quarantine people.

Wednesday, August 16

Spent day interviewing staff members regarding composition and needs of my Army. Selected Army device[i]

Met newly arrived staff members for Civil Govt.

Thursday, August 17

Sent for G2 & G3 and directed them to prepare revised combat plan (largely to test them).

Swam at Haliewa & had supper there with Cowart.

Lt Col Bork, 27th Div came in, played ping pong & talked about a fishing trip with Ralph Smith.

---

i   By "Army device" he means the shoulder patch of Tenth Army, which was two red triangles arranged to form the letter X, the Roman numeral for 10.

Friday, August 18

Welcomed more new staff members.

Pitched a game of softball with my staff and took all the hide off of my elbow sliding 3d base.

Saturday, August 19

Dinner with M. [ ] Henshaws 6:45. Took Post & Arnold. The rest were mostly Navy & Marines including Adm Halsey, Gen Vandergrift,[i] Gen H M Smith. Also a Mrs Claridge from New Zealand and some local civilians including the Phlengers, the Henshaw's daughters, Mrs. [ ]

Sunday, August 20

12:30 PM—Lunch at Club with Hodge. This was attended by a group of visiting firemen from Washington among whom were Gen Hull (OPD) Gen Giles (AF) Gen Bissell (AF).[ii]

Monday, August 21

5:30 PM—Dinner at Officers Club—Jim Bradley.[iii]

12:15 PM—Lunch with Richardson at Shafter.

Much the same crowd as yesterday's luncheon. Gen Hull said he would try to help me get Ambassador Grew for my civil governor.[iv]

Tuesday, August 22

Ralph Smith dropped in. It appears that Gen Marshall has decided to send him to France to relieve situation here. Saw Holland Smith at Adm Nimitz conference and he greeted me without much enthusiasm. (He has probably seen my board report to the effect that Ralph Smith's relief from command was not justified)

---

i   General Alexander A. Vandegrift, commandant of the Marine Corps. He earned the Medal of Honor for his leadership of the 1st Marine Division on Guadalcanal.

ii Major General Barney K. Giles, chief of staff for U.S. Army Air Forces; Major General Clayton L. Bissell, assistant chief of staff for intelligence (G-2), U.S. Army. OPD is shorthand for the Operations and Plans Division.

iii Major General James L. Bradley, commanding 96th Infantry Division.

iv Joseph C. Grew had been U.S. ambassador to Japan from 1932 to 1941, and was repatriated in 1942. A noted Far East expert, he was desirable for dealing with the complexities of occupying parts of Formosa and China. The appointment never came to pass, as other events intervened.

Wednesday, August 23

Targeted in my carbine and sniper's Springfield at 200 yd. Both shoot well.

Thursday, August 24

Hollowed out some carbine bullets 3/16" across 3/16" deep. They expanded well on laundry soap. (Later found that they did not expand on sheep.)

Friday, August 25

At morning meeting at Adm Nimitz office, RAdm [ ] gave interesting talk of 1 ½ hrs on Normandy landing. He was CofS of landing fleet.[i]

12:40 PM left in Loadstar (pilot (B.G.) Moore AC, copilot Col Steele)[ii] with Dr Frank & Lt Comdr Eisler, the former host, the latter an archer. Flew along N.E. coast of Hawaii seeing cataracts, tropical jungle green cane fields & well kept sugar village. Landed at Hilo about 2:00 PM. Col. Muller, C.A. Dist. Comdr[iii] gave us a car & we drove across middle of island over lava flows (delta) and arrived at Wai …[iv] on Parker Ranch at 4:00 PM. Called on ranch mgr. Mr. Carter.

Spent night at Hotel, now converted into an officer's club & mess with rooms.

The [ ] Marine Div commanded by Maj Gen Rockey[v] is moving in to its training center there. Dr Frank says that all the Kanaka ranch girls, about 300, are pregnant to the Marines which he thinks will improve the quality of the next generation of ranch hands.

Saturday, August 26

Maj [ ] comdg local hospital gave us a command car and a Chinese Kanaka. Henry Ah Fong from the ranch joined us at 6:00 AM and we went up Mauna Kea about 7,000 feet. Saw fine Herefords, pigs & horses.

---

i   Buckner is referring to Rear Admiral Arthur D. Struble, on his way to the Southwest Pacific to take up an amphibious command in Seventh Fleet.
ii   Brigadier General Ernest Moore, commanding VII Fighter Command.
iii Coast Artillery District.
iv   Waimea, on the north side of the Big Island of Hawaii.
v   Buckner is referring to the 5th Marine Division, commanded by Major General Keller E. Rockey.

There are 35,000 of the Herefords and ½ million acres in the ranch. On way up we saw pheasants, valley quail, Japanese quail, doves, plover and wild pigeons in great numbers.

Held fire on our first sheep herd trying to let [ ] use his bow, but he missed. Frank missed 3 shots with 250/300 rifle. I did not fire (looking for goose hied). Frank missed 2d flock & changed to Springfield with peep sights which he liked better than savage open sights. On next batch, four went down, I hit one in the head with carbine, Frank got 2 with Springfield & our driver (soldier) got one with 250–3000. Saw another bunch & let [ ] go alone after them. He got one with an arrow. Frank & I went after another group. I got one about 75 yds. Shot 5 times and hit home 4 (2 running). All vital shots but none knocked him off his feet. Bullets did not expand. Frank missed. Frank & I returned to car & I got Springfield with service bullets. Saw 3 more sheep, stalked them & he got 2 and I one with one shot at each. Died in their tracks. The carbine is no gun for game with present service ammunition. No shock. Dragged out sheep, and got back to club about 3:30 PM, leaving most in cold storage.

Had supper at Carters. His sister & Mr & Mrs Fuller also there. Fuller former Pres. Of Bank of Hawaii.

Parts of ranch where we hunted resembled Montana.

Sunday, August 27

Left 8:00 AM and drove via Kilauea crater & coffee plantation to Hilo. Bought palm mats for Adele. Had 12:30 lunch with Col Muller & took off for Hickam Field at 2:40, arriving about 3:35. Put mutton away in cold storage plant.

Monday, August 28

Saw VAdm Turner & RA Hill[i] at conference. Turner coming out to my Hq. Wed and having lunch with me.

Tuesday, August 29

Mentioned to Adm McMorris the desirability of using some of the mainland Marines for island missions. He appeared to be against it but offered no good reasons.

---

i   Rear Admiral Harry W. Hill, commander of a group in Turner's Fifth Amphibious Force.

Wednesday, August 30

VAdm. Turner & some of his staff came out to my Hq. The former gave a talk to our staff & all remained for lunch. Had all their staff there.

Thursday, August 31

Harmon showed me letter re: additional air units. I concurred.

Started sleeping in hammock in my back yard. Supporting strings too weak. Broke on entrance side. Replaced them with Venetian blind cord which worked well, after which the hammock was comfortable. Later found it shed rain well.

Friday, September 1

A few fire trees, shower trees and African tulips still in bloom but going out.

6:00 PM—Dinner with Dr Frank. Bring Westervelt

Met Mrs. Byrnes (Twin) & Mrs. McCauley (Ky & Jax)

Saturday, September 2

Had conference with Adm Nimitz, VAdm Spruance, VAdm Turner & others re: my coming project. Spruance expressed doubt as to advisability of project and suggested a smaller island. Adm Nimitz said that unless our project went through we would be tied to a southern project that would make the war last another year.[i]

Sunday, September 3

Addressed 200 newly arrived staff officers 9:00 AM.

Went to chapel.

Called in evening on Judge Yates & Henshaws—both out.

Monday, September 4

3:00 PM. Flew to Maui to observe landing exercises of 94th [sic—96th] Div (Bradley). Took about an hour, passing Molokai. Met by Zimmerman with whom we stayed. 20 staff officers came along with me. Drove around island with Zimmerman until supper. After supper went to see Robert ("Boy") Von Tempski who gave us some Portuguese Silva's brandy.[ii]

---

i   This is a reference to General MacArthur's desire to liberate the Philippines.

ii   Robert von Tempsky was a prominent rancher on Maui.

Richardson's order assigning me officially to Army published today (at last).

Tuesday, September 5

Arose 4:30 AM & drove to shore where we got in landing boats and watched different stages of landing from water side and then landed and observed it from land side. Water part was better than beachmaster and shore party work. Alligator maintenance was poor. Drivers not well trained.

Returned to Schofield in afternoon, flying over leper colony of Molokai.

Sent in letter asking for Jarman to handle ports & supplies from shore to army. Later to command rear areas.

4:00 PM–6:00—Cocktails at Ft Kamehameha with Woodruff. (Got back from Maui too late.)[i]

Wednesday, September 6

R. Adm Hill, (in chg. landing operations for Turner) called with [ ] in the morning at my office.

4:45 PM. Housewarming of N.A.T.S. Terminal Bldg.[ii] Had aquacade, inspection of post, cocktails, dinner, speech & show at theatre.

Sat between Adm Ghormley & Mrs. Dillingham.

Thursday, September 7

Sherman got back from Washington with no assurance of an early decision regarding my project. Target date now set at 2 weeks later than first planned.

Had "Personal Appearance" troupe in for refreshments after their show. Post Comdr, Post Exec and some staff members, including 2 Marines present. 9–12 PM—Hors d'ouvres, sandwiches & 3 qts.

Girls included:

Mrs Sweet—St Hortense

Dorothy Fay—in charge of party. Played mother part.

---

i   Major General Roscoe B. Woodruff, commanding part of the Hawaiian islands garrison.

ii Naval Air Transport Service Terminal Building.

Martha Shaw—Old Aunt part
Eloise Hardt—
Nancy Lee Worth
Jane Flynn—Carole Arden, movie star.

Friday, September 8

Gen MacArthur sent message to Richardson protesting Dumas' assignment to my staff and insisting that latter be released to him.[i]

Saturday, September 9

Post & Schleiker arrived at 1:00 AM (Sun) with the two girls they had taken to the dance and who couldn't get sleeping rooms at the Turret Club nor go home due to the curfew.

They were in a hilarious mood, pulled me out of the hammock and insisted that I come to the house, have a drink and watch them dance the hula. In due time I returned to my hammock and the girls slept in the spare room as I discovered next morning when I came in to dress at 7:30 and found my bunk gone. Post had apparently put them together as a protection to himself and Cowart.

Sunday, September 10

Waves rather high at Haliewa. One officer had to be rescued by the lifeguard on a surf board.

Called with Post on Wightmans in the evening.

Monday, September 11

11:00 AM—Woodruff to come to army for combat.

1:15 PM—Had meeting organizing Army Hqrs. mess

2:00 AM Bruce talked to staff on Guam expedition where he commanded 77th Div.

6:30 PM—Gen Arnold. Dinner at officer's club.

Tuesday, September 12

1:00 PM—Lunch with Adm. Nimitz at his house. Dinner given in honor of the Army & Navy boards here to investigate the Pearl Harbor

---

i   Brigadier General Walter A. Dumas, who served as Tenth Army's assistant chief of staff for operations (G-3) until the end of the war.

unpreparedness. (Investigation started just before elections evidently to embarrass the President.)[i]

Present at luncheon were British Fleet Admiral Keys,[ii] 4 full Admirals, about five VAdms & 3 Lt Gens. A bomb in our midst would have done a lot for promotion.

Wednesday, September 13

After morning naval conference Adm. Nimitz spoke to me about the Ralph Smith incident & my board report, regretting that Richardson had sent a copy to Washington to Gen Marshall. He wanted it all cleared up here. I agreed with him and called his attention to personalities involved and assured him that no inter service feeling existed in my army. I also mentioned (later) the impropriety of my writing a personal letter to Gen Marshall, thus short-circuiting Richardson. Adm. Nimitz agreed but hoped that Gen Marshall would make it appropriate by bringing up the subject himself.

6:30—Dinner Ft Shafter Qrs #4—in honor of Army Pearl Harbor Board.

Thursday, September 14

8:15 AM—Joined Adm Nimitz at his Hq and boarded new carrier *Hancock* with 880 ft deck, 32K speed & over 90 planes: Fighter, dive bomber and torpedo. 4 destroyers escorted us out of Pearl Hbr. Had AA firing at drones, and rocket firing from planes at towed spar. All planes landed on deck in about 50 minutes and took off in about 30. Fleet Adm Keyes was aboard, now about 71. At 59 he played on a polo team & won a coveted trophy for 2 years straight. He is on his way to Australia.

We returned at 6:00 PM. A number of local civilians were aboard including: 2 Dillinghams, 2 Castles, Allen, Spalding, Thurston.

---

i   Congress directed this joint investigation in June 1944. The Army Board was led by Lieutenant General George Grunert. It reported back in October, but its findings were not made public. A wider public investigation started after the war, and ended in 1946.

ii   Fleet Admiral Baron Roger Keyes, passing through on a goodwill tour through Canada to Australia and New Zealand. He was famous for his roles in World War I and in the early stages of World War II as liaison to the Belgian government and later director of combined operations.

Get–together reception & dance for staff 6–9:00 PM. I took the head nurse (Maj) Gill. Party a great success due to Chap. Hillyer's preparations. We had a representative group of girls and a Samoan hula floor show. The 2 Gowen girls dropped in the house for a short time after the party which ended at 10:00 PM.

During this time, Admiral Halsey's Third Fleet launched airstrikes on Formosa and the Philippines, encountering less resistance than expected. He recommended speeding up the Pacific timetable of advance. After deliberations, the Joint Chiefs of Staff ordered MacArthur's forces to land at Leyte on October 20 and Luzon on December 20, although the latter date slipped to January 9, 1945. The capture of Peleliu and Angaur by Geiger's III Amphibious Corps would occur as planned on September 15, but XXIV Corps' operation against Yap was dropped and that corps assigned to MacArthur for the Leyte landing.

In light of these decisions, Nimitz reconsidered the necessity for Operation Causeway, and asked Richardson, Harmon, and Buckner for their opinions.

Friday, September 15
8:10 AM. Archie Arnold dropped in to say good-bye. I also said goodbye to Bradley at the naval conference.

6:15 PM. Dinner at Adm. Ghormley's. Sat between Mrs Erdman, who said she would arrange for a pheasant hunt on Hawaii and Lady Keyes who plays polo, grows a distinct moustache and has children—unusual combination. Met (BG) Waller USMC there.[i] Also Mrs Van Haf, who says she will invite me to Sunday dinner and swimming sometime. Evening marred by 16mm tragedy after dinner instead of conversation.

Saturday, September 16
10:00 AM—Dedication of Dive Master School.

Sunday, September 17
Took a walk in mountains north of Koli Koli Pass. Guavas ripe.

---

i Brigadier General Littleton W.T. Waller, Jr., commanding Marine forces in the 14th Naval District.

Monday, September 18

10:00 AM. Dedication of Base Command Ord. Motor School. Maj Wine, Comdt of School presided. Burgin[i] made speech, I was shown around by Lt Peterson who did exceedingly well in discussing instruction. He showed me an experimental engine that, after starting, would run with spark plugs disconnected. Worked on a sort of hang fire principle.

6:00 PM—Dinner at Wightmans [ ] Cookes and Post there only.

Tuesday, September 19

12:30 PM—Lunch at Richardsons in honor or Asst Secy of Navy Mr Gates.[ii]

Had a long climb in the mountains before supper.

Rained off and on during night. I enjoyed hearing showers on top of my jungle hammock cover. Have now been sleeping out in my hammock nearly a month and find it very comfortable. The little doves wake me every morning by their loud chatter in the trees nearby.

"Two'—tit-tit-tit-toot'-toot'-."

Wednesday, September 20

Staff went down to present my plan to Adm Turner's staff.

Red Cross director called.

Got directive regarding possible changes in plan due to new situation. Possible speeding up and more of a swing toward my original idea.

Pitched 7-inning softball game against young "Freebooters" team. Won 11–2.

Thursday, September 21

A real thunderstorm 3–4 PM. First I have noticed here. I am told that lightning is unusual here.

Called with Post after supper on Gov. Stainback.

Friday, September 22

At morning naval conference, got first detailed reports of Adm Halsey's strike on Manila. His message wound up, "Nothing left on screen but Hedy Lamar."

---

i   Major General Henry T. Burgin, commanding Pacific Base Command.
ii   Artemus L. Gates, assistant secretary of the Navy for Air.

Called in evening on Miss Myrtle Polson who says that her father was related to and resembled me. Later called on Mrs Keleher where I ran into a large group of young Navy and Marine officers.

Saturday, September 23

At morning meeting in his office, Adm. Nimitz deplored Army–Navy squabbles and showed that he was trying to end them. He read an Army observers report that went improperly into the Army–Marine controversy and told Richardson that such reports should not be circulated since they tend to foster antagonism.

Possible changes in Army plan were indicated as the result of MacArthurs movements.

6:30 PM—Dinner, Alexander Walker, 2616 Nuuanu.

Sunday, September 24

Adm. Halsey's report on the Philippine carrier strike recd in Adm. Nimitz office. Successful beyond our highest expectations. He reports Jap air power in Philippines as "Hollow shell operated on a shoestring."

Adm. Nimitz wants my concise recommendations by Tuesday to give to Adm King.

Monday, September 25

Had staff conference in morning and made decisions regarding paper for Adm Nimitz.

In afternoon attended Little World Series baseball game N-4, A-3. 12 innings.

Tuesday, September 26

(No entry)

On this day General Buckner rendered his opinion on Operation Causeway, adding some details in a follow-up note on October 4. Like Harmon and Richardson, Buckner expressed reservations about the plan. While echoing others' thoughts about geography and the relative merits of the islands, Buckner also noted that there were insufficient service and support troops in the Central Pacific to meet Causeway's requirements. Either troops needed to come from Europe, or the invasion would have to wait for several months, not being feasible much before March 1, 1945.

A few days later Admirals Nimitz and Spruance flew to San Francisco to discuss Causeway *with Admiral King.*

Wednesday, September 27

Climbed to peak above Koli-Koli Pass. 52 minutes from road to top. Could see the ocean on three sides of the island. Beautiful view.

Thursday, September 28

Saw G-3 regarding training directive and gave him my general ideas and some notes.

Pitched softball game against Engr section. Won 9–5.

6:15 PM—Dinner, Alfred T. Castle, 2550 Nuuanu.

Friday, September 29

3:00 PM—Talked to staff on physical fitness.

Took 2-hour walk on Firebreak Trail.

Roused 2:30 AM (30) by air alert and went to office. Alert caused by return of one of our planes with defective radio and unable to identify itself.

Saturday, September 30

Called on Gen Wells in evening.[i]

Sunday, October 1

Attended morning conference at Ft Shafter.

Climbed across ridge north of Koli Koli Pass. Took some pictures. Altitude 2,000 ft.

Joined a party at Nolds house which developed into supper followed by ping pong.

Monday, October 2

6:15 PM—Dinner with Col Daniels at Club for (BG) Hatcher.[ii] A "galaxy" of Red Cross girls and nurses helped the dance.

---

i   Major General Briant H. Wells (U.S. Army Retired), the recently-retired executive vice president of the Hawaiian Sugar Planters Association and prominent member of the Honolulu Chapter of the Red Cross.

ii Brigadier General Julian S. Hatcher, chief of ordnance field service.

Tuesday, October 3

Adm Nimitz got back after his S.F. conference with Adm. King. Looks like our present plan will be changed or deferred for lack of available service troops.

Pitched softball game against [ ]

We won 17–5.

Wednesday, October 4

Directive received deferring our project.

Took physical exam. Blood pressure 120–76. Dr said he could find nothing wrong except danger from Japs.

The directive, made public the next day, shifted the Central Pacific Area's objectives. The three Marine divisions of Holland Smith's V Amphibious Corps would conduct Operation Detachment and attack Iwo Jima on January 20. On March 1, Tenth Army with XXIV and III Amphibious Corps plus attachments, would execute Operation Iceberg to capture Okinawa and surrounding islands. Admiral Turner's amphibious force would support both invasions.

Delays in preparations meant that Detachment started February 19, 1945, and Iceberg April 1, 1945. From this point onwards, Buckner started referring to Iceberg as "my project" in the diary.

Thursday, October 5

6:00 PM—Party (dinner) at club preceded and followed by drinks at my house for Richardson, V.Adm. Towers & all heads of my staff not heretofore entertained. Also McCunniff & Blount.

Friday, October 6

Pitched softball game against Ordnance team—Won.

7:30. Attended Betty Hutton's USO show at stadium. The juggler, [ ] Sitz was the best I have ever seen.

After the show went to DuPree's house where he had a party for the cast. Betty is less rough off the stage than on but still not very smooth.

Saturday, October 7

Adm. Nimitz, after sounding out my attitude on the Smith vs Smith controversy and finding that I deplored the whole matter and harbored no inter-service ill feeling, announced that I would command the new joint project.

Had a good walk in the mountains.

5:30 PM. Dinner at Turret Club with Col Smith Post got girls by assignment and had to take them home to Waikiki. (Mrs Wells and [ ]

Sunday, October 8

Conferred with Adm Turner. He has funds for employing Okinawans. Also will take our staff out on his command ship. Wants my views on our project.

Had a good swim at Haliewa.

Monday, October 9

3:30 PM—Softball batting practice.

5:30 " Dinner, Mrs Keleher, Halikulani Hotel.

Tuesday, October 10

Shafter team postponed our game with them until Thursday.

We played the AAA team and lost 2–3 after playing an extra inning.

Wednesday, October 11

Got authority from Adm Nimitz to organize separate island commander and staff.

Walked from Koli Koli Pass road to peak in 55 minutes—1,400 ft climb.

Thursday, October 12

Played softball at Shafter against Richardson's Hqrs. 3 Gen Officers our team & 2 on theirs. Ruffner[i] & I pitched. Game went 10 innings. We won 5 to 3.

Friday, October 13

Dinner with McCunniff at Outrigger Club preceded by drinks at the Goods. I took Mrs Keleher. Beautiful sunset and good Hawaiian music.

Saturday, October 14

Took off from Hickam Fld with Frank[ii] piloted by Maj Sutterlin (Ky)[iii] and arrived Homestead Fld Molokai 25 min later. The three

---

i   Brigadier General Clark L. Ruffner, Richardson's chief of staff.

ii Dr. Frank, Buckner's hunting partner on the trip to the Parker Ranch.

iii Kentucky was the major's home state.

of us drove by car to top of cliff above leper colony[i] where we were met by horses and pack mules and a Kanaka[ii] horse wrangler, Moki. We rode down zig-zag path 1,500' cut in face of cliff. Stayed in guest house with mgr. of colony, Mr. Waddroup. Two nurses there also, Miss Miller from Bellbuckle, Ark and Miss L [ ] who said she was French and looked East Indian. Had drinks before supper after driving all around colony with Waddroup. About 350 lepers, 60% Kanakas. Mostly with the skin form of the disease. They live very well and many have cars. 29 pronounced cured, can leave but don't want to. Many lepers recover without treatment. The disease is now on the decline here. One man came to the colony with his leprous wife. He had, in all, seven leprous wives without becoming infected. Frank says that Father Damien was a dirty squaw man that didn't mind living with leprous women. He regards him as a much over-rated saint.[iii]

Sunday, October 15

At about 8:00 AM drove in truck along base of cliff to water tanks where we saw over a dozen goats on upper edge of talus. Sutterlin, Moki and I struggled through ¼ mile of lantana and got within about 200 yds of goats which began moving. We opened up at that range. My first shot downed a medium black and white and my second a black and tan. I was not sure of the second but he stopped running and disappeared behind a rock. Sutterlin missed his first shot and began shooting at one that ran off to the left. It fell after several shots and both of us started shooting at a black billy that fell after about three shots from each of us. He probably hit it since it did not drop promptly after my shot and I had soft nose Springfield ammunition and he had service bullets. It later showed a clean hole. I then loaded with service ammunition and we each fired about two clips at another goat that ran to the right. It was hit and lay down or was knocked down several times finally falling for good over 350 yds away. Moki, who was not armed, came up and

---

i   Kalaupapa, closed in 1969 and now part of Kalaupapa National Historical Park.

ii   Native Hawaiian.

iii   The Belgian Jozef de Veuster, or Father Damien of Molokai, a famous Catholic priest who worked at the colony and nearby Kalawao from 1873 until his death from leprosy in April 1889. In 2009 he was formally canonized as a saint.

pushed my big billy which then rolled a hundred yards. It had over 26" spread of horns. Sutterlin's had unusual horns that almost touched for the first 10" before spreading. While I was dressing out my head we each missed a shot on the skyline at over 500 yds. Frank, from below, said that he hit one at 800 yds, My 220gr Peters belted bullet made an exit hole that the goat's entrails came out of.

We went out to the "first valley" and saw Father Damien's deserted churchyard colony.[i] We saw some goats (?) across the valley but too far to shoot or climb. While we were there, two life rafts floated ashore (presumably from the *Antigua*).[ii]

At 2:00 PM we finished lunch at the settlement and started back up the trail mounted. Joined by 3 women and a man. The horses automatically stopped at the halfway point for rest. (Moki charges $4.00 for a trip). A car driven by Sgt Moore (Wis)[iii] met us at the top and took us to the plane and we returned to Oahu, where I worked nearly 2 hrs skimming and fleshing the skull and scalp.

Monday, October 16

12:30 PM—Lunch with Richardson for Sir Philip Mitchell, Gov of Fiji on his way to be Gov of Kenya Colony for about 5 yrs. He invited me to visit him and guaranteed elephant, lion, buffalo and rhino shots.

6:00 PM. Had Adm. Nimitz, Holland Smith, Harmon and a number of Honolulu civilians for dinner at the club: The Wightmans, W. Dillinghams, Alex Walkers, Broadwells, Mrs Erdman, Mrs Keleher etc. Also Charley Ryder and the Franks.

Tuesday, October 17

First good rain since I have been here. Some of the young African tulips still in bloom. The old ones and practically all of the flame trees have stopped blooming. The hybiscus is still blooming but less profusely than 2 mos. ago. The bougainvillea is still in full bloom but had less leaves to be seen a month ago, when it was at its best. Some yellow shower trees still blooming. Ginger & bird of paradise still blooming.

---

i   Kalawao, closed in the early 20th century and combined with Kalaupapa.
ii The transport SS *Antigua* ran aground nearby on October 14, 1944. She was successfully re-floated and returned to duty.
iii The sergeant's home state is Wisconsin.

6:45 PM—Dinner at Ft. DeRussy with Ruffner. Sat next to Mrs Castle & Mrs Ward. Dance party.

Wednesday, October 18
(No entry)

Thursday, October 19
Walked from road to top of Mt. above Koli Koli Pass in 41 minutes.

7:00 PM. Dinner with Herman V. Von Holt. 900 Alewa Drive. Had Hawaiian dance orchestra from the Outrigger Club. Mostly high ranking naval & marine officers there: Adm Nimitz etc. Had Okulihao[i] old fashions.

Friday, October 20
(No entry)

On this day, General MacArthur's forces invaded Leyte. Among the troops landing under General Walter Krueger's Sixth Army was Hodge's XXIV Corps with 7th and 96th Infantry Divisions, both earmarked for Iceberg *once the fighting in Leyte concluded. Within three days, the Americans had a sizeable beachhead and restored the Philippine Commonwealth government in its temporary capital of Tacloban.*

The Japanese sent the bulk of their fleet to stop the invasion. As a carrier force under Admiral Ozawa Jisaburo came from the north to try and lure Halsey's carriers away from the beachhead and Leyte Gulf, surface forces under Vice Admirals Kurita Takeo and Nishimura Shoji moved to converge on the beachhead from north and south, respectively. After two days of air and submarine attacks on October 23 and 24, Halsey headed north to smash Ozawa's force, but left San Bernardino Strait, Leyte Gulf's northern entrance, unguarded.

When Halsey announced his intentions, his message was written in such a way that Vice Admiral Thomas Kinkaid believed San Bernardino Strait was guarded by part of Halsey's fleet. Kinkaid's Seventh Fleet ships, in Leyte Gulf protecting the invasion fleet, turned on Nishimura's force at Surigao Strait, the southern entrance to Leyte Gulf. In the early hours of October 25 the Americans sank every one of Nishimura's ships except a destroyer. Meanwhile, Kurita had come through San Bernardino Strait, surprising a force of light carriers and escort

---

i   Okolehao, a Hawaiian spirit.

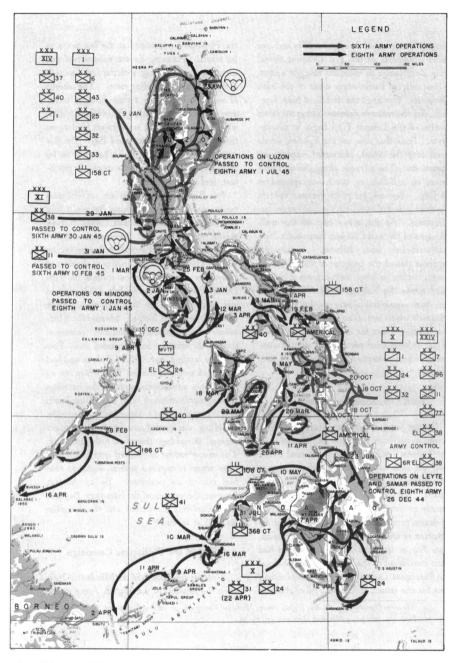

The Philippine liberation campaigns, 1944–45. Leyte and Leyte Gulf are covered by arrows dated October 18 and 20. Note the presence of XXIV Corps and 7th, 77th, and 96th Infantry Divisions, all units earmarked for Tenth Army on Okinawa. *U.S. Army*

ships. The Americans fought back tenaciously over three hours against very high odds. In the confusion, Kurita failed to realize his advantage, and broke off the action before retiring the way he had come. Capping the day's action, Halsey's planes sank all four of Ozawa's carriers before turning back in a vain attempt to stop Kurita's retreat.

The battle of Leyte Gulf was the largest and bloodiest naval battle in history, and the last time battleships fought each other. It ended in a major U.S. victory, and crippled the Japanese Navy for the rest of the war. Halsey's decisions at the battle have been controversial ever since.

Saturday, October 21

Took Maj Fletcher over skyline walk in 1 ½ hours. He was pretty badly blown when he got to the top, where I had to wait a while for him.

Sunday, October 22

With staff shot carbine on range. Mine shoots about true at 100 yds with normal sight. At 200 yds had to use wind sight and aim at bottom of target.

2:00 PM—Went to luau beyond the Pale with the Franks.

Monday, October 23

Staff presented first study of new plan. Col Shaw made splendid presentation.

Took 10 staff members over skyline walk. Went slowly and had to wait for them. Took two hours and even then 2 fell out and had to turn back before going half way up.—My staff need hardening up.

This staff study, which Nimitz's headquarters issued to all commands on October 25, became the basis for planning Operation Iceberg. It would be updated throughout the next two months as more information became available, and underpinned Tenth Army's tentative plan for the invasion.

Iceberg's objectives were in the Ryukyu Islands, deep in Japanese territory and the closest to Japan's home islands yet attempted. Okinawa and its surrounding islands were 350 miles from Kyushu, southernmost of the home islands—well within range for Japanese land-based planes. It was about the same distance to Japanese bases in Shanghai and 500 miles to Japanese airfields in Formosa. The nearest American bases, by contrast, were 900 miles away in Leyte or

1,200 miles away in the Palaus and the Marianas. Honolulu and Pearl Harbor were 4,100 miles to the east of Okinawa, with San Francisco another 2,100 miles beyond that.

The Ryukyus formed a Prefecture of Japan, with representation in the Japanese Diet. Okinawa's Shuri Castle had been the seat of the independent Ryukyu Kingdom, and was visited by Commodore Matthew Perry's squadron in 1853. Japan had ruled Okinawa and the Ryukyus since 1879, although the Japanese treated the Okinawans as second-class citizens.

Okinawa was the largest and most populated island in the Ryukyu chain. It stretched 60 miles on a roughly north to south axis, varying in width from two miles to 18. The terrain was flat in places, especially in the island's middle, but mostly it was rolling and frequently wooded. Most of the island's 400,000 residents lived in the southern third, which included Okinawa's two largest cities, Naha and Shuri. Existing and potential airfield sites dotted the middle and southern part of the island.

Iceberg contemplated a three-phase conquest of Okinawa and the surrounding areas. First, Buckner's forces would secure southern Okinawa in Phase I, followed by the island's northern third and nearby Ie Shima in Phase II. Phase III would follow, subdivided into IIIa through IIId, and envisioned capturing more islands further north using troops from Tenth Army and the V Amphibious Corps. After completing each phase, the captured territory would be developed as a base for future operations. The goal was to accommodate an air force of 650 planes, plus anchorages for shipping needed to support an invasion of the Japanese home islands. All of these objectives were expected to be completed within 120 days.

Island government and development would fall under an Island Command (abbreviated Iscom). Iceberg would also have its own land-based air force based around the 2nd Marine Aircraft Wing, known as Tactical Air Force (TAF). Both Iscom and TAF fell under Tenth Army, giving General Buckner a broader scope of responsibilities than any previous Pacific army commander.

The study also called for Spruance's Fifth Fleet to support all operations by providing air cover, shore bombardment in support of ground troops, and carrier air strikes on Japanese bases in the home islands.

Tuesday, October 24

First news of naval battle in Philippines arrives. Situation still not clear.

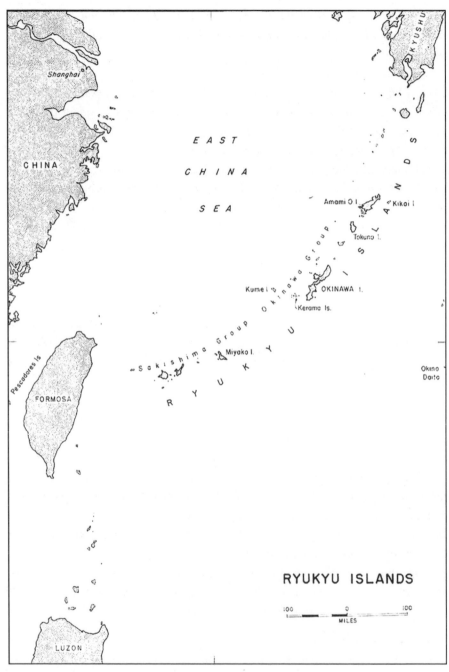

The Ryukyu Islands. *U.S. Army*

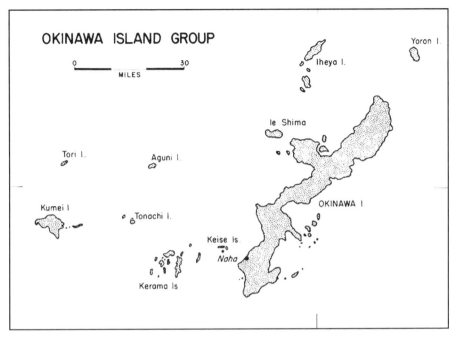

Okinawa and surrounding islands. *U.S. Army*

In afternoon flew to Kauai to see tank test in rice paddies. Stayed with Harvey and Zimmerman of [ ] Div.[i] Took about an hour to fly over. Kauai is called the "garden island." Peculiar air currents cause an annual rainfall on part of the island of 640 inches, while other parts of the island are dry enough for mesquite and cactus.

Schick, Cowart and I lived with Harvey in the plantation house. We had drinks before dinner and movies afterwards.

Wednesday, October 25
Saw the tank demonstration in the morning, at lunch and then drove.[ii]

Thursday, October 26
Philippine situation still not entirely clear except that Japs got the worst of it. We also suffered but they withdrew with many cripples that we may still get.

---

i   Major General Arthur M. Harper and Brigadier General Wayne C. Zimmerman, the commander and assistant commander respectively of the 98th Infantry Division.

ii Incomplete entry. He returned to Oahu during the day.

Got my new pointer bitch from Frank.

Played IX Corps softball team. Beaten 10 to 0.

Went to stag dinner at Burgin's house, (the Fagan house) on Diamond Head—a beautifully developed place on the sea. Jack Colliday turned up there from Saipan.

The dog kept me awake most of the night eating up slippers etc and playing with my wrist watch.

Friday, October 27

2:00 PM. With Cowart, went through the obstacle course in 49 minutes. Post informed me that many staff members are unable to get more than half through the course—poor condition.

Dinner 6:30 PM with (Priscilla) Ward [ ] Mocla St

Met Dr & Mrs Judd.

Saturday, October 28

Deer hunt with Frank called off.

Staff made final presentation of plan to me.

Final score of Philippine sea fight shows a badly crippled and defeated Jap navy but not a destroyed navy.

Sunday, October 29

Frank came out in morning to target in his scope (Noske). Later we went into Koli Koli Pass to take pictures to illustrate his article on our Hawaii hunt. We used his mounted ram head to pose with. Also his goat.

Swam in evening at Haliewa and learned to "body surf," coming in on the front of waves without a board.

The dog kept me awake off and on throughout the night.

Monday, October 30

6:00 PM—Dinner, Mrs Keleher. Take Mrs John Macauley, 746 Ferdinand St. Tel 97414. (Near 2900 block of Upper Moana Valley Rd). Pick her up 5:45 PM—Met Mr. Ewing there (news commentator) and his wife. Found that Mrs. Macauley is Gen Helmick's daughter. Saw the latter & Mrs Helmick at the house.[i]

---

i   Major General Eli A. Helmick and his wife Elizabeth. Helmick commanded the 8th Division in World War I, and retired in 1927 as inspector general of the Army.

The dog chewed up my slippers and got a good start on my hat. Also kept me awake in other ingenious ways.

Tuesday, October 31

Played softball against Engineer team. We played worse than ever before but won 10–9.

Wednesday, November 1

Adm. Mitcher[i] Attended morning naval prayer meeting and told Adm. Nimitz that he believed Adm. Halsey was unduly optimistic in his report of enemy vessels sunk.

Adm. Spruance told me that he though [thought] Adm Halsey should never have permitted the Jap fleet to pass through San Barnedino St.

In afternoon took 2 ½ hour walk to top of mountain south of Koli Koli Pass with dog.

10:30 AM—Presented my combat plans to Adm. Turner & Adm Spruance.

Thursday, November 2

10:30 Attended Harmon's and Ruffner's conference on my project & Holland Smith's at Shafter. Had lunch with Harmon at Hickam Field.

Friday, November 3

1:00 PM—Flew to Hilo with Frank, called on base Comdr, Col Miller and got car driven by Pvt. Wyatt and started out Kammela Road along shore for Leighton Hind's ranch, 90 mi away.

Broke down half way but got into a command car and went to officers club at Wanamea Hospl, Lt Col Askins (Ala)[ii] Comdg where we spent night. Wyatt came along later with new car. We telephoned to Hind who said that 8 aviators had just dropped in for the night and that he was a little crowded. He entertains a number every weekend without charge and gives them horses to ride and lets them shoot game, including wild peacocks.

Mauna Loa was smoking and snow covered the top of Mauna Kea.

---

i   Vice Admiral Marc Mitscher, commanding the carrier force. Under Halsey's Third Fleet, it was known as Task Force 38. In Spruance's Fifth Fleet, it was Task Force 58.

ii The officer's home state is Alabama.

Saturday, November 4

7:00 AM. Started for Hind Ranch, 15 mi off, and found horses saddled, 3 big dogs ready and two Kanaka cow punchers to accompany us, one the foreman, Kamaki Lindsay. The ranch has 19,000 acres, 4,000 head of Herefords and 100 horses.

We rode over old lava flows. Saw small crows, rusty looking raspberries and 3 peacocks (wild). Could have gotten at least a dozen pigs but killed only two. Frank shot a large boar with fine tusks as a trophy 200 lbs and Kamaki roped a fat 100 pounder to eat. I passed up several boars that were big but had small to medium tusks.

The dogs did remarkably. They could bring the biggest boar to bay and hold him there by working on his hind legs. Smaller hogs they held by the same. About 1 dog in 10 survives his first year at this. When they had a pig they could be called off without dismounting. While alone I followed one dog that bayed a 75lb sow too lean to eat. I dismounted a la Ft Benning and tackled her hind legs. The dog then left & joined the others that were roping another pig. When I released mine, it charged me 4 times and I saved my legs by bringing one foot down on her snout as I jerked the other away. Finally I got her by the hind legs again wedged her under a log and got to my horse before she got up.

We returned to the house by 3:00 PM, had a drink with our host and drove back to Wanamea where we called on Mr Carter, Sr, Mgr of the Parker Ranch. His son was away. We joined the medicos in a party and dance after supper and turned in by 9:30. Put pig in ice plant.

Sunday, November 5

8:00 AM. Drove to Hilo by same road we came out. Many large streams & waterfalls. Pandanus palms all along cliffs. African tulips still in full bloom. Arrived Hilo before 11:00. Plane picked us up at about 1:00 and took us back to Hickam Fld. My car met us there. We took the pig to the cold storage plant and Frank went home and I to the office.

Saw "Mrs Skippington" at the movies that night, played by Bette Davis.

Monday, November 6

Speck Wallace[i] arrived as my island Comdr. His oldest son has just been killed in France, so I swung letting him go home to see his family

---

i   Major General Fred C. Wallace.

for two weeks, meanwhile getting him oriented here and in touch with Colladay who has Saipan experience.

Tuesday, November 7

At the morning naval conference three ship Comdrs described their experiences in the recent Philippine naval battle. One said that the escort carrier force was fired on 5 minutes after they first saw the Jap fleet. No radar warning.

In afternoon took entire skyline trail walk in 56 minutes. Reached highest point in 37 minutes. Betsy [dog] was with me.

After supper listened to election returns until Roosevelt's election was assured and conceded by Dewey.[i]

Wednesday, November 8

Went in afternoon to Halikulani Hotel to take picture but wound up by taking shelter from a rain storm at Missy Keleher's cocktail party and took her afterward to dinner at Chinese Restaurant.

Returned to her house after dinner where the hotel mgr, Mr [ ] joined us and loaned me a book on Hawaiian flora.

Thursday, November 9

My observers beginning to get back from Leyte. DeWitt was in this morning.

Had practice softball game in afternoon. Won 6–5.

Friday, November 10

Took a walk in the hills and gathered leaves to take home and identify from my flora book.

Saturday, November 11

Ambassador Grew was at the morning naval conference. Craigie[ii] was also there and wants to command my fighter wing.

Had staff discussion of Adm Turner's first draft of his order. He scattered too much. I prefer greater concentration on the main objective.

6:00—Pig barbecue at Franks'.

---

i   Franklin D. Roosevelt won a fourth term over New York Governor Thomas E. Dewey.

ii Major General Laurence C. Craigie, U.S. Army Air Forces.

Sunday, November 12

Mr Grew discussed Japs at morning conference. Doubts that leaders will admit defeat until army is bested in the homeland.

1:40 PM—Attended Shriners' benefit football game between Rainbows and Helianis. Former won 21–7. Sat next to Adm Furlong and won $1.00 on game. We bet merely for the purpose of being able to root for someone.

Monday, November 13

Mr Grew discussed Chinese situation and Chiang Kai Shek.

Took 8 mi walk with staff representatives on Martin's course. Lost dog and had to leave group and return by same route followed out. Found dog in car on my return after following its tracks several miles.

Tuesday, November 14

Capt. McKenna told of the sinking of the *St. Lo* which he commanded.[i]

3:30 PM—Softball vs AAA. Lost 7–11.

6:45 PM—Met McCunniff at his Hq to see "snooperscope." It has decided possibilities on a larger and more powerful scale.

Wednesday, November 15

12:30 Lunch with Richardson for Amb. Grew. After supper, Comdr O'Keefe formerly at Adak, now exec of *Wisconsin* called.

Thursday, November 16

6:00 PM—Dinner dance at Club by Arty, Sig Cr, OD & QM, Tenth Army (Edwards, Ashton, Pulsifer & Daniels).

Friday, November 17

5:15 PM—Dinner, Mrs Bowen, followed by Hamlet. The latter played very well by Maj Maurice Evans an enlisted cast.

Saturday, November 18

Walked in the hills before supper. Printed pictures 6:30–11:00 PM, mostly for Franks article on our hunting trip.

Sunday, November 19

After returning from naval conference, watched preparations for Club luau. Pigs being stuffed with hot rocks and buried in fire pits.

---

i   The aircraft carrier *St. Lo* was sunk October 25, 1944.

Capt Dillon (Ala) naval air base Comdr, reported. Luau, preceded by drinks at Nold's, continued until about ten. Very good hula dancing. About 3,000 attended.

Monday, November 20
Naval officers from escort carrier force in Leyte battle described fight during morning naval conference.

Took colored pictures of Halikulani hybiscus. Some unusual and exceptional specimens. Had cocktails with Mrs [ ] who loaned me some interesting horticultural books on Hawaiian flora.

Took Missy Keleher, who helped me with photographs, to dinner at Chinese restaurant.

Missy wangled a photo of myself and asked me to autograph it with an appropriate message. I did "To Missy with misgivings."

Tuesday, November 21
Capt Orr came through from Leyte. On way home to get married. Completed skyline hike in 47 minutes.

Wednesday, November 22
Maj Gen Mulcahy, USMC reported for duty. Wants Carr for CofS.[i]

Thursday, November 23
11:30 AM Made Thanksgiving address to command. Ate two Thanksgiving dinners with a 9-mile walk in between. In evening went to Shafter with Pulsifer to attend Powell's weekly Sig Cr meeting had movies and discussions after dinner. Lt Col Munsen showed his movies for troops occupying Germany. I was called on for a speech—told "Orator" story. Got home 12:30 and was kept awake by the dog, Betsy. She also got lost during my afternoon walk and tried twice to get into the town bus.

Friday, November 24
Saw Harmon and Hale Re Carr. Also discussed staff echeloning with Turner.

---

i   Major General Francis P. Mulcahy, who would command the Tactical Air Force in support of Tenth Army. He requested Brigadier General Lawrence J. Carr of Seventh Air Force to join his staff.

Saturday, November 25

12:45 PM—Flew to Molokai with Frank and Mr Lenox, head of Forest Reserve in the Hawaiian. Drove to Kaunakakai (domain of the cock-eyed mayor of K). Met there by a Portuguese ranger named Flavius Peter with 4 saddled horses and a pack horse. We climbed for 3 ½ hours up a steep trail to a little rangers cabin on top at about 3,500 ft. On the way up near the head of a canyon we saw some goats. Lenox and I opened up with the Springfields at from 500 to 700 yds at the goats which were running. We had to chase them. I had good luck and killed 4 in 9 shots. (Sniper's rifle, 180 gr Peters belted ammunition). Lenox's 1918 ammunition mostly misfired, I gave him some of mine. He killed 1. Frank was on higher ground and got no shots. We were thinning out goats to prevent over-grazing and erosion, already very bad.

Picketed one exhausted pony ½ hr from top.

After unsaddling, we hunted at dusk for the old wild bull that we had come for but didn't see him.

Returning at dark we had some hot buttered rums & filet steaks, fried potatoes, onions, canned peaches and tea.

After 2 rums, Frank insisted that there were five of us and started to prepare five plates for supper.

The night was clear, cool and bracing. Two of us slept in wall bunks and 2 on the floor.

Sunday, November 26

Rose before dawn and, after a cup of tea & some canned peaches, went after our old bull. Saw tracks not more than 24 hours old. About sunup could see whole string of islands as far as Hawaii. Still clear. No bull. Saddled up and started back for Kaunakakai at 10:15. Saw more goats in canyon and all shot a number of times 500–800 yds. I got 1 of the two killed. Picked up rested strawberry mane pony as we descended. Left horses & Flavius Peter at place where we first got them. Met a man there named Anderson interested in getting Italian queen bees sent to the islands. Took us 2 hrs to get down the mountain. Much over-grazed by cattle.

Met my car at 12:00 PM and drove to air range to look for deer. Saw a few tracks, but no deer. Returned via Maui to Hickam Fld, arriving about 5:00 PM. We left at Maui.

Monday, November 27

Drew Pearson's article Re walrus in Star & Bulletin today. Naval officers say my only mistake was failing to shoot Pearson.

Tuesday, November 28

Adm Richardson and his board for post-war defense organization arrived.[i] Says Army generally favors complete unification, Navy non-committal. Jimmy Roosevelt[ii] ordered home (election over).

4:00 PM—Softball vs Ordnance—Won 8–5

Staff had conference with ComGenPOA's[iii] staff today on service troops and Post reported a much more co-operative mood than heretofore.

Wednesday, November 29

2:00 PM—Joint conference with Adm Turner Re our operations—His Hqrs.

Thursday, November 30

Baseball—Ordnance 4:00 PM—Won 13–6 but couldn't go.

5–7 at Halekulani, Mr O'Dyer, British Consul. Cocktails. Supper later at Chinese place with Gen Waller & Missy.

Friday, December 1

Missy came out to target her rifle. Had her, Mrs Sweet & Cowart for supper at club.

Saturday, December 2

Most A&N morning activities suspended until Army-Navy football broadcast was over A-23, N-7.

Walked in mountains looking for a new course for my staff. They are still talking about the last one. Many are nervous over crossing the narrow hogbacks.

Sunday, December 3

Swam at Haliewa. First time in a long while.

---

i   Admiral James O. Richardson, former commander of the Pacific Fleet.
ii Lieutenant Colonel James Roosevelt USMC, President Franklin Roosevelt's eldest son.
iii A shorthand acronym for General Richardson's headquarters.

Monday, December 4

Yellow candle bush in full bloom.

5–7 PM—Wightmans—Cocktails to meet plantation owners. Met the Kearneys (She dances exceptionally well) Mrs Bond from Ewa says she will invite me to dinner shortly.

Plantation Mgrs were an interesting group.

Tuesday, December 5

Saw Emmons & F.J. Fletcher at Pearl. Corlett[i] to arrive today for Conf. Saw Clancy at Ft Kamehameha.

6:30—Mrs Gisela Corbett, 3030 Puiwa Lane Supper. Bring ~~Com. Bassett~~ Mrs Keleher.

Wednesday, December 6

Pistol practice in afternoon.

Pete Corlett & Roy Craft called in evening. Here with F.J. Fletcher & Emmons on N. Pacific Conference.

Thursday, December 7

Went after naval conference to Shafter to see Emmons. Saw his CofS, Bathhurst,[ii] who discussed Alaska gossip. He expressed dislike & distrust of Gov Gruening.

Noon Adm. Nimitz talk at Pearl Harbor Navy Yard followed by lunch there with Adm ~~N~~ Furlong.

Friday, December 8

Met H.R.[iii] Naval Affairs Committee at Naval Conf. Photographed with Adm Nimitz Adm Fletcher & Emmons after conference for deceptive publicity purposes.

11:30 AM. Went to Shafter and had teletype conversation with Claiborne at West Point. Messages came through promptly and accurately.

---

i   Major General Charles H. "Pete" Corlett, who had commanded in the Aleutians, Kwajalein, and later XIX Corps in Europe.

ii Brigadier General Robert M. Bathurst.

iii U.S. House of Representatives.

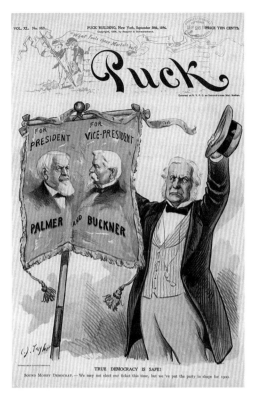

Simon Bolivar Buckner Sr. in 1861. *Library of Congress*

An 1896 broadsheet about the Palmer–Buckner Gold Democrat ticket. *Library of Congress*

Glen Lily, as seen in 1940. *Library of Congress*

The West Point Corps of Cadets on parade for Theodore Roosevelt's inauguration, 1905. Standing in the ranks as a plebe was Simon Bolivar Buckner Jr. *Library of Congress*

West Point cadets on parade, 1910. *Library of Congress*

The main parade ground at West Point, 1910. *Library of Congress*

Union and Confederate veterans at Gettysburg Battlefield, 1913. *Library of Congress*

John L. DeWitt (left) speaking to President Franklin Roosevelt in 1942. *U.S. Navy*

The tent city at the Fort Richardson site outside Anchorage, winter 1940–41. *Wisconsin Veterans Museum*

Anthony Dimond, Alaska's delegate to the U.S. Congress (left), confers with Alaska's Governor Ernest Gruening (right). *Library of Congress*

Buckner (left) decorates Colonel Benjamin B. Talley (right) for his achievements in Alaska, as a staff officer looks on. *Library of Congress*

Leslie Gehres in Alaska. *U.S. Navy*

Officers' quarters at Fort Richardson. *Wisconsin Veterans Museum*

Alaska Department Headquarters at Fort Richardson, as it appeared in early 1944. *Wisconsin Veterans Museum*

Bulldozers at work in the Adak lagoon. *U.S. Army*

Troops of the 7th Division come ashore at Massacre Bay, Attu. *U.S. Army*

Lieutenant General Simon Bolivar Buckner Jr. *U.S. Army*

Unalaska Island during the winter of 1943–44. *Wisconsin Veterans Museum*

Buckner confers with senior officers in Hawaii. Left to right: Admiral Chester Nimitz, Lieutenant General Delos C. Emmons, Vice Admiral Frank Jack Fletcher, Admiral Raymond A. Spruance, and Buckner. *U.S. Navy*

Robert C. Richardson. He inscribed this portrait as a gift to Admiral Nimitz. *U.S. Navy*

Holland M. Smith. *U.S. Army*

Ralph C. Smith. *U.S. Army*

Richmond Kelly Turner. *U.S. Army*

Roy Geiger of III Amphibious Corps, the man who succeeded Buckner as Tenth Army's commander. *U.S. Army*

Andrew Bruce of the 77th Infantry Division (right) confers with a staff officer on Guam. *U.S. Army*

Marc Mitscher. *U.S. Navy*

Buckner in 1945, as Tenth Army commander. *Smithsonian Institution*

American troops come ashore on Okinawa on L-Day, April 1, 1945. *U.S. Navy*

The following images were taken by General Buckner on Okinawa with his personal camera:

The invasion fleet as seen from a landing craft heading ashore. *Courtesy William C. Buckner*

A damaged building on Okinawa. *Courtesy William C. Buckner*

Okinawan refugees. *Courtesy William C. Buckner*

U.S. tanks go into action against Japanese positions. *Courtesy William C. Buckner*

Soldiers at a frontline observation post along Okinawa's east coast. *Courtesy William C. Buckner*

Okinawan landscape. *Courtesy William C. Buckner*

A tree on Okinawa. *Courtesy William C. Buckner*

American vehicles, including General Buckner's jeep, bogged down in deep mud. *Courtesy William C. Buckner*

Nimitz, Spruance, and Buckner (left to right in center) walk with their staffs, April 1945. *U.S. Navy*

Buckner (foreground holding camera) watches the 6th Marine Division in action. Beside him holding the cane is Major General Lemuel Shepherd, the division commander. *U.S. Marine Corps*

Buckner (right) with senior officers of the 8th Marines, June 18, 1945. Colonel Clarence Wallace, the regimental commander, is in the center with his operations officer, Major William Chamberlin, to the left in sunglasses. Minutes after this photo was taken, Japanese shellfire struck the hill, killing Buckner. *U.S. Marine Corps*

General Buckner's funeral on Okinawa, June 19, 1945. *U.S. Marine Corps*

Buckner's grave after the funeral, taken with his camera. Note the dog tag affixed to the cross, just like any other soldier. *Courtesy William C. Buckner*

Adele Buckner, as next of kin, receives her husband's Navy Distinguished Service Medal for the Okinawa campaign. *U.S. Navy*

Simon Bolivar Buckner's final resting place in Frankfort, Kentucky, as seen on August 1, 2021. *Photo by Author*

Interviewed new aide, Maj Hubbard[i] and notified him of his appointment.

Post got back from Saipan about 8:30 PM.

Saturday, December 9

11:00–11:45 AM—Testified before Adm Richardson's board Re: reorganization & consolidation of services after the war. Expressed myself as favoring unification. Adm R. said that most of Army was similarly minded but Navy, while not definitely opposing it, were not convinced. Nelly Richardson was an exception and feared consolidation.

Sunday, December 10

2:30 PM—Started on firebreak Trail Rd, climbed to crest above Koli Koli and followed ridge line west and then north to high peak [ ] (2 ½ hours). Luxuriant tropical vegetation on peak, tree ferns etc. Took 2 ½ hours to get back to car, last half hour in dark, making progress slow down steep ridges. Took many pictures and had a good work-out.

Monday, December 11

Gen Maxwell (Dr)[ii] reported as Iscom. Surgeon.

1:30—Had conference with my staff & Gen Geiger's outlining general plans to the latter.

6:00 PM—Meet at Nold's Qrs. before 6:30 party at club by Engr, AAA (Pick up Missy at Halikulani 5:30 with flowers—by way of scandal) Worried her to death by making her think they were geraniums.

Tuesday, December 12

6:15 Ewa Airfield. Dinner Gen Mulcahy's mess.

Wednesday, December 13

11:00 AM—Col Blanchard USMC[iii] who was at Kodiak '40 will pick me up at office for lunch. (Called me up at 3:15 AM last night in true Alaskan form)

---

i   Major Frank R. Hubbard.
ii   Brigadier General Earl Maxwell.
iii Colonel John D. Blanchard.

Thursday, December 14

12 noon—20-min talk to Wahiawa Rotary Club, Mr. Seger. (Quoted Eskimo verses & told Old Yukon bear story)

Dinner, McCunniff—4 Coms. Pick up Mrs John Macauley at 5:00 PM.—Orchids, by way of decoration.

Club beautifully decorated by Mrs Keleher and jungle school personnel. Negro orchestra.

Friday, December 15

1:00 PM—Grenade practice—live grenades.

My new aide, Maj Frank R. Hubbard, Cav., appointed and moved into the house.

He and Cowart working on my Monday party.

Saturday, December 16

(No entry)

Sunday, December 17

12:30 PM—Lunch, Adm Nimitz for British Adm. Sir Bruce Fraser.[i] Adm. Mitsher given two decorations after lunch.

3–6:00 Drop in to Koala Club opening. Rec. Center.

5:30 PM—Mrs Ewing, 6021 Summer St. Tel. 78901 (Ewing is the local news commentator—radio)

Monday, December 18

Naval Affairs Committee of house at Pearl Harbor.[ii]

6:00 PM—My dinner and dance at the Club. Room decorated with ti, palms, ginger, and bamboo. Armoured force orchestra. Dancing after dinner. Old fashions, champaign & highballs. Guests were: R.Adm. Davis,[iii] R Adm Blandy,[iv] Maj Gen Leavey,[v] Maj Gen Wallace, Maj Gen

---

i   Admiral Fraser commanded the British Pacific Fleet 1944–45.

ii   This is a reference the Naval Affairs Committee of the U.S. House of Representatives, which made a visit to Pearl Harbor.

iii Rear Admiral Arthur C. Davis, Spruance's chief of staff.

iv Rear Admiral William H. P. Blandy, commanding an amphibious group under Turner.

v   Major General Edmond H. Leavey, chief of logistics for U.S. Army Pacific Ocean Areas.

Geiger, Com Theiss, B.G. Fielder,[i] BG Post, B.G. Smith,[ii] BG Crist,[iii] BG Nold, BG Harris,[iv] BG Dumas, Com Bisset. BG Ruffner, Capt Chaplin (N), BG Silverthorne (M),[v] Col Schick, Adm Spruance, VAdm Turner, Mr Ward, Maj Cowart, Maj Hubbard.—Mrs Leavey, Mrs Ward, Miss Helene Gowen, Miss Mildred Gowen, Mrs Erdman, Mrs Keleher, Mrs Lyman,m Mrs Bowen, Mrs (Mayfield) dropped out, Mrs Macauley, Mrs Branneman, Mrs Dillingham, Mrs Mackey, Mrs Ackerstrom, Mrs Mitchell, Mrs Graham, Miss Crewes.

Tuesday, December 19

Cowart relieved as aide today so as to devote all time to duties as Secty of G.S.[vi]

6:00—Capt C.J. Wheeler,[vii] USN cocktail supper for Adm. Fraser G.C.B. Pick up Missy 5:30.

Hawaiian dancers etc. Leis presented to the Admiral with appropriate pictures. He ate it up.

Met Mrs Baldwin of Maui. Rides Arabian horses and ropes cattle.

Also met Mona Holmes.

Wednesday, December 20

Walked in the hills.

Projected slides after supper—mostly flowers.

Thursday, December 21

Saw "Fighting Lady" movie at Pearl.

Went to Shafter to intercede with Richardson in behalf of Schick's promotion.[viii] Met new Gov of Fiji there.

---

i   Brigadier General Kendall J. Fielder, chief of military intelligence for Hawaii and U.S. Army Pacific Ocean Areas.
ii Brigadier General Oliver P. Smith, USMC, senior Marine staff member assigned to Tenth Army headquarters.
iii Brigadier General William E. Crist, chief of Military Government Section, Tenth Army.
iv Brigadier General Charles S. Harris, commanding antiaircraft units for Tenth Army.
v   Brigadier General Merwin H. Silverthorn, III Amphibious Corps chief of staff.
vi Secretary of general staff for headquarters Tenth Army.
vii Captain Charles J. Wheeler, U.S. liaison to the British Pacific Fleet.
viii This request was successful, as in January 1945 Schick was promoted to brigadier general.

2:00 PM—Took 1st Anti scrub typhus inoculation.

6: [unintelligible] at Club. [erased text]

6:30 PM—Mrs Bond dinner Ewa Plantation. All Marines except Millers & one other civilian couple. (Quoted "Friendly Arctic" & Man of War story).

Friday, December 22

Discussed soldier eqpt. with staff.

Sweetheart vine in bloom.

Saturday, December 23

Gen. Truesdale,[i] Comdt at C&GS School spent morning discussing my organization & staff methods. Says MacArthur wants all and troops in Pac. Under one man—(obviously himself).

Hubbard and I took the Gowen sisters to the Turret Club dance. Flowers for each.

Sunday, December 24

An officer at Pearl Harbor discussed his experiences on a destroyer in the recent disastrous Philippine typhoon. His ship rolled 73 [degrees] repeatedly.[ii]

5–10:00 PM—Van Holt elastic dinner. About 200 of Honolulu's "400." Met Duke Kahanamokie. Went to Harmon's later.

Monday, December 25

7:30. Breakfast with Mrs Ankerstrom's—Batter bread, sausage and Tom & Jerry.

Two-hour walk.

4–6—Dillingham—egg nog. Take Cowart.

6:00—Dinner Frank.

Tuesday, December 26

Went with Mr. Baugh into the shaft from which the post water supply is pumped. Water 70 [degrees] F. Took Nold & Hubbard.

---

i   Major General Karl Truesdell, commandant of the Command and General Staff School.

ii   This is a reference to Typhoon Cobra, which struck Third Fleet on December 17 and 18, 1944, and caused significant damage and loss.

Wednesday, December 27

Noon—lunch at Kanialua with Blanchard

Take Col McDougall—start at 11:00 (Had to drop out due to Sig. O.[i] conference. [)]

Thursday, December 28

Second anti-typhus shot.

Visited Maj Frase and Lt Jinkins in Hospl.

6:30 PM—Tenth Army party at club.

Friday, December 29

Attended soldier presentation of the Mikado. It wasn't bad at all.

Saturday, December 30

Inspected anti-aircraft field exercises. Found positions too symmetrical and conspicuous. Told them so.

Brought Betsy back from Vet. Hospl. Her broken leg seems to have healed well.

Sunday, December 31

6:00 PM. Went to K. Ruggles' party at her aunt's [ ] Valley Road over waterfall. Took three members of the orchestra, the bull fiddle and a naval officer home about 1:00 AM. House where party was given was built over a pool with a 10-ft waterfall with a hillside garden behind. Owner, and artist. Many good and some bad pictures there.

---

i   Signal officer.

CHAPTER 4

Preparing Tenth Army: January–March 1945

1945

Monday, January 1

10 AM—Post, McCunniff & I went to Mrs. Ackerstrom's house for batter bread breakfast. 12 ft torch ginger in yard.

Took a walk in the hills and at 5 PM went to Mr Seger's egg nog party in Wahaiwa. Meanwhile Betsy ran away again. She has neither sense nor character. She wanders aimlessly and gets lost. When brought back she is enthusiastically affectionate but won't stay. She tears out screens if left in the house.

Tuesday, January 2

Betsy was brought back, still limping but improving.

6:00 PM—Mrs [ ] Saks luau near Kok Head. She dressed us up in native mother hubbards. Adm Towns & Furlong hated it. Danced after dinner to Elmer Lee's orchestra.

Wednesday, January 3

(No entry)

Thursday, January 4

6:30 PM—Took Mrs Walter Dillingham to the Wards for dinner. Adm Nimitz, the Walkers, Harmon, Ruth Dillingham, Douglas King & Comdr Lamar there. The Adm & I got to story telling. I told the celery, rejuvenation and "spruceefigue" yarns.

Betsy tore out another window screen and is gone. I am not hunting for her.

Took my final anti-scrub typhus shot.

Friday, January 5

Post & I had supper with Ed. C. Chester at the Moana. He is now on Harbor Board here and mgr of a sugar co. Knew him in Alaska.

Saturday, January 6

Took an hour's climb in the hills. Found a 155mm dud. Left it alone.

Approved tentative order for my operation. Annexes later.

The final plan for Operation Iceberg, *which was the basis for Buckner's "tentative order," called for Tenth Army to land 183,000 men at Hagushi on Okinawa's west coast on April 1, 1945. The forces assigned to Buckner's army included both U.S. Army and U.S. Marine Corps troops. The Army contingent consisted of Hodge's XXIV Corps with Major General Archibald V. Arnold's 7th Infantry and Major General James L. Bradley's 96th Infantry Divisions, plus Major General Andrew D. Bruce's 77th Infantry Division. Major General George Griner's 27th Infantry Division was in floating reserve, with Major General Paul Mueller's 81st Infantry Division available upon request to Nimitz. Geiger's III Amphibious Corps with Major General Pedro del Valle's 1st Marine Division, Major General Thomas L. Watson's 2nd Marine Division, and Major General Lemuel Shepherd's 6th Marine Division provided the Marine contingent.*

In support of Tenth Army were the 1,000 ships of Admiral Raymond Spruance's Fifth Fleet, which would support and protect Buckner's operations. Vice Admiral Richmond K. Turner directed all amphibious operations and the several task forces bringing the ground forces to Okinawa. Buckner would report to Spruance and Turner for the first stages of the battle, later answering directly to Nimitz. Major General Fred C. Wallace led Island Command (Iscom), and Marine Major General Francis Mulcahy oversaw the Tactical Air Force.

A week prior to the main assault, Bruce's division would secure Kerama Retto as a fleet anchorage. The Hagushi landings would be accompanied by Watson's division demonstrating off Minatoga on Okinawa's southeast coast.

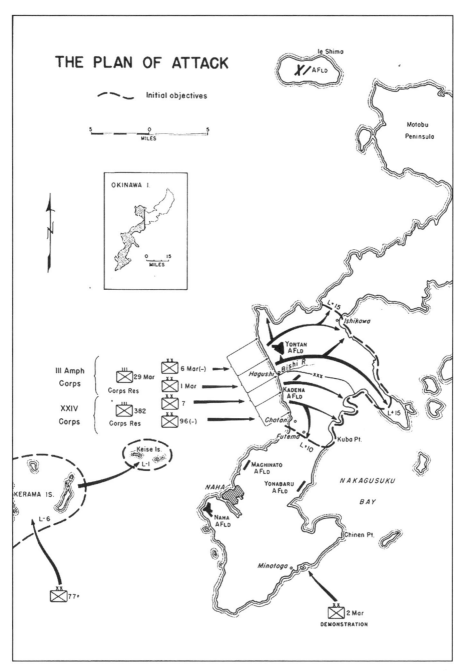

The final landing plan for Operation *Iceberg*, with the main landing at Hagushi on the west coast and the diversion at Minatoga. *U.S. Army*

After landing at Hagushi, Tenth Army was to fight its way across Okinawa to cut the island in half, a task expected to take up to 15 days. After that, XXIV Corps would execute Phase I and capture Okinawa's southern third. When Buckner decided the time was right, III Amphibious Corps and other available units would attack northern Okinawa and the surrounding islands as part of Phase II. The follow-on operations in Phases IIIc and IIId (IIIa and IIIb being dropped during planning) would see three divisions of V Amphibious Corps and one of Tenth Army capture Miyako and the Kikai Islands further north. The sequence and timing of the Phase III attacks would be ordered by Admiral Nimitz.

Opposing Buckner on Okinawa was Lieutenant General Ushijima Mitsuru's Thirty-Second Army of two divisions, a brigade, a tank regiment, Okinawan militia, and attached units totaling 120,000 men. To provide maximum delay and opportunity to damage U.S. forces, Ushijima chose not to defend on the beaches. He deployed most of his forces in a series of fortified defense rings centered on Shuri, leaving detachments in central and northern Okinawa.

American intelligence picked up much of Ushijima's preparations and gave a basic understanding of Okinawa's geography. However, it was deficient in two key respects. First, detailed maps covering all of Okinawa were lacking. Second, estimates of Ushijima's strength credited him with between 60,000 and 70,000 men—numbers that would be believed until late in the battle.

Sunday, January 7

Hear that Hodge & some of his staff will soon arrive here from Leyte.

Dumas suggests recorded speech to men on ships en route.

3 PM—Football game at Furlong Field between Air Corps & Navy teams. Most of players all-Americans or professionals. Navy won 14 to 0. A good fast game comparable to good professional football.

Recd. a telephone message that Betsy was at one of the barracks. Sent for her but found that she had already gone. Rather glad she was.

Monday, January 8

2 PM—Presented alternate plan to Adm Turner who accepted it.

Had dinner and dance at post club.—Steak, old fashions, sparkling burgundy & highballs.

Guests were:

Adm Nimitz	Col. Ashton
B.G. Chaney[i]	Col. Heard
B.G. Mulcahy (M)	Mr & Mrs Ewing
Mrs Van Holt	Col Keleher
Maj D. Burgin	Col Daniels
BG Post	Miss H Gowen
Vice Adm Hall[ii]	Miss M Gowen
B.G. Maxwell	Miss Crews
Mr & Mrs W. Dillingham	Mrs. Ackerstrom
Ruth Dillingham	Mrs Erdman
Col Pulsifer	Mrs Lyman
Col Edwards	Miss Keleher
Mr & Mrs Bond	Mrs Graham
Col Jones	Mrs Mitchell
Col Blakelock	Mrs Wodehouse
Col Shaw	Mrs Ruggles
B.G. McCunniff	Mrs Branneman
Capt Little (N)	Maj Hubbard
	Maj Cowart.

Tuesday, January 9

Inspected AAA units. Lunch with B.G. Handework.[iii] Most units looked well. Group Hq need more training as soldiers.

B.G. Garvin[iv] CofS of XXIV Corps & several staff members arrive from Leyte to discuss plans. Sent message asking Hodge to join them. I shall postpone my planned trip of Jan 16 to see him but go a few days later to inspect my Divs. Looks as though our troops loaned to Gen MacArthur for the Leyte campaign would be difficult to get back. I cautioned Adm Nimitz of this when the XXIV Corps was sent there.

---

i   Brigadier General James E. Chaney, island commander-designate for Iwo Jima.

ii   Vice Admiral John L. Hall, commanding the Southern Attack Force for *Iceberg*, charged with landing XXIV Corps.

iii   Brigadier General Morris C. Handwerk, commanding the antiaircraft training center on Oahu.

iv   Brigadier General Crump Garvin, XXIV Corps chief of staff.

Wednesday, January 10

Sketch

6:30 PM—Adm. Spruance dinner at his Qrs. After dinner he showed the film "Woodrow Wilson," a good historical movie (2 ½ hours long)

Thursday, January 11

Morning taken up at Pearl Harbor presenting by all concerned every phase of Detachment and Iceberg.

Saw Ozzy Coldclough on his way to command a new battleship.[i]

After the conference, detailed training and final preparations could begin for both Operations Detachment and Iceberg. For Buckner, this meant a lot of travel and coordination over long distances, as his forces and supplies were scattered all over the Pacific. Some supplies were in Seattle and San Francisco, while other troops were in Hawaii. His main combat units were also dispersed, with Watson's division in the Marianas, Geiger's corps on Guadalcanal and nearby islands, and Hodge's corps still fighting on Leyte. The first time Tenth Army came together as a complete formation was on Okinawa.

Friday, January 12

Made a recording of my talk to be given over the loud speaker systems of every transport on the way to the objective.

Inspected Army signal units. Not at all satisfied with appearance of men, their discipline or the condition of their area. Said so.

6:30 PM—Gen Goodyear (Red Cross) dinner at his house. He is also connected with the movie industry. Present were Mr. Mayer (Red Cross & movies), Mr McCoy (ARC), Mr Pettit (ARC) of S.C. and Post. Our host spent most of the time persistently trying to persuade me to write about Alaska from a military standpoint. I did not agree.

Saturday, January 13

Made talk at opening of 1st 3 grades NCO Club of my Hq.

Curry dinner at Mrs Ackerstrom's followed by club dance & night cap at my qrs. Also ping pong.

---

i   Captain Oswald S. Coldclough, on his way to assume command of USS *North Carolina.*

Sunday, January 14

Went to enlisted men's picnic at Kanalua USO & returned via the Pali.

Monday, January 15

Gen Hodge arrived. Told of Japs eating our dead on Leyte.

Had supper with Adm Murray[i] on in honor of [sic] Asst Secty for Air Gates of Navy. Sat at small table with Adm Mitcher, Adm Sherman and Mr [ ] asst to Mr Gates.

Tuesday, January 16

Inoculated against cholera, bubonic plague and pneumonic plague.

6:00 PM—Dinner, Harmon, Hickam Off Club lanai. Call for K Ruggles, 226 Wylie St Nuuanu Valley. Ten Hon 69802. Orchids, by way of adornment.

Sat next to Marion Worthington

Met Mr & Mrs Kays.

Wednesday, January 17

Took Hodge to see Adm Nimitz and had conference there regarding service units and rehabilitation of XXIV Corps.

Adm Nimitz decided to send a message to Gen MacArthur insisting that the latter live up to his agreement regarding the release of the Corps. Also decided to send Gen Felman[ii] to Leyte as his representative and Gen Englehardt[iii] as Gen Richardson's.

Got letter from Richardson intimating that he did not have full confidence in Wallace as my island commander, that he had not been the former's choice and asking that I state in writing whether or not I felt satisfied with him. (Evidently an attempt to shift the blame to me if he did not do well.) I replied by stating that my only dissatisfaction with his work was the result of Richardson's being slow in furnishing him with an adequate and competent staff—thus dropping it squarely back

---

i   Vice Admiral George D. Murray, commanding U.S. Naval Air Forces, Pacific Fleet.
ii Brigadier General Herman Feldman, executive assistant to the assistant chief of staff for Logistics in Nimitz's headquarters.
iii Brigadier General Francis A. Englehart, chief of ordnance for U.S. Army Pacific Ocean Areas.

into his lap. I also asked for Richardson's suggestions in the event that Wallace should not prove satisfactory just to see if he had a candidate.

Thursday, January 18 (Friday, January 19)[i]

Left Hickam Fld in 4-motored transport plane at 8:10 AM with B.G. Smith, Ely, Hubbard & Capt Houghton (ATC).

Pilot: Capt Hatch (Chicago) Copilot Capt Turner Flt. Trip Clk, Cpl Elliott.

Av. Tarawa 12 hours later. (2 ½ hour time change) Met by Capt Gillespie USNR (md) the island Comdr & Maj Byarts (ATC). Smith & I stayed at former's house. Island well cleaned up now. Military population 2,000, and dwindling. British Govt. handles the natives. Houses of thatch. Drove around island with Gillespie & went to outdoor movie after supper.

Friday, January 19 (Saturday, January 20)

Skipped a day. Got up at 6:30 and walked over the island looking over the old Jap defenses which were strong. Guns well sited to cover obstacles. Took off at 8:20. Crossed Equator.

At 1:10 flew over Tukopia[ii] a jewel of an island with the most beautiful coloring I have ever seen, particularly the blues. Photographed it in color. Sparsely populated and owned by England.

Sighted a steamer at 1:20 PM.

Av. Espiritu Santo six hours after starting. Met by Gen Griner & some of his staff. Drove to 27th Div camp, went swimming with Col Ovenshine CofS[iii] and others, took ride in Navy speed boat and Engr skip-jack, attended a reception & cocktail party followed by dinner and a dance (about 15 Red Cross girls & nurses & a French trader & his wife hosted—Rolande, coconut planters).

Learned that Chap Hillyer had made a bad impression here by announcing that CO's didn't know how to manage chaplains.

Saturday, January 20 (Sunday, January 21)

Rose at 6:00 and had a swim. The island industries are coconuts and cocoa. The inhabitants Melanesians with their kinky hair stained red

---

i   Buckner has again crossed the International Date Line.
ii A reference to Tikopia Island.
iii Colonel Richard P. Ovenshine, 27th Infantry Division chief of staff.

with lime. Tonquinese[i] are imported by the French planters to do useful work. They are brought over on 5-year contract. There are no towns on this island and the native villages are very small.

At 9:30 AM, reviewed and inspected 27th Div. They look well but are more concerned with furloughs than fighting.

The weather was hot and humid and the rain about to start. The soldiers were enjoying swimming, fishing, and sailing. They had made every known kind of a boat, including one constructed of three belly tanks and an old jeep engine.

At 2:00 PM we flew over to New Caledonia where it was much cooler. Cattle, horses and goats were grazing. Good pastures and many eucalyptus trees. Industry: mining.

Met Gen Mueller of 81st Div & Pat Gilbreath.[ii] About 25% of Div now here. Drove over to Mueller's qrs with Blakelock and Dumas, whom we had picked up at Espiritu Santo. Had drinks & supper with Mueller & spent night there.

Sunday, January 21 (Monday, January 22)

Rose at 6:00 and took a walk up the hill. Pretty view. At 9:30 AM made a brief talk to an assembly of Div staff and others and wound up by pinning DSM on Mueller for Angaur campaign.

At 1:15 PM drove to local air strip and flew in small planes to Numea [Noumea] (about 20 min). Met by Pat Gilbreath. Called on Pat's office to discuss training of service troops and then called on VAdm Newton, ComSouPac.[iii]

Put up at Grand Hotel Central (leased by Army) and took a walk about town. Melanesians with blondined hair (lime) Javanese and French. The latter sloppy and greasy looking. French colonial architecture (unsightly) and ill-kept gardens. Vegetation similar to Hawaii. Tall royal palms. Roses.

Fine climate, fishing, deer hunting, sailing & swimming, everything needed for a tourist resort.

---

i   Tonkinese, people from the Tonkin area of French Indochina (now Vietnam).
ii Major General Frederick "Pat" Gilbreath, commanding South Pacific Base Command.
iii Vice Admiral John H. Newton, commanding South Pacific Area.

Monday, January 22 (Tuesday, January 23)

Rose at 6:00 and walked around town until 8:00 when we drove in cars to Tontouta airport (1 ½ hrs). Took off at 9:45 for Guadalcanal. On way passed the island of Tuomkew[i] occupied by unspoiled Polynesians. Looks like an atoll but lagoon is fresh water. Thatch villages and primitive looking island. 3:30 PM arrived at Guadalcanal. Met by Geiger (3d Phibcorps) Max Murray (Iscom) and del Valle 1st Mardiv and Shepherd 6th Mardiv.[ii]

Had beautifully appointed dinner with Geiger followed by a good movie "Horses in Indiana."

Tuesday, January 23 (Wednesday, January 24)

Spent day inspecting the 6th Mardiv field exercises & qrs with Gen Shepherd. 29th Reg had sloppy qrs & apparently poor discipline but splendid weapon teamwork in Det & Co attacks.

Bn exercise got out of hand. Tanks & men exposed themselves instead of using cover. Individual camouflage good. Arty (155 hows) were slow getting on target in direct anti–cave fire. 29th Regt, a new one, seemed behind the others.

Had lunch with Gen Shepherd near beached Jap ship.

Returned and went to movies after supper. Old fashions before and Benedictine afterwards at Geiger's mess.

Wednesday, January 24 (Thursday, January 25)

Got up at 6:00 and went swimming out of an amphibious jeep which had to be pulled ashore later by a wrecking car. Geiger and our respective aides went along.

Observed Arty CP prevent Regtl attack★ problem by 1st Mardiv & tanks. Too much exposed and halted.

12:30 PM flew in P.B.Y. with Gen del Valle to the Russells (1 ½ hour) and saw his Div (1st) camps. Training facilities none too good—very little terrain variety. Flew along Guadalcanal shore, lined with sunken Jap barges. Also several beached Jap ships and a submarine. Passed Henderson Field & "Ironbottom Bay" where our four cruisers were sunk. Saw

i   A reference to Taumako Island.
ii   Shorthand for III Amphibious Corps, 1st Marine Division, and 6th Marine Division.

Montague, 1st Div. Got back about 5:00 PM & after a shower drove to Iscom's Hq for dinner with Max Murray. After dinner saw Hedy Lamar in "The Conspirators" for the second time.

★Capt Porch[i] of Anniston, del Valle's nephew came to see me and remained for lunch. Has son from last Dec whom he has not yet seen.

Thursday, January 25 (Friday, January 26)

As usual, got up and found the ground covered with fragile aromatic flowers that disintegrated with the morning sun. Ginger of several varieties bloomed everywhere. Also on the Russells, one entire coconut grove had every trunk covered with yellow orchids about the size of violets.

Took off at 8:00. Passed Finchaven[ii] 4 ½ hours later. After 8 hrs flight stopped an hour at Hollandia the rear echelon of SWPac administrative Hq under Brig Gen Baird.[iii] Dumas saw him about an officer we wanted but "The records had just gone to forward echelon." High mountains, waterfall, large lake and ground littered with destroyed Jap planes.

Flew on about an hour beyond Hollandia & landed at Biak. About 68,000 Mil. Pop. Including 41st Div (Jens Doe)[iv] about to leave. Met by Doe & Col. Kirrick, Engrs, in chg of construction. Smith, Dumas & I had dinner with him at the latters house in a quiet little cove. Returned to ATC Comdr's Col Estelle [ ]. Found two nurses and an aviator there. One nurse simply & clingingly slushy over the flyer. The nurses went to a dance with their men & we went to bed. About 400 nurses & Red Cross girls on this Is. & Japs still being captured. One Jap admiral reported at large. Jens Doe was loading his 41st Div. For landing on Luzon.

Friday, January 26 (Saturday, January 27)

Wakened early by the garrulous squawking and whistling of a large black-and-white bird. Parrots joined later. Our host produced a Papuan

---

i   Captain Ralph D. Porch.

ii   A reference to Finschafen in New Guinea.

iii Brigadier General Harry H. Baird, deputy chief of staff, U.S. Army Forces Far East, the headquarters which administratively controlled all Army troops in MacArthur's Southwest Pacific Area.

iv Major General Jens A. Doe and his 41st Infantry Division, shortly to participate in the liberation of the Philippines.

called "Sgt. Yoyo" and had him sing "Pistol Packin' Mama." We took off for Leyte at 8:00 AM. Landed on point near Tacloban. Field littered with our planes destroyed by Jap raids. No dispersion yet. Planes parked wing to wing. Beaches still congested.

Drove to XXIV Corps Hq. Natives in barrios along road. Women now wearing American dresses and hair dues, but roosters and bare feet still in evidence. Went over Leyte campaign map with Hodge. His success was due to fast advance and quick control of road net. 6th Army took most of his corps troops and equipment consistently. 7th Div. still "rehabilitating" by attacking Comote Is. Eichelburger[i] has just left to see another landing in Luzon at Subig[ii] Bay.

Looks as though SW Pacific is not forethoughted in planning details. Hodge considers our staff far superior in this respect. Hodge's corps will get no real rest nor rehabilitation before next campaign and their equipment is badly in need of repair, but they are good fighters.

Took swim before supper. Plan visiting all his Divs. I have great confidence in both my corps.

Saturday, January 27 (Sunday, January 28)

Got up early and had a swim in the surf.

Gen's Feldman & Englehardt from CincPoa & ComGenPoa arrived and we had a conference at Hodge's Hq with his staff preliminary to tomorrow's conference with Gen MacArthur's rear echelon relative to getting XXIV Corps shaken loose and prepared for Iceberg operation. The XXIV Corps has been shortchanged in everything for the benefit of the Sixth Army by lack of forethought, loose promises and selfish motives. Gen MacArthur, I hear, is very irate over Adm Nimitz message accurately describing the status of XXIV Corps and requesting that his agreement with Gen MacArthur be lived up to. At the conference I urged that we avoid recriminations over the past but bend every effort toward pooling all efforts so as to improve the readiness of the Corps for its coming operation for which I am responsible to the JCOS.[iii]

---

i   Lieutenant General Robert H. Eichelberger, commanding Eighth Army.
ii   A reference to Subic Bay. XI Corps of Eighth Army was scheduled to land there.
iii Joint chiefs of staff.

Visited Jim Bradley's Div (96th) with Hodge. Bradley looked sick. I left him a qt of bourbon. Returned 18 mi. in our jeep. Plenty of carabaos along road but almost no horses and very few pigs. Women's clothes not native costume but looked like Jap imitation of white women's costumes. Fighting cocks in evidence everywhere.

Learned from Garvin, CofS, XXIV Corps that it was intimated by Gen Chamberlin, Dep CofS, SWPac[i] that my presence at tomorrow's conference was not desired. I shall, therefore, attend to say whatever they seem afraid for me to say.

Sunday, January 28 (Monday, January 29)

Took an early swim. Haven't seen the sun since arriving in Leyte. Air alarms last night and night before. 7th & 77th Divs killed over 520 Japs yesterday trying to reach west coast.

Conference with G.H.Q. SWPac[ii] was quite satisfactory. Chamberlin, (Dep) conducted it and Byers,[iii] CofS Eighth Army was there. Felman from Adm Nimitz & Englehardt from Richardson's office were there. Also Hodges & his CofS: Garvin. For the first time, they showed a cooperative spirit and promised 1st priority above everything else to getting the XXIV Corps ready. I had carefully prepared appropriate remarks if this had not been promised.

After lunch drove down beach and inspected loading areas and beaches for the Corps with Garvin.

Adm. Hall and staff arrived meanwhile. He is to transport the Corps. Got some "ofud" from a coconut tree for salad.

News arrived of an unopposed landing by a Div & a Regtl combat team near Subig Bay on Luzon.

Still no sun but rain, rain, rain.

News from prisoners indicate that the Japs expected to go to the west coast of Leyte on Jan 29 and be evacuated by ship on Feb 14.

---

i   Major General Stephen J. Chamberlin, assistant chief of staff for operations (G-3), Southwest Pacific Area.

ii   General Headquarters, Southwest Pacific Area.

iii   Brigadier General Clovis E. Byers, Eichelberger's chief of staff.

Find that the American dresses worn by native women were sold to them by the civil government. The most ornate are made from our colored parachutes traded to them by soldiers.

300 Japs killed today and about 1,000 other found dead from starvation or disease.

Monday, January 29 (Tuesday, January 30)

Opened the day with a good swim. Rain continued with rising winds. By noon there were 50-mi gusts accompanied by deluges of rain, preventing my flying to other side of island.

Took final cholera and plague shots.

Adm Hall moved into tent with us.

Road bridges all washed out across rivers along both sides of island.

Hodge showed Hall and myself photographs of remains of our soldiers butchered and eaten by Japs. Patrols reported human flesh in officers' mess pans. He also showed a picture of the massacred natives in the church on the Comotes. They were told to assemble there for evacuation and were machine gunned to death, men, women and children.

Tuesday, January 30 (Wednesday, January 31)

Saw sun finally at sunrise, the first time since arrival. Soon obscured by scattered showers. With Hodge flew to other side of island and saw Arnold with 7th Div & Bruce with 77th. Had lunch with latter. He is being relieved by Americal Div whose G3, Gee was making arrangements. Bruce wants to send back men over 38 and get replacements from amtrack Bn now being made into Port Co.

Flew back via Baybay and Abwyog. Could see patrols burning shacks in mountains where Japs were. A number of native women recently reported raped and then bayonetted by Japs. One brought in alive. All were bayonetted just above the vagina, through the womb.

Visited P.T. boat base at Ormoc. They raid Cebu. Stole barge from Jap beach.

Started raining again when we got back to Hq. XXIV Corps which was near Rizal.

Bruce looked badly, having had some sort of dysentery for a week. He said a Jap document had been captured stating that American prisoners, after being questioned, should be taken to some secluded spot out of sight of civilian witnesses and there disposed of.

Looks as though SWPac aid to XXIV Corps is minimum they can get away with. Englehardt wants Tenth Army to have a base echelon at Leyte. This is a Comgenpoa job. 1,700 of Hodge's men are unloading LSTs on Bataan.

Another air alert but no bombs. 630 Japs killed today.

Wednesday, January 31 (Thursday, February 1)
Took off at Tacloban 8:20 AM. Circled Pellelieu[i] 4 hrs later. Flew over Ulithi and saw a tremendous amount of shipping and, after about 9 hours flying altogether, landed on the Depot Field at Guam. Enormous strides made in the development of the island since I was here last. A number of B-29s on the fields and extensive road, storage and harbor development. Maj Gen Larsen USMC is island commander. We had supper and stayed with him.

Hear Adm Nimitz has moved out here but may be off on a trip tomorrow.[ii]

Thursday, February 1 (Friday, February 2)
Felman was back and joined my party in a conference with Adm Nimitz. The XXIV Corps situation was discussed and it was decided that no present action would be taken in view of SWPac's promises but that the latter would be watched closely check fulfillment of promises and action taken if any promise were not lived up to. I expressed myself as preferring to enter the campaign on time but not entirely ready rather than postpone D-day and give the Japs more time to prepare defenses. In other words, time is working for the Japs, therefore hurry.

Went with Gen Erskine to see Bn problem by his 3d Mardiv & had lunch with him.[iii] He gave me a Marine water bag. Inspected a Bn combat problem. He turned out a Bn as guard of honor.

---

i   A reference to Peleliu Island.

ii Admiral Nimitz moved his headquarters from Pearl Harbor to Guam on January 27, 1945.

iii Major General Graves B. Erskine, commanding 3rd Marine Division.

Returned & took off at 2:45. Pilot was about to fly low over Rota when I reminded him that 5,000 Japs were there with anti-aircraft guns. He changed course just in time.

Landed at Saipan & met by Jarman, Colladay & Gen Watson, Comdg 2d Mardiv. Drove all over island with Jarman (his $10.00 tour). Remarkable progress since my last visit. B29s there in large numbers.

Jarman took Dumas to stay with him in his futuristic house built like a partitioned V-shaped porch. Had us all in for highballs & dinner.

Friday, February 2 (Saturday, February 3)

Spent the whole day with Gen Watson inspecting the 2d Mardiv. They appear well trained and well disciplined. I was greatly impressed with the quality of his battalion commanders. Training facilities were meager but the 2d appears to be, superficially, the best of the Mardivs. Watson showed that he is a disciplinarian.

Jarman mentioned to me twice that he was all through with his constructive work as island commander. Richardson told me that on his recent visit to Saipan Jarman had expressed lack of confidence in Wallace. Initially I had asked for Jarman as my island commander and been turned down by Richardson. Gilbreath of New Caledonia is also in the picture somewhere or wants to be. Griner, at Espiritu Santo doubted Wallace's ability in talking to me. My request for Richardsons suggestions will probably smoke the situation out.

Gen Goodyear, A.R.C., was at Saipan trying to get authority to visit Leyte but Gen MacArthurs Hq delayed action so long that he started back for Oahu yesterday. Permission came today.

Saturday, February 3 (Sunday, February 4)

Took off at 8:30 AM (Isely Field, No 2). Flew over a couple of irridescent atolls and landed at Kwajalein about 8 hrs later. Met by Brig Gen Ross,[i] island commander and Maj Gen Wood USMC.[ii] The latter commands the local Marine air units that are keeping neighboring Jap islands neutralized.

---

i   General Ross had been reassigned from the 27th Infantry Division to be Kwajalein's island commander.

ii   Major General Louis E. Woods, commanding 4th Marine Aircraft Wing.

Went to the guest house and saw Brig Gen Randall[i] of the 77th Div on his way back from my Hq to his. Went to movie "The Animal Kingdom" before retiring.

Sunday, February 4, Repeated Sunday, crossed 180th Meridian. A pious week with two Sundays.[ii]

Took off at 8:20 AM. The crew immediately got busy having us sing their short snorter bills. Some of these were strings of bills three feet long.

Reached Johnson Is (1x1/2 mi) in 7 hrs 50 min. Heavy traffic here—a gas station. Is. surrounded by a broad fringing reef with good fishing.

Maj Lowen, in charge of ATS met us and took us to the house of the Is. Comdr, Capt [ ] USN, and gave us a highball before supper at the mess. Heard that Manila had been taken without a local fight.

A Marine 2d LT drowned while swimming at Johnson today. Blakelock was met by his son in the ATC here. The former has just been promoted to B.G.

Took off for Hickam Field at 5:45 PM.

Arrived Hickam 4 hrs later, local time 12:15, met by Cowart.

Monday, February 5

Answered a large pile of accumulated mail. Packed bedding roll for shipment.

Tuesday, February 6

Had meeting of chiefs of all staff sections at which each took inventory of his state of readiness and explained it to the others.

Post had McCunniff, Mrs Ackerstrom, Miss Cresor & myself in for supper followed by "Doughgirls" at the movies after which we went over to the McCunniffs and communed for about an hour, following which they took their girls home and I continued packing.

Wednesday, February 7

Saw Adm Halsey at the Pearl Harbor conference.

Got my trunk and bedding roll shipped. Bought some fishing tackle.

---

i   Brigadier General Edwin H. Randle, 77th Infantry Division's assistant division commander.

ii   Buckner again crossed the International Date Line on his way back to Hawaii.

Visited four of my staff in the hospital.

Sent letter through Richardson to Adm. Nimitz asking that Gen. Geiger take over the Tenth Army should I become a casualty. His reaction will be entertaining since he mortally fears and distrusts the Marines.

Thursday, February 8

Told Gen Goodyear, ARC, that I could give him no "top secret" information, that he could not come along with me on either of the command ships but that if Gen Richardson agreed for him to go with my expedition, I would be glad for him to accompany one of the Divs in reserve that were coming later.

Went swimming at Haliewa.

Attended Gov. Stainback's dinner 7:00 PM. Met the Richards there. Hawaiian orchestra and dancing. Sat between Mrs Kay and hostess. Also met Mr. & Mrs. Waterhouse. It was the Kays' 19th wedding anniversary. Mrs Stainback had a black eye and wore large smoked glasses until I had an unveiling ceremony and got them removed.

Friday, February 9

8:00 AM. Assembled my entire staff and addressed them with expressions of appreciation of their splendid work in the planning stage of our project and confidence in them during the execution stage.

Had a long interview with the Chaplain, who brought in Chap. Of the III Phibcorps and Chap. Of the 1st Mardiv.

Adm Cobb[i] and his CofS, Capt [ ] reported officially for duty.

Adm Wright[ii] called to discuss his part in the landing.

Took Mrs Keleher's .22 rifle back to her, photographed the coconut tree—Diamond Head view in color, saw Miss Fidler who reminded me that I had won a 10 [cent] bet from her New Year's Eve and wound up by having dinner at the Halikulani with Missy.

Hubbard got me a crash knife from Hickam Field.

---

i   Rear Admiral Calvin H. Cobb, commanding Naval Forces Ryukyus.
ii Rear Admiral Jerauld H. Wright, commanding Task Group 51.2, responsible for Watson's demonstration.

Saturday, February 10

After lunch took the No 1 mountain walk with Betsy, who had just returned.

5:30 PM. Dinner with the Gowen girls at their house followed by the regular post hop at the club. Met Miss Fairweather and Mr [ ] and Mrs [ ] She is a bride from Australia.

Sunday, February 11

Went to the Halukani and had a swim with Mrs Keleher, took some colored pictures and then drove with her to the officer's club at Kaneoe[i] for cocktails, dinner and a dance on the open-air floor with Capt Dillon, U.S.N.[ii] He had Elmer Lee's Hawaiian orchestra and the best singer and hula dancer in town. The host and some of the girls among the guests danced the hula also. Met the new Mrs Squeaky Anderson.[iii] Also saw, for the first time since 1912 at Stotsenburg, Helen Nicholson, now Mrs Cream and a Capt of Marines.

Betsy was brought to the Vet. Hospl. yesterday. I took her home and she was gone again when I returned from today's party, for which I was thankful.

Monday, February 12

I was awakened at 5:30 AM by a whimpering outside my window. It was Betsy.

Secty. Navy Forrestall[iv] arrived for the morning Pearl Harbor meeting.

Attended lunch by Adm Towers in honor of the Secty and sat next to the latter who was pleasant, easy and appeared to have a good grasp of things. He leaves tomorrow to see Adm Nimitz. Adm. Halsey expects to leave in a day or two for a "rest." He says that his favorite form of rest and recreation is killing Japs so he looks forward to the end of his leave.

Attended Co. officer's dance at post club. Saw the new Mrs "Squeaky" Anderson. In one breath, she said that she and Squeaky "clicked,"

---

i   A reference to Kaneohe Marine Corps Air Station.

ii Captain Wallace M. Dillon.

iii Captain Carl E. Anderson, formerly stationed in Alaska and beachmaster-designate for the Iwo Jima landing.

iv James V. Forrestal, secretary of the Navy.

mentioned a Brig. Gen. of my acquaintance who still loved her but was unhappily married and couldn't get divorced to marry and an A.C. Col. who loved her and had just written that he was sick of his 3d bride (offered to show me the letter) and wound up by saying "while I don't exactly love Squeaky, he has a heart of gold and I'll never let him down, no, never let him down." She told Post that Squeaky had willed her a lot of money—Hence the "heart of gold." She was fairly well lit up.

Betsy is gone again.

Tuesday, February 13

Secty Forrestal is still here.

Col Ristine, Insp. Gen's. Dept.[i] arrived here to take my testimony regarding charges made against me by the Interior Dept. for violation of the laws protecting walrus. He was sent to St. Lawrence Is also from Washington. While the Interior Dept. knows that others have been on walrus trips similar to mine, they have paid no attention to these but are still trying to get something on me as a result of spite over my winning two cases in court against them in getting an Alaska resident hunting license.

Daughtery had previously written me that Jack O'Connor had spent three weeks at St Lawrence Is. trying to get something on me but had said that my only law violation was taking "unprocessed" tusks out of Alaska. Since the tusks in question are still storied in Anchorage, it appears that I am guilty of no violation whatever. Maj [sic] Ristine, while noncommittal, appeared to understand the situation. I gave him all facts concerning my trip and was able to go into complete detail by referring to my diary. After Drew Pearson's article and the misleading innuendo regarding my hunting I am very glad to have an opportunity to present the facts.

Warrant Officer Geo. Monick accompanied Col Ristine to prepare the record.

Wednesday, February 14

Secty Forrestal has left to see Adm Nimitz.

---

i   The U.S. Army's Inspector General Department, headquartered in Washington.

Thursday, February 15

Ristine told me today that Secty. Ickes[i] had sent charges against me to the Secty of War asking that "appropriate action" be taken and also requesting that within three years I be returned to Alaska, surrendered to the game authorities for fine or imprisonment and that my rifle be confiscated, since I had shot a walrus with it.

Ristine asked if I thought that I was being discriminated against and I said that I would like him to recall me as a witness and ask me that question tomorrow and I would give him a chain of events from which conclusions could be drawn.

With this in mind, I have made notes and dug up Daugherty's letter of October 8 mentioning "two fine gentlemen on a mission of spite."

Word has just arrived of Adm Mitcher's carrier strike against Tokyo this morning.[ii]

Friday, February 16

Gave additional testimony to Ristine. Mentioned Mr Ickes' statement to Asst. Secty. of War McCloy[iii] regarding "that damned man Buckner." Wound up my testimony by saying that from the foregoing occurrence it seems that is "not that they loved walrus more but 'that damned man Buckner' less." I filed Daughtrey's letter of October 8, 1944, with my testimony. It showed that Dr Gabrielson had sent his agents to investigate me personally rather than general conditions as others who were doing the same thing that I was at the same time.

Saturday, February 17

Richardson returned my recommendation, through him to Adm Nimitz, that Geiger be my replacement if I should become a casualty during the coming engagement. His indorsement said it was inadvisable to forward it and directed that neither I nor any member of my staff mention the subject to Adm Nimitz nor his staff. Richardson said he had taken the matter up with the War Dept.

---

i   Harold L. Ickes, secretary of the interior.

ii   This was the first aircraft-carrier-launched attack on Japan since the Doolittle Raid in April 1942. Because of the International Date Line, it occurred on February 16 in Japan.

iii John J. McCloy, assistant secretary of war.

I returned the letter to him for reconsideration stating that it was an opportune time to heal differences and bad feeling between Army and Marine services. I also said that I felt it my right to talk directly with Adm Nimitz on this subject but under present conditions, would be guided by his expressed desires.

Sunday, February 18

Took Mrs Keleher to Gen. Perkins' party (a good dinner spoiled by a bad movie afterwards instead of conversation). She was a little on edge, knowing that her husband's battleship was in the fleet attacking Tokyo today. She also knew that this was D-day for the attack and landing on Iwo Jima—a leak in secret information somewhere.

On February 19 (February 18 in Hawaii), the Marine V Amphibious Corps landed at Iwo Jima while the Fifth Fleet launched attacks against the Japanese home islands. The Marines secured the island in five weeks of fighting, ending March 26, but at great cost: 26,000 casualties, including over 6,000 killed, against over 24,000 Japanese dead. The battle was the bloodiest in the Marine Corps' history, and was immortalized by Joe Rosenthal's famous photo of a flag-raising on Iwo's Mount Suribachi.

Monday, February 19

First definite news of the Tokyo and Iwo Jima operations arrives—all good.

My party at the club came off nicely. Guests were: V. Adm. Murray, RAdm Cobb, Lt Gen Richardson, Capt Dodge (N), Gov. & Mrs Stainback, Mr. & Mrs. Ward, Dr & Mrs Frank, Mr & Mrs Wightman, Mrs Sack, Cap & Mrs Wilson (N), Col Green, Col Ely, Capt Dillon (N), Col Garfield, Col Harper, Comdr Kirtland, Col. Bentley, Col Raney, Col Smith, Col Bridgett, Col Schleicker, Chap Hillyer, Col Buchanan, Col Carlton, Col Westerveldt, Col Finney, Mrs Lyman, BG. McCunniff, Miss Crews, Mrs Branneman, Mrs Keleher, Mrs Graham, Mrs Ruth Dillingham, Miss H Gowen, Miss M Gowen, Miss Rogers, Miss Walsh, Mrs Ackerstrom, Post, Cowart & Hubbard. Mrs Mayfield and Mrs Erdman had to fall out at the last minute (packing & sick baby). Armadier orchestra, champaign, old fashions and highballs afterwards during dance and at the house. Case and a half of bourbon and [ ] bottles of champaign.

Total cost—$282.90.

Tuesday, February 20

Had photographs, for official use, taken of me at the Shafter studio. Had supper with Dr Frank, where he had members of the game conservation club of which he is President. They had a very interesting discussion and made definite constructive plans. Among those present were Elmer Mullinix, Magoon, Lenox (founder), Case (?)

During the morning Mr Griffis of the Red Cross dropped in and said he didn't want Gen Goodyear to be in charge of Tenth Army ARC affairs on the target due to his age and his approach to the target with the 27th Div at Espiritu Santo. I told him that I concurred if that was what he wanted.

Wednesday, February 21

Rr. Adm Combs,[i] supply man from Washington dropped in.

5:30 PM. Mrs Ackerstrom's party in honor of the promotion of Schick and Blakelock, followed by dance at the club. I produced some large tin stars which the girls pinned on with appropriate solicitations.

Thursday, February 22

Wrote birthday letter to Gen Connor.[ii] Gen Goodyear called at 11:30 AM and got his assignment. Took the No. 1 mountain walk in 51 minutes.

Attended Iscom dinner and dance at club.

Friday, February 23

My three Press Relations Officers reported for duty: Army—Lt Col Davidson

Navy—Lt. Comder Banks

Marines—Capt. Merrillat

Took Nina Crews to Wightman party. Cocktails at their house and turkey supper and dance at Outrigger Club. Elmer Lee's orchestra serenaded me and tried to get me to dance the hula with their singer, but without success.

---

i Rear Admiral Lewis Combs, deputy chief of civil engineers. He is known as the creator of the Construction Battalion units, known as "Seabees."

ii Major General William D. Connor, superintendent of West Point when Buckner was commandant of cadets. Connor was born February 22, 1874.

Met the swimmer Bill Smith Jr. His father is in the orchestra and sings. Guests at dinner were also:

Post [ ] Mrs Carson

Mr Bridge [ ] Mrs Allen (Maui)

Saturday, February 24, K-1?

Attended dedication of Hickam Field Passenger Terminal. Richardson & Ryan made good speeches. We inspected planes and facilities and refreshments were served. About 200 guests. 4:00 PM.

From there I drove to the Halikulani, picked up Mrs Keleher and took her to McCunniff's party (dinner & dance) at the Wheeler Field Officer's Club. When this was over, we went to McCunniff's quarters for a nightcap, after which I took Mrs Keleher home and found it was 2:00 AM when I got back.—Moral: Don't take girls to parties who live too far away if you want any sleep.

Sunday, February 25

5:00 PM Took Helene Gowen to the Oden Smith's dinner at Wahaiwa. Helene lives just outside of the post. Guests also were:

Post and Mrs Ackerstrom

Mr & Mrs Galloway, she from Ketchikan.

Monday, February 26

11:00 AM. Presented trophies to:

Mr Sgt. Bernarding—A.G. basketball winner, 1945.

Pfc. Rodeo—   "   softball   ",   1944.

T. Sgt. Gagner—   HQ Co   "   ",   1945.

Attended "wetdown" promotion party by Schick & Blakelock followed by dinner at club with the latter.

Tuesday, February 27

Harmon reported 24 hrs overdue in plane returning from Kwajalein.[i]

Had lunch with Corinne and drove out beyond Diamond Head to take colored pictures of the breakers. Short of color film but got a few good shots and wound up with black & white.

---

i   General Harmon's plane disappeared returning to Hawaii from the Marianas. No
    trace was ever found.

Returned to post for supper and spent evening in office balancing financial accounts and writing letters.

Wednesday, February 28

Still no word from Harmon.

Subscribed to *Time* for 3 years.

Took Nina Crews to Harris' Garret's dinner and dance at the Connor Club preceded by cocktails at Mrs Mitchells. She gave me her picture, flatteringly inscribed—probably because of her unique experience in being taken home without being pawed to death.

Thursday, March 1

At the conference this morning were Pat Hurley (Ambassador to China), Gen. Wedemeyer, Adm. Cook (CofS to Adm King) and Wild Bill Donovan.[i] The first three were on their way back from the Roosevelt-Stalin-Churchill conference in Crimea.[ii]

Had lunch with Richardson who had all of the visiting firemen there. Afterward had conference with Gen Donovan in Fielder's office. He wants to send representatives with the Tenth Army. I questioned him on what service they could render but was noncommittal and told him that it was a matter of policy that Adm Nimitz would have to decide.

Got measured for glasses & spare pants.

Friday, March 2

Had Gen Maxwell, Faymonville[iii] and their group including Gail and six or eight others from the W.D. in for lunch after which they had a conference with heads of my staff. After the general conference Maxwell came to my office and said Hildring (Civil Gov't head)[iv] wanted me to understand that he received so much advice and assistance from high War

---

i   Major General Patrick Hurley, U.S. ambassador to the Republic of China; Lieutenant General Albert C. Wedemeyer, commander of China Theater; Rear Admiral Charles M. Cooke, chief of Naval plans; Major General William J. Donovan, director of the Office of Strategic Services.

ii   This was the Yalta Conference, which occurred February 4–11, 1945.

iii   Major General Russell L. Maxwell, assistant chief of staff G-4 of the War Department General Staff; Brigadier General Philip R. Faymonville, office of the chief of ordnance.

iv   Major General John H. Hildring, director of the War Department's Civil Affairs Division.

Dept. and Gov't. officials that it was difficult for him to seem consistent or logical to those in the field. He also said Surles[i] wanted newspaper men to be well looked after. Maxwell also hoped that I could at some time make a place for Phil Faymonville.

Saturday, March 3

Told Adm Towers that I might use some of Bill Donovan's agents as secret service after Phase I. Willing to take one man and try him out. Could take him on March 15 APA.[ii] Expressed no great enthusiasm but willing to try him.

Spent night until late cleaning up at office and writing letters.

During the forenoon, Pope Gregory, (Q.M. Gen) and Gen. Kirk, (Surg Gen)[iii] with a large retinue from Washington dropped in to say "Hello." The Washington climate is very disagreeable in February & March, hence the visiting firemen.

Sunday, March 4

Wound up with dentists: Maj Carroll and Capt Dunwoody.

Unable to call Mrs Dillingham to cancel dinner engagement, wrote her a note: "Please forgive me for bowing to the inevitable but be assured that I bow to you as the incomparable." Also called Ruth D. and Mrs Ward. Will have to write the Franks a letter.

Called on Richardson who said he was still awaiting word from the War Dept regarding command succession in case I became a casualty (pocket veto.)

Had several of the neighbors in for a nip before supper.

Took a long, hot, tub bath before retiring, probably the last for many months.

Monday, March 5 and Tuesday 6

Rose at 5:30 AM and went to Hickam Field with Schick, Smith, Cowart, Hubbard, Dumas, Bissett, Louper. Had breakfast there. Richardson and Ruffner were there to see us off. The former gave me

---

i   Major General Alexander D. Surles, director of the War Department's Bureau of Public Relations.

ii An attack transport (APA) leaving March 15 for Okinawa.

iii Major General Edmund B. Gregory, quartermaster general of the Army; Major General Norman T. Kirk, surgeon-general of the Army.

a farewell gift of a quart of Scotch and a copy of "Behind the Japanese Mask"—Steiner. Took off at 8:30 AM in a C-54E.

Av Johnston Is at 12:15 (Hon Time) had lunch there and took off an hour later. (My fountain pen is squirting as the plane climbs.) Finished Richardson's book shortly after lunch.

We have crossed the 180th Meridian so it is now Tuesday on Monday.

Landed at Kwajalein 9:00 PM (Honolulu Time) a 12 ½ hour trip. The search for Harmon was still in full swing with no real news but the usual hallucinations of tracers. Signal lights, rockets, Jap planes, submarines etc. One pilot distinctly saw a brown Jap plane land and taxi on a field situated on an island where no field existed.

We reached Kwajalein before the message announcing our departure from Hickam got there. We saw a Maj Borne who took us to the ATS house where we put up for the night.

Brig. Gen. Ross took us to the movies, which were bad. He said that there were about an average of 200 landings & take-offs at the field every day.

Wednesday, March 7

Having slept so much on the plane yesterday, we were all slept out by 5:30 AM and got up.

Maj Borne took us for a jeep tour of the island after breakfast, winding up at the plane. We took off at 8:12 AM. Maj Gen Wood, Comdg the Marine air wing saw me off.

8 hours later, arrived at Guam. Schick, Dumas & I were given Lamar's house next to McMorris' at Cincpac's Hq, and the others were billeted with the Island Comdr, Gen Larsen.

Saw McMorris, Adm Spruance & his CofS, Adm Davis at the first-named's house.

After supper there Adm Spruance, Adm's Davis & McMorris had a conflab with us on air command relationships which was entirely satisfactory and flexible enough for all purposes. Spruance got aboard his flagship after supper with a view to sailing in the morning.

Thursday, March 8

Looked over Phase II study handed us by Gen Mondell.[i]

---

i   Brigadier General Harold C. Mandell, assistant chief of plans, U.S. Pacific Fleet.

After lunch met plane with Post, Wallace, Blakelock, Davidson, Nold, Harris and others.

Expect Turner's ship in Mch [March] 10.

Post brought a bottle of crème de menthe from Mrs. Ackerstrom and a walrus tooth Eskimo carving of a death mask from Charley Madsen.

The Navy lives well ashore. They make themselves far more comfortable than the Army. Their houses are better, they are well furnished, including rugs, curtains double & single beds, wicker and overstuffed furniture, mess china, mess boys and every comfort. At Adm Nimitz' mess now presided over by Adm. McMorris, the officers assemble at 6:30 for cocktails and have a very gay party before 7:00 PM ("1900") dinner.

Adm Wright was in for dinner tonight.

A Harmon search plane reported that at about noon today he saw two life rafts tied together between Johnston Is & Oahu with gulls and debris around them and at least one living man on a raft. He circled and observed carefully in conditions of low visibility. A destroyer is on its way to the scene.—Probably imagination like similar reports in past.

Friday, March 9

From Leyte comes word that S.W.Pac. has declined again to live up to agreements, this time regarding replacements for the XXIV Corps.

Saturday, March 10

Nothing seems to have materialized from the Harmon clue of two days ago.

A good report came from the 300-plane bombardment of Tokyo this morning by B-29s.[i]

Rear Adm. Perry,[ii] formerly at Kodiak, arrived today. He expects to be with us in charge of an escort carrier division.

Arranged for press conference tomorrow with all war correspondents who are to accompany us.

---

i   This was Operation *Meetinghouse*, the first major fire raid on Tokyo by 334 U.S. B-29s. It was the most destructive single airstrike in history, killing over 83,000 people. Over the next months, a succession of raids would cripple Japan and its urban areas.

ii Rear Admiral John A. Perry.

On March 11, Buckner directed the Tenth Army's tentative order from January 6 to be put into effect as the final plan for Operation Iceberg.

Sunday, March 11, <u>started taking atabrine</u>

The life rafts and living survivor reported on Mch 8 turned out to be two kapok life preservers from a wrecked Navy plane and no survivors at all. People's eyes fool them when they are excited.

Had 11:00 AM press conference. Laid emphasis on equal publicity for all services and the desirability of reaching down as far as possible to lower units and N.C.O.s. Also including staff officers, who are usually overlooked.

Adm. Turner came in on his flagship at noon. He had dinner with us at Adm. McMorris mess. Afterwards we saw colored movies of the Iwo Jima fight. Someone brought in four Red Cross girls for the movies. I was invited to join them on another party later but declined.

We expect to board Adm Turner's ship tomorrow.

(On the way back from the office this afternoon I met 1st LT Herman who lived with Buckey[i] at Valley Forge. I told him I would give him Buckey's address if he came at 9:00 AM tomorrow.)

Monday, March 12

Herman didn't show up for Buckey's address.

Adm. Creasey[ii] of the British Navy, their head submarine officer, and some of his staff were in for lunch. After lunch we went out with Adm. Turner in his barge and boarded our command ship the *Eldorado* (Capt [ ]).[iii] We sailed shortly before six, a long looked-forward-to occasion.

After sailing, Turner took me aside and dwelt on the difficulties and uncertainties of our mission which he characterized as a "son of a bitch" and asked what I thought about it. I expressed confidence and started to argue him out of his misgivings. I found then that he wasn't worried at all but was trying to find out if I was.

After supper, Turner talked to Post and myself about the shore party set-up of the Marines whom he has less confidence in along these lines

---

i   Simon Bolivar Buckner III, General Buckner's eldest son.

ii   Rear Admiral Sir George E. Creasy, flag officer submarines for the Royal Navy.

iii   Captain Jesse R. Wallace commanded *Eldorado* from late 1944 until July 27, 1945.

than he has in Army units. He said that the Marine shore party work at Iwo Jima was poor, particularly that of the V Corps & the 4th Div.

We heard this afternoon that Adm Oldendorf[i] and his chief of staff had been badly injured at Ulithi when their small boat collided with a buoy. Oldendorf was to have been our gun support officer.

Buckner letter to Adele Buckner:
March 12, 1945
Sweetheart:

The anticipated regulation prohibiting the dating of letters was not put into effect, and, apparently, will not affect me no matter what the situation. So far, my trip has been intensely interesting, more so in fact than any of the others.

Admiral Nimitz, as you have seen from the papers, has been in Washington so I have not seen him at his forward command post. However, I have had very satisfactory conferences with his staff and others in his command with whom I have associations.

Eddie and a number of my crowd came out here in the most luxurious passenger planes that I have yet seen. The old governor's house where we were entertained on our bridal trip and where you selected the dinner guests in accordance with rank is now a heap of battered ruins as is the town in which it was located. However, order is coming out of devastation and the island is a beehive of construction and activity. We get a great kick out of seeing the big flights of B-29s take off for Tokyo and eagerly await their return with encouraging and satisfying reports of the results of their bombings.

We are all deeply distressed at Harmon's loss. So far there has been no trace of him. We lived in the same house together as 2nd Lieutenants in the 9th Infantry and owned a model T Ford in common on the Mexican border.

My present trip is not yet finished, but I shall probably travel by water during the rest of the journey. What, when and where are matters that I cannot yet convey to you. Suffice it to say that I am full of enthusiasm, just as when we boarded a transport in this same harbor nearly three decades ago.

---

i   Vice Admiral Jesse B. Oldendorf, U.S. Navy.

My love, my hopes and my happiness rest in you.
Bolivar

Tuesday, March 13

All day the *Eldorado* zigzagged westward escorted by the destroyer *Putnam*. Some of the gun crews drilled with dummy shells on a dummy gun, the idea being to acquire speed in loading. The skies are clear, the trade wind is with us and a moderate swell gives a little life to the ship. The destroyer stays about a mile ahead of us.

During the morning I finished "Japan and the Japanese" and spent a while on the "flag bridge" with Adm. Turner.

We had cooked breadfruit and Guava beans for lunch. During the afternoon I read most of "The Pacific World"—Osborne.

There is very little life in the sea—no birds and only an occasional lonely flying fish.

After supper, Adm Turner repeated his conversation of last night almost verbatim. He is still leary [sic] of shore parties and thinks the Marines know little about moving their supplies off the beaches and won't take experienced advice.

He doesn't consider Gen's Geiger nor Schmidt very intelligent. He regards Erskine as the best Div. Comdr in the V Phibcorps and doesn't admire the other two.

Wednesday, March 14

A couple of small balloons were released before lunch and shot at by the anti-aircraft guns aboard. The shooting was rotten.

Finished reading "The Pacific World" and started "Mountain Growth"—Hobbs—a very enlightening discussion of present island, mountain and volcano development in the Pacific.

Thursday, March 15

Adm Turner didn't show up for lunch.

Flying fish in considerable numbers seen. Also one white gull-like bird passed us going east. He was barely visible and did not sail much.

A P.B.Y. plane flew over us. Another was reported yesterday but I didn't see it.

Smoothed out the trigger pull on my pistol.

Turner missed supper also.

After supper I read and also got about caught [up] on letter writing if such a thing be possible.

Friday, March 16

About 9:30 AM we came into Leyte Gulf and went to a berth opposite Adm. Kincaid's Hqrs of the 7th Fleet. Harbor full of ships of all kinds.

Adm Davis, Comdg a sort of amphibious rear echelon came aboard with some of his staff including Jimmy Roosevelt.

After lunch, Post, Hubbard & I went with Adm. Turner and called on Kincaid and on Gen MacArthur's Hq. He was away and represented by Gen Steph. Chamberlin.

Turner left us and returned to the ship while the rest of us called on Eichelberger's Eighth Army Hqrs where we saw Eich. & his CofS, Clovis Byers. We then drove out to XXIV Corps Hq. The Corps & most of the staff were on amphibious rehearsals but we saw Gen Garvin, CofS, and Talley[i] and some of our staff.

At 6:00 we went to Kincaid's for dinner. Adm Kaufman,[ii] Comdg the Naval District was there. There was much speculation as to the future command setup in the Pacific and whether MacArthur would take over for the eventual attack on Japan. Kincaid thinks he is very sound strategically but overlooks important operational details.

Saturday, March 17

During the morning, we went over to where the XXIV Corps was having a landing rehearsal with the 7th & 96th Divs. A hard rain came up and made it impossible to carry out air support missions.

After lunch, Adm. Hall and Hodge came aboard.

Capt Whitehead (N) air support liaison officer, Rr Adm Pride (his understudy) and Col Shaw arrived from Ulithi. Pride had seen the suicide plane, with crew of three hit the carrier [ ]. He said that ships were lighted up in spite of the fact that the plane was picked up on the

---

i   Colonel Benjamin B. Talley, commanding 1st Engineer Special Brigade.
ii   Rear Admiral James L. Kauffman, commanding Philippine Sea Frontier.

screens 80 miles away. Another plane dived into an island. It was about 9:00 PM.

At 7:30 PM I went to the ship's movies which were interrupted by an air alert at 8:00—a real blessing.

Sunday, March 18

Gen Bruce, Comdg 77th Div, came aboard in the morning for an hour's visit.

During the afternoon, the rest of my staff and Hq enlisted force came aboard from the XXIV Corps Hq where they had been awaiting our arrival.

We saw copies of an affidavit by an escaped prisoner from a sunken Jap boat showing that the Japs crowded prisoners into a ships' hold with the deliberate idea of suffocating them and had killed about half that way when the ship was sunk by aircraft. The conditions described made the black hole of Calcutta seem almost mild by comparison. When the ship was sinking the Jap sentinel fired into and hit ten of the survivors.

Monday, March 19

During the morning our staff manned battle positions and we observed another amphibious landing by the XXIV Corps. They were 15 minutes late crossing the line of departure and Adm Turner said he was going to relieve the L.S.T. Div. Comdr. responsible for the delay.

Gen Mulcahy (USMC) Comdg my land based aircraft arrived from Honolulu and joined us aboard.

I told Dumas that he might go in Manila to see his sister-in-law who had been a captive in Jap hands since the outbreak of the war, provided he could fly up tomorrow and return next day. He wants to supply her with funds. She is still at Santo Tomas, where she was confined.

Tuesday, March 20

Dumas couldn't get plane transportation to Manila, after all.

The morning was uneventful, except for a visit from Gen Bruce (77th Div) and Rr Adm Kiland[i] who is taking him to his objective. Bruce, as

---

i   Rear Admiral Ingolf N. Kiland, commanding Task Group 51.1, the Western Islands Attack Group, for *Iceberg*.

usual, is rarin' to go and is looking well ahead for action. I much prefer a bird dog that you have to whistle in to one that you have to urge out. He is of the former variety.

Clovis Byers came aboard just before noon with an invitation to dine with Eichelberger on Thursday, which was accepted.

Turner, Post, Adm Hall & I dined with Hodge at Rizal—a delightful dinner. We got back aboard by 9:00 PM via duck [DUKW], P.T. boat and Admiral's barge.

I gave Hodge a quart of Scotch and a pistol slide with a stainless steel front sight. He let me have the second volume of Lee's Lieutenants by Freeman to read. I started it when I was last with him in Jan.

Wednesday, March 21
Today the 77th Div (Bruce) started for the target. At last our advance guard is headed for the enemy with no intermediate stops. Bruce is rarin' to go.

From 2 to 5 PM we went to the *Teton*, Adm Hall's flagship and listened to a critique of the amphibious rehearsals. There was a general feeling of confidence and assurance at the meeting. I saw Arnold (7th Div) and Jim Bradley (96th Div) at the meeting. After the first hour, the benefit accrued from critiques progresses in accordance with the law of diminishing returns.

Don Prior of the combined American radio networks wants me to go on the air with him and Adm Turner when we are on the target, just as he did with the latter, Holland Smith and Schmidt at Iwo Jima. I would much prefer to keep quiet, but saw no way out of it since Turner accepted.

Thursday, March 22
Had a rough, rainy trip to and from Eichelberger's diner. He had just returned from the Iloilo expedition. The Japs left the city and took to the hills. About 2/3 of the city and all of the waterfront has been burned. Eich. drove into Iloilo in a jeep. Maj Gen Irwin[i] and an Australian brigadier were also at the party. Byers was away. On the way back the

---
i   Major General Stephen F. Irwin, British Army.

cockswain of the Adm's barge got lost in the rain and Adm. Turner took over and got us back.

Friday, March 23

We steamed over toward the Samar coast this morning and took on fuel from an oiler.

Further details came regarding Adm Mitcher's strike in the Japanese Inland Sea. The fact that he could cripple warships there is a real landmark in this war. It means that the Japs now have no safe anchorage anywhere in which they can restore or hide their fleet. Their intelligent men can't help realizing this.

Saturday, March 24

Today was spent having a command post exercise using the actual messages that were sent during the first Iwo Jima assault day. It was an excellent way to shake down the staff and teach them what to expect.

Messages were picked up to the effect that the Japs had located some battleships near Okinawa and that they had made at least one air attack on our minesweepers. Nothing came directly from our forces, although the sweeping and bombardment were to have begun today.

Sunday, March 25

Our LST's and tractor outfits moved out this morning. Being slower than the transports, they need a head start. They will meet us on the objective.

On March 26 Bruce's 77th Infantry Division attacked Kerama Retto, securing the island group on March 29 with little loss.

Monday, March 26

Early morning messages indicate that the bombardment, minesweeping and air attacks came off as scheduled. U.D.T.'s report only 1 moored and 6 floating mines and beach conditions in the Kerama Retto about as expected. Only rifle fire at UDT's and only 1 casualty.

10:00 AM we had a demonstration of the use of 5lb T.N.T charges against Jap underwater swimmers. We dropped one in 60ft of water and killed a great many small fish.

Intercepted local messages indicate that the 77th has a good foothold in the Kerama Retto but nothing direct from him.

A message from Adm. Mitcher says that Okinawa is honeycombed with caves, tunnels and emplacements and predicts a very tough job for us. Tomorrow we start on a great adventure.

Buckner letter to Adele Buckner:
March 26, 1945
Sweetheart:

I have just finished tonight's installment of a long letter to you. I can't mail it yet and probably won't be able to for some time. However, in due time it will tell you of my present movements and probably those of some days to come.

I am wondering if Mrs Mayfield, wife of a Naval Commodore, looked you up as she passed through San Francisco. She had a war job of some kind in Honolulu while her husband was in New Caledonia. Now the two of them are going to Chile. She promised to see you if possible.

I have seen a good deal recently of Eichelberger who commands the 8th Army here. He is busy mopping up the southern islands. Clovis Byers is his chief of staff. Eichelberger looks well but is irritated over having to do the cleanup job after Krueger has had the interesting part of the campaign period. I hope to have better luck with the Tenth. There is plenty of fresh ground to be broken and some of it is none too soft. The fighting will be more and more interesting as we press forward into the Mikado's domains. Iwo Jima is an example of how heavily a small island can be fortified. The Marines had a tough time there because every inch of the island was defended by solid rock and concrete emplacements. The Marines did a good job in taking it and its capture compensates for the heavy losses. In actual numbers the Marine casualties equal those of Lee at Gettysburg. This will give you some idea of how heavy the fighting was.

The Philippines will never be the romantic spot of our last stay there. However, the natives are still up to some of their old tricks. They stole so many rations and pieces of equipment here that the provost guard inspected every native who went down the road with a bag, or bundle.

It suddenly occurred to the provost marshall that the number of funeral processions seemed to be excessive. When he started opening coffins he found the sacred remains of many of our looted supply dumps.

I miss your arms and your lips. It will take a long time to get caught up when I get back. Goodnight dear.

Bolivar

Tuesday, March 27

At 10:45 AM our convoy weighed anchor and moved with an air of dignified confidence on its non-stop trip to close with the enemy.

When we were well started a message came to the effect that a sailor in the *Eldorado's* crew had just been designated to attend an officer's training school. We signalled to a P.T. boat which came alongside. The sailor slid down a ladder which we lowered, someone threw his bags into the PT boat after him and the little craft took him smiling toward shore.

In the afternoon we briefed all the war correspondents aboard and had some anti-aircraft practice at sleeves towed by planes from our escort carriers.

Just before supper, word came from Bruce that the landing of the 77th Div in the Kerama Retto was progressing well and that he had captured 38 suicide boats hidden in caves.

Wednesday, March 28

Finished reading the third volume of Freeman's "Lee's Lieutenants"— Gettysburg to Appomattox. A tragic epitaph to a nobly defended cause.

Thursday, March 29

The gun crews of the ships in the convoy practiced following planes from the carriers that simulated straffing attacks. Our ship also launched its paravanes to see if they were in order and that the crew knew how to use them.

Adm Turner now spends all his time and takes his meals on the flag bridge. His staff said that he had never messed with the troop commander's staff until the two weeks he was with me from Guam until the convoy left Leyte.

Friday, March 30

No. of suicide boats captured in Kerama Retto now reported as over 300.

Had abandon ship drill in PM.

Had a submarine contact and passed one or more floating mines. During the afternoon a destroyer came alongside and delivered mail via breeches buoy.

Saturday, March 31

Ely came aboard from a destroyer in a bricches buoy. He had just left Adm. Blandy's task force with the 77th Div and had the latest pictures and U.D.T. reports.

Tomorrow is Easter Sunday, my father's birthday and the day of my first battle. I hope that I shall be able to look back upon it with the same degree of enthusiasm with which I anticipate it.

Attended Easter services at 8:15 PM and turned in early so as to be fresh for tomorrows events.

CHAPTER 5

The Battle of Okinawa, April 1 to June 17, 1945

On April 1, 1945, Tenth Army landed on Okinawa. The invasion date was code-named L-Day, or "Love Day" using the phonetic alphabet of the time, a somewhat ironic choice that generated much comment.

Sunday, April 1

Rose at 4:30 and had hot cakes for breakfast by way of getting fortified for a day of fighting.

The weather was good and the golden sunrise was not for Japan. Shortly before six some Jap planes attacked. Seven were shot down. Apparently we shot down an eighth that was ours.

The crescendo of the bombardment, culminating in the rocket discharge was a magnificent spectacle. From start to finish the landing was a superb piece of teamwork which we could watch from the 50-yd line in the command room or on the flag deck.

We landed practically without opposition and gained more ground than we expected to have for three days, including the Yonton [Yontan] and Katena [Kadena] airfields. Arnold's 7th Div made the farthest gains and got half way across the island. The weather continues good and we have nearly 60,000 troops ashore with negligible casualties.

At about dusk several suicide planes came in. The *West Virginia* and one other ship were hit. We set up a smoke screen around our ship—Tonight the sky is constantly lighted by star shells.

The Japs have missed their best opportunity on the ground and in the air. When their counter-attack comes we will be holding strong ground.

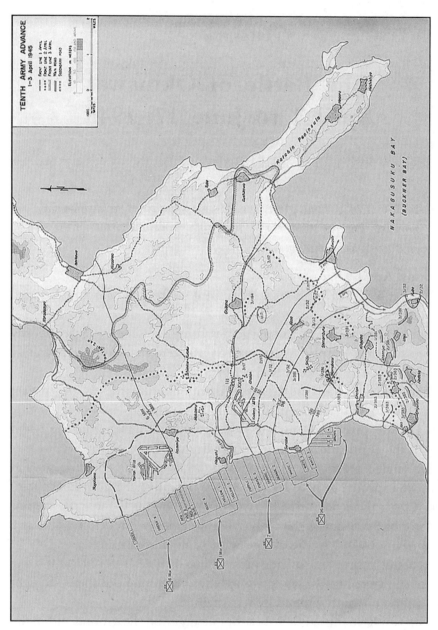

Tenth Army's landing and actual progress, April 1–3, 1945. *U.S. Army*

Monday, April 2

A Jap plane was shot down by AAA.

The 7th Div got entirely across the island today. Being well ahead of the 1st Mardiv on its left, it could not turn south abreast of the 96th Div which was attacking in that direction against gradually stiffening resistance. Some opposition was met by the left of the III Phibcorps. Weather excellent.

I have decided to order up the 27th Div from Ulithi to land on the east shore about Apr 10. Hodge came aboard during the afternoon.

Adm Spruance is trying to hurry us in the capture of Ie Jima [Ie Shima]. This would gain no time in completing the field and would use up the army reserve before the main fight starts.

Main Jap forces are apparently in the south and heavy fighting should start within two days.

At dusk 12 suicide planes came in—2 shot down by fighters, 2 by AAA, and one damaged an LCI attacked Kerama shipping. They struck and damaged 4 transports. Ships in our vicinity put up a smoke screen.

A slightly injured Jap plane landed today by mistake on a field that we had captured. He was shot when he started to run and the plane was captured.

On April 3 Buckner signaled to Geiger, "All restrictions removed on your advance northward." Buckner thus activated Phase II much earlier than planned. This was an important and overlooked decision, but one that showed considerable initiative and aggressiveness. The diary entry from this day reveals that Buckner also was entertaining other possible maneuvers.

Tuesday, April 3

Yesterday 11 women armed & in Jap uniforms along with some soldiers tried to attack a 96th Div FA position & were killed.

Disapproved Hodge's request to have 77th Div land and cover his rear. (He probably wants to assure himself that it will remain in his corps.)

All units progressed satisfactorily. The 7th Div got turned south and the 1st Mardiv reached the east coast. Resistance still light.

The 27th Div was sent for to land on the east coast about Apr 10. It is at Ulithi.

The 2d Mardiv ordered to land Apr 5 on beaches north of those now used by III Phibcorps. Geiger came aboard after lunch in fine spirits.

At sundown our fighters reported that 25 Jap planes started toward our ships but after 13 had been shot down, the rest left.

Buckner letter to Adele Buckner:[i]
March 13, 1945
My darling:

I am beginning this letter now and including news that cannot be released at present. This permits me to write things down as they happen and to mail the letter when the news can appropriately be divulged.

Yesterday I left Guam with about a dozen key members of my staff on board the joint command ship from which I will eventually disembark when my army goes ashore to fight. With me is the Vice Admiral Turner who will command the amphibious expedition, put us ashore, give us supporting gunfire and support us with escort carrier planes until we can take enough airfields to stand on our own feet and fly in our own planes in and support ourselves. The command ship and the admiral are just back from Iwo Jima where they performed a similar service for the V Marine Corps.

Major elements of my command will be an army corps of three divisions, a marine corps of three divisions and some more army divisions in reserve to be landed when and where the situation demands. In addition, there will be numerous corps, army and service troops to support the combat elements and air units to join when we capture or build the necessary fields. My divisions are composed of seasoned and experienced troops. In fact, I seem to be the only raw recruit in the crowd when battle experience is considered. However, the others should raise the average.

We are headed for the Philippines where I will watch some amphibious rehearsals of our landing operations and pick up the army corps in time

---

i   He started this letter in March and finished in early April before mailing. He offers
     a day-by-day account to Adele of his activities in the weeks before the Okinawa
     invasion. His descriptions of the past few weeks offer additional perspectives to
     the diary.

to start for the objective. The marine corps embarks elsewhere and joins us. I have already visited both corps.

Escorted by a destroyer, our ship has been plowing westward all day through a moderate swell, constantly zigzagging to worry any Jap submarine that may try to torpedo us. I have seen only three flying fish since leaving Guam and no birds of any kind. I finished up a book called "Japan and the Japanese" and got a good start on "The Pacific World." When I finish writing this, I shall look over plans for what I shall probably have to do if I accomplish my present mission satisfactorily.—Good night.

March 17 (St. Patrick's Day)

We got into Leyte yesterday and I saw Admiral Kincaid of the 7th Fleet; Eichelberger, commanding the Eighth Army, and his Chief of Staff Clovis Byers. The last two sent you their very best. Today I watched amphibious rehearsals for my landing and saw General Hodge, commanding my XXIV Corps and Admiral Hall who takes this corps to our target. Tomorrow, some more members of my staff will come aboard. We were blessed by a brief air alert this evening which had the virtue of breaking up the ships movie which I had made the mistake of attending.

(Running short of paper).

March 21

For several days I have been watching practice landing exercises on the beaches here, attending critiques and getting impatient to move on. Last night, I had dinner ashore with General Hodge commanding the XXIV Corps. Archie Arnold, Jim Bradley and Bruce are the division commanders in this corps. Tomorrow night, Admiral Turner, Eddie Post and I dine with Eichelberger. He is off today watching a landing to mop up Japs on another island. The Japs fortify the old Spanish towns and we have to destroy them to get at the Japs. I am afraid that Manila, Zamboanga, Cebu, Ilolio and Ilo will all be gone before the Japs are destroyed. Large parts of these towns have already been burned by the Japs.

Today was a great day. I saw the convoy with my leading division move out on its nonstop trip to strike the enemy. Those of us who are to follow for the main landing got a great thrill out of it. Mulcahy, a big red-faced Irish Major General of Marines who commands my land based air force was standing near me when the convoy slowly steamed by with its escort of destroyers darting about on the watch for submarines. He looked up with a broad smile and said "Here goes the kickoff for the big game."

March 23

Six of us had a most enjoyable dinner with Eichelberger last night. He had just flown back from the capture of Iloilo. The Japs took to the hills leaving the entire water front and two-thirds of the city destroyed.

March 25

Yesterday my staff manned all their positions on the command ship and had a command post exercise using the actual messages sent and received during the first days attack and landing on Iwo Jima. It gave them all a good idea of what kinds of messages and events are likely to come up on the day of our main landing.

Our carrier force and battleships have struck our objective and our mine sweeping was due to begin today. Tomorrow, my leading division lands to secure the Kerama Retto, a group of small islands just southwest of Okinawa. We will forfeit strategic surprise by this but it is necessary for the fleet and will strengthen the main attack and landing.

We are now having an air alert in San Pedro Bay—possibly a Jap snooper trying to check the movements of our big fleet here at dusk. This is our third since we have been here.

March 26

Fragmentary messages tell of a foothold on the Kerama Retto by our leading division. Admiral Mitcher also says that recent air reconnaissance shows Okinawa to be honeycombed with fortifications. He predicts a tough job for us.

March 28

Word came that the Kerama Retto had been occupied according to plan with very few casualties. 250 1-man "suicide" attack boats were captured in caves along the shores. 12 strangled native women were found in one cave.

March 30

A submarine contact and a couple of floating mines were reported by our escort vessels.

March 31

Colonel Ely, my G-2 and son of General Hanson Ely, came back from the Kerama Retto on a destroyer and boarded us with the breaches buoy. He had the latest pictures and reports of the landing beaches. These, he reported, had been distributed to every battalion that is to land tomorrow. With members of my staff, I am attending Easter services this evening. Tomorrow is our big day—incidentally my father's birthday.

April 1

From the opening bombardment and air attack to the landing of the last tank and gun our assault against Okinawa today was as beautiful a piece of teamwork as I have ever seen. Opposition was light, the Japs evidently having expected us to land elsewhere on the island. We gained more ground today than we had hoped to get within three days. This included two air fields. Some of our ships were hit by planes but none sunk. The enemy has launched no counter-attack so far, but we have gained ground that will give us strong positions that we should be able to hold and later expand. I consider the day highly successful. We have nearly 60,000 troops ashore and will land more tomorrow.

April 2

We got across to the east coast of the island today, cutting it in two. Resistance is stiffening somewhat on both flanks but the Jap commander failed to counterattack this morning. A slightly damaged Jap plane landed today on a field that the pilot did not know we had captured. He was "very sorry please." So far, the Jap's apparent misconception of our plan, his failure to oppose our landing and his concentration near our pretended landing have made things easy for us, but very hard fighting against a strong system of concrete and underground defenses is still ahead of us. However, we are here to stay.

April 3

Good progress continues against light resistance. Main defenses appear to be in the south and heavy fighting will probably begin tomorrow or next day. About 13 planes were shot down while attacking our ships today at sunset and others driven off. No ship was hit.

I have written this letter from day to day as a sort of running account of events as they happened. Now that these events have been made public,

I can mail the letter but you will probably be some time in receiving it and the press will have given you this and much later information.

Everything is now going well and so far my opposing general has not displayed any noticeable degree of military brilliance. At least, he has not yet done any of the things that I hoped he would not think of. I hope he keeps this up.

Thoughts of my responsibility for so many lives are always sobering, but the fine fighting qualities of my men fill me with enthusiasm in my present task. However, my enthusiasm for your love is always my brightest thought.

Bolivar

Wednesday, April 4

Air raids reported so far have come at dawn or dusk, many by suicide planes. Numbers as follows:

Apr 1—15 attacked, 11 shot down.
"   2—30   "   12   "   "
"   3—71   "   26   "   "

Wind today shifting to north and slightly slowing up unloading. Work progressing on air fields.

Hodge, Geiger and Adm Reifsnider[i] came aboard.

I was unable to go ashore as I had planned due to two conferences on future operations.

Troops are beginning to develop enemy positions to the south. Bradley well ahead of Arnold. The latter in very rough ground. The Marines cleaned up everything to the north and started up the isthmus practically unopposed. Some evidence of looting and vandalism. I issued further instructions to stop this.

Handelman of the Int. News Service wanted a statement from me to issue on "VE" day. I told him I knew nothing of VE day and wouldn't tell anybody if I did. Too many people have already talked too much on that subject.

---

i   Rear Admiral Lawrence F. Reifsnider, commanding Task Force 53, the Northern Attack Force for *Iceberg*.

Thursday, April 5

Cold north wind, rain and some swell. Very little unloading as the result. No planes attacked this group.

Had conference with Geiger and Adm. Reifsnider regarding Phase 2. Also conferred with my own staff regarding Phase 3 and what is to follow.

Sherrod,[i] who was in Alaska as a correspondent came to see me. He is on his way to N.Y.

The 3d Mardiv [sic-III Phibcorps] continued to advance northward against negligible resistance. A few Okinawans had been given guns. They don't know either how to fight or how to surrender. They shoot a few rounds and go into caves but won't come out and have to be killed. The 7th & 96th Divs moved slowly against increasing resistance.

The civil population seems docile. Two men who killed their wives because the Japs told them they would be raped to death became very hostile to the Japs when they surrendered themselves and found this not to be true. One attacked a Jap prisoner.

Am preparing to land a reconnaissance group on Ie Jima. The eastern islands are being reconnoitered today by the Marine Recon. Bn.

On April 6 and 7 the Japanese mounted their first major response to the Okinawa invasion from bases in Kyushu and other home islands. On April 6 the first mass kamikaze attack, known as Kikusui (Floating Chrysanthemum), struck Spruance's fleet, hitting 22 and sinking 11 American ships, mostly destroyers and transports. Many damaged ships underwent repairs at Kerama Retto before sailing out of the battle area. Significantly, one of the two ammunition ships supporting the invasion was among those sunk, which led to ammunition shortages ashore for several weeks.

On April 6, a task force including battleship Yamato, the most powerful battleship afloat, plus one light cruiser and eight destroyers, set sail on a one-way mission to attack the American shipping off Okinawa. This operation, known as Ten-Go, ended April 7.

Friday, April 6

The Japanese cabinet fell today.[ii]

---

i   War correspondent Robert Sherrod.

ii   The Japanese government changed as a result of news from the battlefront.

The northern flank continued to advance without opposition and the southern force to develop a strong Jap position.

During the morning Adm Spruance came aboard and with Adm Turner and myself conferred on the next phase of the campaign. We all were in agreement.

Adm Spruance's flagship had recently been hit by a suicide plane whose bombs went completely through the ship, broke a propeller shaft and exploded on the other side of the vessel. He is now on the *New Mexico*.

From 3:00 PM on we were under constant air attack largely by suicide planes. Six or seven ships were hit, mostly destroyers in our picket screen. Also an ammunition ship which was abandoned.

Very few planes got to the transport area. I saw only four hit the water near our ship. The carrier planes and anti-aircraft report that they shot down [ ]

An ammunition dump blew up on Katena airfield and a gasoline barge burned on shore—possibly from falling anti-aircraft shells that shot down a friendly plane and caused 41 casualties in shore parties.

Saturday, April 7

Went ashore in barges "Annabelle the Whore" and "Bertha the Vicious Virgin."

Yesterdays reports indicate that between 3:30 PM and dark our shipping was attacked by 182 planes of which 116 were either shot down by our planes and AA or dived at or into ships. There were 22 separate groups attacking. 22 got in far enough for suicide dives and 14 ships were hit by 18 planes. Most hits were on destroyers. Two ammunition ships were hit and blew up at Kerama Retto.

This morning at 7:30 I made (reluctantly) a 2-minute Army Day talk over the radio.

News came of Gen MacArthur's being put in command of all Army troops in the Pacific. Adm Nimitz will retain naval command.[i]

From 10:00 AM to 5:00 I was ashore visiting the CPs of the XXIV Corps, the 7th Dv and the 96th Div. From a hill watched as the Div. Bn attack a hill. Had lunch at Arnold's CP.

---

i   These assignments were made in preparation for the invasion of the Japanese home islands. The orders also stipulated that current command arrangements would remain in effect until a time agreed between Nimitz and MacArthur.

Saw Bradley in his CP at the Agricultural School. Very luxuriously furnished.

Visited Katena airfield—It is ready for planes except for gas and ground crews which should arrive in a day or so. Saw some suicide rocket planes with 2000 lb warheads. 4 Marine fighter squadrons occupied the Yonton field today. There was little enemy air activity today.

Adm Spruance carrier planes sank BB *Yamato*, 1 cruiser & 3 destroyers and damaged other destroyers near Kyushu today.

Sunday, April 8

Very little air attack today. Adm Mitcher's carriers finished off a light cruiser and two or more destroyers of the fleet hit yesterday.

Went ashore and spent today visiting III Phibcorps, 1st Marine Div and 6th Mardiv. Had lunch with Gen Del Valle who had fresh pork for which I took him to task.

6th Mardiv advancing rapidly into Motobu Peninsula killing about 50 Japs a day. Slight resistance against disorganized groups, some from Navy.

Some sniper fire against 1st Mardiv HQ at night.

Okinawa civilians, a pathetic lot, coming out of holes carrying children, old people, and few belongings. They seem docile and often smile and wave as we pass. They seem to dislike the Japs. Many of their villages are destroyed but they accept it stoically. Some say they are glad we are here and give us information about the Japs.

The XXIV Corps advanced about 1,000 yds against increasing resistance. I am going to land the 27th Div. to give impetus to its attack and use the 77th to take Ie Jima after the 27th lands. Part of the 27th, meanwhile, I shall use to secure the eastern islands.

Buckner letter to Adele Buckner:
April 8, 1945
Darling:

While my Hq. is still afloat, where I am in better communication than I could be on shore at present, I have spent the past two days ashore visiting all my Division and Corps Headquarters and watching the progress of the fighting. All units are doing splendidly but heavy resistance is developing in the south as I anticipated. We have a deep area of concrete and steel to break but we can break it. Casualties so far have been light, but will be heavier from now on.

The Okinawan civilians are coming out of their holes and being taken over by the civil government section of my command. They are a pathetic lot, small, dark and heavily bearded. It is pitiful to see what modern weapons do to civilian communities harboring enemy defenses but it is necessary to shoot the enemy out of whatever positions they hold. If we were not doing it here they would be doing it in our country and with their characteristic barbarous savagery.

The Jap soldiers told the Okinawans to kill their women rather than let us take them. A few of them did so and, after finding that we treated civilians well, they are most hostile to the Japs. The Okinawans are a docile people who have always been looked down upon and mistreated by the Japs. I passed streams of them on the roads today carrying their babies and their few household possessions. Many of them smiled and waved at us. In contrast, a good many Jap women have infiltrated into our lines at night with weapons and explosives and tried to blow up our equipment.

This morning I saw an old man toddling down the road with a heavy sack on his shoulder. He looked scared to death and was passing a halted line of trucks and Jeeps. As he passed each he would hold his free hand high above his head to show that he was unarmed. Then he got opposite the Jeep in front of mine, the soldier in it made a quick move and reached in his pocket. The old man thought his last moment had come and stood petrified with terror as the soldier whipped out a large cigar and presented it to him. He dropped his bundle and began to smile and bow. When I last saw him he was still smiling and bowing himself into a state of utter exhaustion.

We have had intermittent dawn and sundown air attacks daily against our large fleet offshore in the process of unloading but two days ago we were under constant attack from shortly after 3:00 PM until after dark. In all, twenty-two groups of planes totaling about 182 in all came after us. Some ships were hit but our planes and anti-aircraft shot down 116 that we counted, and a good many others may not have gotten back to Japan. I have had great thrills in duck blinds but none comparable to that of seeing an enemy plane shot down when it was heading directly at our ship.

The success of our operation here has overthrown the Japanese cabinet and, considering their recent sea and air losses, it will be difficult for them to find another militant cabinet willing to take the responsibility for conducting a losing war. Nobody wants to take command of a sinking ship. Consequently, unless the whole nation becomes fanatical, it is not unlikely that the next cabinet may be made up of a conservative group that will try to salvage what they can by making peace feelers before long. However, the Japanese mind seems to work in an unpredictable manner. We can only fight and see.

Meanwhile, happy days to you and Mary. All my love,
Bolivar

Monday, April 9

Gen. Griner came aboard after breakfast and conferred regarding his landing. He was attached to the XXIV Corps and landed on western beaches this afternoon except 1 reinforced regiment that is to capture the eastern islands tomorrow.

I spent the afternoon visiting the wounded hospital ships: *Comfort* and *Solace*. Sailor badly burned by suicide planes.

Our first mail arrived but none from home.

Heavy resistance with increasing Arty, mortar and rocket bomb fire encountered on the southern front. Our advance slow.

Tuesday, April 10

Spent the day ashore. The enemy in front of the XXIV Corps is superbly fortified and probably outnumbers our attacking Divs. Our 96th is receiving a considerable number of casualties. The 27th Div landed today but rains have bogged it down and held up Arty. ammunition which is now short on our southern front. I told Hodge that a heavy attack would not be profitable until the 27th reached his front line at which time he should make it. I also told him of my plan to turn over the 77th to him after it took Ie Jima about Apr 16. I am trying to arrange with Adm. Turner to make a demonstration against the southern part of the island at the time of Hodge's attack so as to contain or divert reserves of the enemy.

Went to 96th Div CP and took Bradley up to Col. Dill's [ ] Regt where an O.P. overlooked the enemy position but it was too rainy and foggy to see anything. Coming back the roads were so bad we had to substitute a weasel for our jeep. Hubbard was with me.

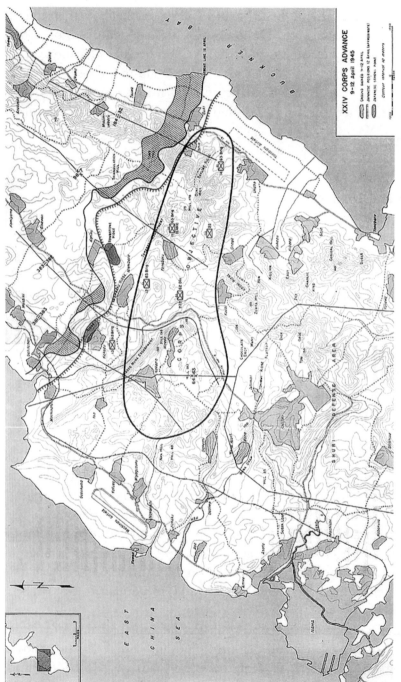

XXIV Corps' advance against the first Japanese outpost positions in southern Okinawa, April 9–12, 1945. *U.S. Army*

More mail came today with a letter from Adele mailed Mch 24.

Sent a message to Gen MacArthur by way of greeting our new over-all commander.[i]

Wednesday, April 11

Received a gracious reply to my message to Gen MacArthur.[ii]

A Bn. Of the 27th Div took the eastern islands off Nagaksuko [Nagakasuku] Wan yesterday. They were lightly held. Only 150 Japs killed. One of our destroyers was hit 6 times by a 75mm gun during the landing.

Weather again prevented unloading on western beaches today. Slight resistance found in northern part of Motobu Peninsula but 6th Mardiv continues its advance.

The XXIV Corps continues to consolidate preparatory to an attack after the 27th Div gets on the line.

Bruce came aboard to arrange details of his attack on Ie Jima. As usual, he is rarin' to try a landing behind the Jap main position in southern Okinawa.

Adm. Sherman came aboard representing Adm Nimitz to confer regarding airfield development here, the rehabilitation of divisions here and Phase III of this operation. He agreed with our recommendations on the last 2 items. We must await further reconnaissance before we are ready to make final airfield recommendations.

9:00–9:15 PM, watched plotting of a bogie's course, the vectoring of an angel until the latter reported visual contact and then the report "one bogey splashed."

---

i   "All members of 10th Army are happy to greet our new theater commander with deep faith in your brilliant leadership and assurances of enthusiastic loyalty in carrying out to the utmost of our ability any task that may be assigned us. We share with you [a] solemn determination to avenge [the fall of] Bataan in Tokyo."

ii   "(Personal for General Buckner) Deeply grateful [for] your fine message. I am looking forward with keenest pleasure to association with your magnificent command."

Thursday, April 12

Several plane attacks about 4:30 AM. Flak fell on our deck wounding 1 man. 7 planes shot down near us.

Spent entire day on board the *Eldorado*.

Conferred with Adm Cobb in the morning regarding his future duties and with Hodge in afternoon regarding his coordinated attack to be made in conjunction with a demonstration. Arty. ammunition shortage due to bad unloading weather and muddy roads makes it desirable to have him attack after Ie Jima is captured.

We were under constant air attack from about 1:45 PM until dark, mostly by suicide planes. Some battleships (2) and (7) radar pickets were hit. Apparently one sinking. I saw only one get to the transport area and it splashed. Another fell in flames over the island opposite our anchorage from so high a point that we couldn't see it start down. Preliminary reports indicate over 100 planes shot down. (Final score: 128)

Some small counter-attacks against 6th Mardiv in Motobu Penn.[i] No appreciable gains in the south. Japs bombed Yonton and shelled Katena fields without serious injury.

40 tons of ammunition blew up in the XXIV Corps' sector as the result of enemy shelling.

President Franklin D. Roosevelt died at Warm Springs, Georgia, on April 12, 1945 (April 13 Okinawa time). Vice President Harry S. Truman succeeded him.

Friday, April 13

Press asked me to "make a statement" regarding the President's death, which I did, chiefly to get rid of them.

Spent most of the day ashore visiting the III Phibcorps and 6th Mardiv. The latter has reached the extreme north of the Motobu Penn, but must still reduce a center of resistance in the center estimated variously as from 1,000 to 2,500 Japs.

Civilians are pouring in by the thousand and being taken over by the civil government. Had a talk with Crist who has started them to harvesting the ripe barley at my suggestion. The women seem to be doing all the

---

i   Motobu Peninsula.

work. It is almost incredible to see what burdens they carry on their heads. In addition most of them have babies strapped on their backs.

Visited Mulcahy and Dillon at the Yonton airfield. The latter is on crutches from a sprained knee damaged by his jumping into a foxhole when a 20mm shell went through his tent.

Cargo is going ashore rapidly again and the roads have dried out.

No appreciable progress in the south.

Post woke me up about midnight with the news that the war in Europe was over. This misinformation resulted from a garbled message to prepare speeches to be broadcast "when" VE day came. The "When" was garbled.

About a dozen planes shot down today.

Saturday, April 14

Spent day ashore. Visited new CP site, went to see Iscom and Talley to speed up ammunition unloading. Saw Hodge and Griner at XXIV Corps Hq. Also went to the 7th and 96th Div CPs. Bradley was sick in bed, apparently with nervous indigestion from his long strain. Easley though [thought] that all he needed was a rest.

6th Mardiv reached north end of island with patrols. XXIV Corps still preparing for attack. 27th Div partly in line on the right.

Bradley reported killing about 600 out of 900 counter-attacking him two days ago. No counter-attack against Arnold.

Only 6 or 8 planes shot down today. 1 picket boat hit by suicides.

Buckner letter to Adele Buckner:

April 14, 1944 [sic]

Sweetheart:

Your letter of March 24 has just reached me and was most cheering. Claiborne seems to be safely started and over the toughest part of his course. I wrote him a long letter a couple of days ago giving him an account of what is going on here as far as conditions will permit.

We have now finished our second week of battle and have all the northern part of Okinawa plus some outlying islands both east and west. In the south, we are up against the most formidable defenses yet encountered in the Pacific, well backed up by artillery and Navy mortars.

Since we have all the airfields that we need to work on for the present, I am not hurrying the attack on the south but am greatly reducing casualties by a gradual and systemic destruction of their works. This we are doing successfully and can, I feel confident, break their line in ample time for our purposes.

While I go ashore every day and visit the front, my headquarters is still afloat so as to work with the Navy which is giving us splendid support and protecting our beaches and ship unloading.

We are constantly under air attack but our carrier planes and my own operating from captured fields have done a splendid piece of work and shot down several hundred of the attacking planes. The quality of Jap pilots is deteriorating and those recently encountered show evidence of hasty and inadequate training.

We were all grieved over the President's death and still feel some concern over his successor's lack of diplomatic experience. We are relieved, however that Wallace was not Vice President.

In spite of the bad name given to Okinawa as a snake infested, malaria ridden pest hole, everyone here find it finds it the best island we have yet taken from the Japs. The climate has been delightful, the island picturesquely beautiful, the flies, snakes and mosquitoes almost nonexistent and the country fertile, well drained and healthy.

Evidently there are occasional typhoons since the houses are built to resist high winds. They are in small groups surrounded by stone walls about 5 feet high. Planted along the walls are hedges of topped banyan trees, so trained as to make the pendant roots grow along the wall and form a palisade of trunks close together and surrounding the compound. The houses are mostly of coral rock with roofs of thatch or tiles. There are almost no doors or glass windows but sliding panels instead.

The hills are all terraced, the land divided into tiny cultivated plots like flower beds and not a weed to be seen anywhere. The hillsides are full of ancestral tombs and interesting structures are built of concrete and stone over the wells and Springs. Cattle, horses, pigs and goats are running loose everywhere and getting fat on the barley, comotis, soy beans, sugar cane, cabbage, Chinese radishes and other abandoned crops. The barley is now ripe and I have gotten the civil government people started on harvesting it with the 75,000 civilians now in our care before it spoils. The Okinawans are now coming out of caves and holes and are giving no trouble. They are apparently a mixture of Ainu, Mongol and Malay. They are even smaller than the Japs and are somewhat darker. The Japs have conscripted and taken away all men of military or useful age, so we have a somewhat helpless crowd on our hands. Eventually we will have well over 400,000.

So far, everything is progressing well, the men are in good spirits and the fight is past its most critical stage. We will have some tough going but it is getting progressively tougher for our enemies. Incidentally, Jap claims of ship sinkings are absurdly extravagant as usual.

Affectionately,

Bolivar

Sunday, April 15

Spent the day ashore visiting the III Phibcorps, the 6th Mardiv and a civil affairs unit. Saw too much wanton destruction by Marines and told Sheppard[i] and Geiger so.

Went to front-line O.P. in 6th Mardiv with Sheppard and looked at enemy position in center of Motobu Penn. Remnants of Jap forces seem to be digging in on a hill there. 6 Bns will attack tomorrow.

Saw two Marines holding a goat, a third trying ineffectually to milk her and a small kid nearby squalling for its lost dinner.

Saw my first two snakes. Birds seem few in number and species. Have seen 2 small Japanese quail, 2 white herons, half a dozen crows, some swallows, 3 doves, a few English (?) sparrows and a dozen slate-colored birds with black wings and tails about the size of shrikes. Also a beautiful small deep blue kingfisher.

Air raid against Yonton field at sunset and at dark. Not much damage done by Jap raid but a good many casualties and damaged planes by our own AA fire. The ships fire low and toward shore. They also burned two gasoline dumps.

A few hostile planes were shot down.

---

i   Major General Lemuel Shepherd, commanding 6th Marine Division.

Monday, April 16

Spent day visiting CPs of XXIV Corps, 27th Div and 96th Div. Also went to 2 forward Ops in 96th area to look over enemy positions.

Saw Bradley who appears in better health and spirits than he was two days ago.

The general situation on the N and S fronts remains unchanged. Attacks being prepared.

The 77th Div was landed on Ie Jima at about 8:00 AM after having put Arty ashore on Minna Jima. Very little opposition on beaches. Airfield taken and garrison retired to the hill at east side of island. Numbers estimated from 200 to 1,000. Attack will continue against them tomorrow. Only 2 RCTs of 77th Div were landed.

Our new CP ashore is now partly occupied and will be ready in a couple of days.

I told Griner to seal up all tombs in his area.

T.F. 58 reported shooting down 166 planes.

Tuesday, April 17

Very little change in general situation. TF 58 reported "another good day" after saying they were under attack. Saw a picket boat with a suicide plane stuck into its bridge.—Captain and 30 of crew killed.

Visited 1st Mardiv and spent rest of day in civil government camps. Lt Comdr Fraser (Mass lawer)[i] has Shinubaru camp well organized and doing useful work.

Watched civilians also on Penn. between Chinu and Nagasako Wan[ii] where about 40,000 of them are left practically to their own devices.

Buckner letter to Adele Buckner:
April 17, 1945
Dearest:

Heretofore I have been spending most of my days ashore but sleeping on the command ship with Admiral Turner. Tomorrow I will move permanently ashore, now that I have all my wire lines and other communications installed. I was in my command post today and it is a

---

i   Buckner is noting that this officer was a lawyer from Massachusetts.
ii   Nakagusuku Wan, later known as Buckner Bay.

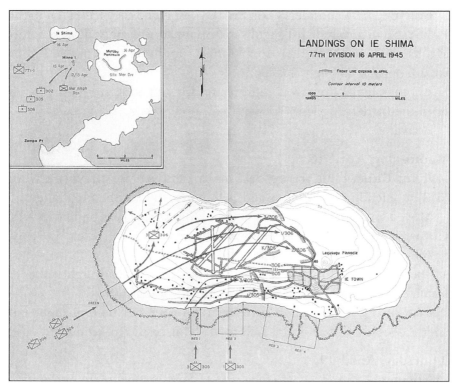

The 77th Infantry Division's landing and advance on Ie Shima. *U.S. Army*

pleasant spot with a lovely view except on occasions when unpleasant things are dropping into it from guns and planes at which time I have a dugout to retire into.

I spent the day visiting and inspecting my civil government camps. Our men are doing a good job in handling the natives and making them as self-sufficient and healthy as possible. They have been living in caves and dug-outs for some time and need a lot of cleaning up. They say that we will give them more and better food than they have gotten since the war started.

The general situation here is little changed except that we took an airfield on Ie Jima yesterday and expect to clean up the rest of the garrison by tomorrow or next day. They are well dug in on a Hill, but I landed enough troops to handle them without difficulty.

Everyone here considers Okinawa the best island they have seen in the Pacific. Strategically it [is] highly important to our air and naval forces as a base to prevent further trouble from starting in the Orient. I hope we are sensible enough to keep it.

Another letter from you came yesterday and took my thoughts far from the battlefield. They are with you now.

Bolivar

Wednesday, April 18

Adm. Turner came aboard. Says his carrier flyers are carrying a heavy load in defending themselves and helping us and are showing fatigue.

Moved my CP ashore after lunch. Got settled and visited XXIV Corps CP. ~~Also visited 7th and 96th Divs.~~

All set for tomorrow's attack.

Took Hubbard forward to the 7th Div CP to spend night so as to watch jumpoff tomorrow from forward OP in that Div.

One of our 155mm gun batteries fired over our tent all night but after a couple of hours I got used to it and it ceased to keep me awake.

Thursday, April 19

Got up at 4:35 and went to forward O.P. with Arnold. Arty. preparation and later use was beautiful. Very little Jap counter fire. Watched flame thrower tanks which seem very effective.

Very little resistance to start with. Men did not advance quite fast enough at first.

At about 9:50 left Arnold and went via 96th Div CP to OP of Col Dillon[i] 96th zone. Resistance much stiffer there. Returned via 27th Div CP to my own.

Result of day's operations: a gain of about 8 to 1200 yds on our right and left leaving a salient in the heavily-fortified escarpment area in the center. Expect to work on flanks of Jap salient tomorrow. Progress not quite satisfactory.

Heavy thunderstorms during afternoon.

---

i   Colonel Macey L. Dill, commanding 382nd Infantry Regiment.

Visited Hodge before supper and told him to speed up advance. 7th Div too cautious.

Friday, April 20

Visited 27th Div in the morning. Saw Col Stebbins[i] of 105th. He was slow in getting his attack off this morning—Jap Arty. concentration and shot out bridges given as reason. Too many reasons and not enough advance. Told him so. Also saw Col. Kelly[ii] of 165th Inf and urged him toward a faster pace: to go where the going is good and pinch out pockets of resistance.

The Katena airfield was straffed and bombed about 8:30 or nine in the evening. One plane was injured by falling AA shells. A bomb hit one shelter and killed 8 men and wounded 17.

Later in the night, about 4:30 AM I think, seven or eight shells, about 155mm size, fell not far from our CP.

Saturday, April 21

Visited Bn OP in [ ] Regt of Col. Halloran.[iii] His right Bn Comdr thinks 27th Div on his right is not helping him as much as contemplated. I then went to 27th Div CP and found that the left Bn of that Div had been driven back, inexcusably I think, by a counter attack. There was also some mystery about loss of tanks that I could not fully get explained. The right of the 27th had progressed fairly well.

In the afternoon I went out to the *Eldorado* to see Turner and discussed the general situation and the coming of Adm Nimitz tomorrow.

Communications with the 77th Div on Ie Shima have not been good but today Bruce sent a staff officer over to say that all organized resistance was over and that he had killed over 1,900 Japs. Probably 500 more to kill. His total killed & wounded: over 800.

After dark a number of Jap planes came in off and on until midnight with lots of antiaircraft firing and some bombing and strafing.

---

i   Colonel Albert K. Stebbins, commanding 105th Infantry Regiment.
ii   Colonel Gerard W. Kelly, commanding 165th Infantry Regiment.
iii This is a reference to the 381st Infantry Regiment, commanded by Colonel Michael E. Halloran.

The last ten days of April were a transition point in the fighting on Okinawa. Formal resistance in northern Okinawa ended April 20, a day before Bruce declared Ie Shima secure. These victories freed up Geiger's corps and Bruce's division for employment elsewhere.

During days of discussions, several officers pushed for one division to make a landing at Minatoga and envelop the Japanese position at Shuri. Others correctly pointed out that XXIV Corps was exhausted and depleted from the recent fighting, and needed reinforcement. After some consideration, Buckner ordered Geiger's corps and Bruce's division to reinforce the fighting line opposite Shuri. Buckner called a Minatoga operation "another Anzio, but worse"—a reference to the landing and siege of the Anzio Beachhead in Italy from January to May 1944, which was expected to be a quick victory but instead bogged down Allied forces near Cassino and Rome.

A close reading of the diary also shows Buckner feeling a need to keep forces available for Phases IIIc and IIId, landings on nearby islands to secure airfield sites. He appears reluctant to overcommit his army on Okinawa when those operations remained to be completed.

Buckner also faced pressure from Nimitz to keep moving. On April 23, Nimitz told him, "I'm losing a ship and a half a day. So if this line isn't moving in five days, we'll get someone up here to move it so we can all get out from under these damn kamikaze attacks."

Buckner's decision to eschew a Minatoga landing, a point of contention at the time, remains the most controversial aspect of his conduct of the battle of Okinawa.

Sunday, April 22

Hodge called up early and confirmed my observations regarding the left of the 27th Div and their poor use of tanks. He had sent BG Bradford[i] to coordinate between the 96th and 27th Divs.

Adm Nimitz, Gen Vandegrift, Adm Spruance Adm Sherman & others arrived by air at noon. I took them sight seeing. Adm. Nimitz discussed Phase 3, the rehabilitation of units here, the transfer of Okinawans from the Marianas back here, the future of the island and succeeding operations against Japan. Phase 3 may be abandoned if sufficient fields can be found

---

i   Brigadier General William B. Bradford, the 27th Infantry Division's assistant commander.

here to fulfill air support requirements.—Arranged for further trips tomorrow to the northward. Adm Nimitz presented me with a bottle of liquor which I told him I would open when all organized resistance here had ended.

During the night our land based planes here shot down 32 attacking "Vals", losing only 1 plane and no pilots. Most of the Vals were shot down just before dark.

Buckner letter to Adele Buckner:
April 22, 1945
Dearest:

Eddie Post and I are now established in a pyramidal tent at our new command post ashore. We have a convenient dugout nearby into which we slide when Jap planes are overhead and fragments from anti-aircraft shells are raining scrap iron.

Practically every day I get to some part of the forward regiments and watch the fighting. In this way I get a good idea of the situation at first hand and I'm in a ~~good~~ position to make necessary decisions. The Japs here seem to have the strongest positions yet encountered in the Pacific and it will be a slow tedious grind with flamethrowers, explosives placed by hand and the closest of teamwork to dislodge them without very heavy losses. In the meanwhile, however, we are making great headway with the part of the island we have and are developing splendid air facilities that we are already using. We will be wise to hold this island after the war under conditions that will permit us to have military control without incorporating the Okinawans into our population as civilians free to enter the U.S.

Buckey's expressed desire to live in Europe after the war is interesting, but he has never tied it in with anything definite as to where he wants to stay or what he expects to do for a living. Just now, he can live like a millionaire compared with the local people but this condition will cease when he is mustered out without a job. I hope he is not unduly optimistic. His knowledge of languages may help him to be the European agent of some American business concern but he will have to make a decision and start laying his foundations soon. All of this I wrote him in one of the many letters he has never answered.

We have now taken Ie Shima with a splendid airfield somewhat mined and ditched at present by the late garrison. We killed over 2,100 Japs on the island and there are probably 500 snipers still hiding in caves that will have to be accounted for. They won't surrender but they skulk around at night and shoot, throw grenades and try to blow up ammunition dumps, weapons and supplies. They expect to die but try to do as much damage as possible first. They present a considerable problem.

Today we had a very distinguished visitor so I spent a good deal of the time taking him sightseeing and discussing the local and future situations, all of which was very satisfactory.

Another letter from you arrived yesterday. Our mail service is splendid and letters are most cheering. I am distressed to hear of your arthritis and trust that you may soon find some complete cure. I am delighted to hear that Mary can play the guitar and sing. It will be a great source of pleasure to her. I wish she could write letters. I have heard from her only about four times in 21 years.

The artillery is beginning to roar down at the front and parachute flares are lighting up the whole sky. This probably means that the Japs are putting on a night counter-attack. I hope so, since this will bring them out of their caves and pillboxes where we can use our artillery on them with good effect.

I have twice had to stop writing this letter due to Jap planes that made it necessary to turn out the light. Their raids seemed now to be over for the time being so I will try to catch some rest.

Devotedly,
Bolivar

Monday, April 23
Spent the day taking Adm Nimitz to the north to see air field sites and visit III Phibcorps and 1st Mardiv. Had lunch with Geiger.

Told Adm. Nimitz that Okinawa should be retained by us as a means of access to the China sea, a flanking position against north and south movements along the China coast, a check against further aggression by Japan and as an outpost to prevent Russia from expansion into the Pacific from Chinese ports that she might acquire at the end of the war by occupying them under the pretext of helping us against Japan. I made this suggestion with the proviso that we should control this island as a "protectorate," "mandate" or some other name that would leave the Okinawans as aliens not permitted to enter our country as citizens and add to our already complex race problems.

Tuesday, April 24

Some progress on southern front—Hill 178 taken and a foothold gained on the Escarpment. Japs apparently retiring to another strong position. Heavy Jap artillery fire.

Very little air attack last night and anti-aircraft today.

Inspected unloading at beaches. Labor crews at the dumps appear to be the bottleneck.

Adm Nimitz left this morning, apparently well pleased.

Richardson published a "newsmap" on Okinawa without mentioning anything but major <u>Army</u> units and their commanders. Wrote him an official letter urging him to give due credit to my <u>Marines</u>. Richardson is always a menace to good relations between the services in the Pacific. Adm. Nimitz knows it.

Wednesday, April 25

Flew to Ie Shima in a cub plane and saw Bruce. Island about cleaned up and 77th Div will be completely loaded by Apr 27 to move to Okinawa and be attached to XXIV Corps. Unfortunately, Bruce blew up all tombs on the island as a precaution against their use by snipers, a most unnecessary piece of vandalism committed with pious intentions.

Slight progress on southern front and preparations for another coordinated attack tomorrow. Visited XXIV Corps, 96th Div and 27th Div CPs in the afternoon.

After supper, assembled my staff and started them to work on my tentative plans to put into effect when and if Phase 3c is called off. Adm Nimitz has recommended against 3c as unnecessary since adequate airfield sites are available here without it.

Thursday, April 26

Adm Spruance and Adm Halsey came to my CP just after lunch and went off on a sight-seeing expedition.

The rest of the afternoon I spent with Arnold on Hill 178 which gave me a beautiful panoramic view of most of the battlefront. Our troops made considerable advances and broke the enemy's hold on one end of the escarpment.

From 3:45 to 4:00 this morning about 8 155 shells fell near our CP but did no damage.

Buckner letter to Adele Buckner:
April 26, 1945
Sweetheart:

Yesterday I flew over to our newly captured island of Ie Shima in a cub plane and landed on a small strip of the Jap airfield that had not been heavily mined, dug up and booby trapped. This island has great potentialities for air development and my engineers are working like beavers behind the bomb disposal unit that is clearing up the mines. The first bomb disposal squad, a small unit, all got blown up themselves but we have had no fatalities yet in the second group. In taking the island, we killed about 3,200 Japs and interned over 1,500 civilians. There are probably about 100 Japs still concealed in camouflage caves but it always takes time to clean these out. They are still finding them on Guam, Saipan and Tinian in large numbers.

This morning we made another coordinated attack in the south against the enemy's second position. We have broken their first position but they have many heavily fortified lines for us to contend with.

All the northern part of Okinawa and the neighboring small islands are now ours and we have counted over 20,000 good Japs. Many others, no doubt have been killed behind the enemy lines by artillery and air bombardment.

For several mornings, a long range Jap gun has been dropping shells near our CP between 3:45 and 4:00 o'clock. We can hear the whine of the projectile on its way toward us, followed by the "crump" of the explosion and whistle of fragments and several seconds later by the distant report of the gun. So far he hasn't hit anything or anybody. We are sound-ranging on this battery and have him about located, so our counter-battery will probably get him before long. Apparently he is firing from the mouth of a cave.

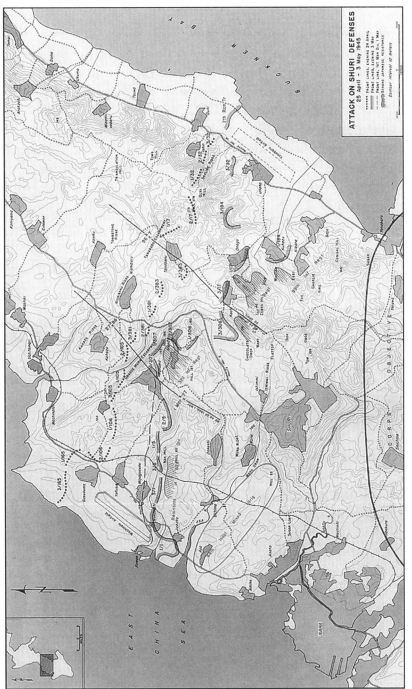

The attack on Shuri's outer defenses, April 25–May 3, 1945. Shuri Castle and Ushijima's headquarters are in the lower center. *U.S. Army*

We have had a couple of rainy days that have discouraged Jap air attacks but it is now clearing so that we can expect more of it. One advantage in establishing ourselves here consists in forcing the enemy to expend his aircraft on us. His air losses are far beyond ours so we're wearing him down. For instance, two days ago our planes based on captured Jap fields here shot down 32 enemy planes in a couple of hours with the loss of only one plane and the pilot of the lost plane was rescued by a seaplane. The Jap seems to be getting low on trained pilots and constant attention keeps him from getting caught up.

Due to the publicity given to the Okinawa campaign, I am getting a deluge of trash mail from cranks, collectors and chiselers. Many ask "Please write me a letter for my collection." Some run about like this "Ever since I read about the brilliant exploits of your Tenth Air Force in New Guinea I have been an ardent admirer of yours and prayed for you every night. Won't you answer my prayers by sending me your Insignia, an autographed photograph and a few little battlefield souvenirs such as Japanese flags or perhaps a light machine gun. Congratulations on your brilliant strategy which I think is swell. They say generals aren't human but I know you are."

"May God bless you and don't forget to send the trophies. We need people just like you." etc etc. This is no exaggeration.

Evangeline Atwood sent me a letter recently faithfully bringing me up to date on Alaskan affairs. John Manders is the new mayor of our city, B. Platt will have another baby in September. Alaska will vote on statehood in the fall of 1946, my recent set-to with Mr Ickes has enhanced my prestige in the territory, Evangeline is in Juneau collecting data on statehood for Bob to publish in the Anchorage Daily Times, Gov and Mrs Gruening are making much of her in view of Bob's editorial potentialities and most important of all, Evangeline has a new hat. There is perhaps no other hat like it. I hope not.

Your letters are coming promptly and keep my thoughts going back a long way from Okinawa.

I look forward to the glorious day of our reunion.

Bolivar

Friday, April 27

At a staff meeting in the morning I announced my decision regarding the use of the III Phibcorps immediately after receipt of word that Phase

3c had been called off. My decision was at variance with my staff's recommendations.

Adm Halsey left in the afternoon.

Still very little progress in the center of the line but some gain on both flanks. Part of 77th Div has arrived behind the 96th.

I visited Iscom and the 1st Mardiv.

Two snipers with telescopic sights killed last night at the Yonton airfield. Infiltrators also caught in rear of 7th Div with orders to look for CP's and kill senior commanders. A prisoner said that his CO drew lots and the half who "won" were privileged to <u>have</u> to do this.

Buckner letter to Adele Buckner:
April 27, 1945
Sweetie:

Your income tax advisor was very expensive for $5.00. I had counted Mary as a dependent since if I drop her I drop the tax and surtax from a more highly taxed bracket. I can drop about 35% of the amount exempted whereas you can drop about 8% of it. In other words, it costs over $100.00 more for you to call her a dependent than for me to do so. I suggest that you write to the collector and say that I will drop her as my dependent when I pay my tax and ask how much more you will have to add to your tax. I will reimburse you for that amount.

Admiral Nimitz seemed well pleased with his visit here a couple of days ago. He left me a bottle of liquor that I promised to open on the day that all organized resistance here was over. I am getting thirsty.

We are now picking up numerous snipers behind our lines but so far they have done little damage. We wounded and captured one yesterday who said that his company had drawn lots and the half who "won" were privileged to <u>have</u> to infiltrate into our lines, look for command posts and kill senior officers. I think we have killed all those who "won." Two were shot last night way back on the Yontan airfield with telescopic sights. They never got to use them. Our rear elements are no longer alarmed when they hear firing behind them; they merely feel satisfaction in the thought that our "anti-termite" patrols have shot another Jap.

Yesterday I had the rare experience of finding an observation point that permitted me to observe the entire battle front. Action was lively all along the line since we were putting on a heavy attack and the whole thing was visible. It was really a superb spectacle—plane strikes, artillery concentrations, smoke screens, flame throwers, tanks and the steady determined advance of the infantry closing with the enemy. Along with this were the crash of bombs, the screech of projectiles, the whistle of shell fragments, the sputter of machine guns and the sharp crack of rifles. I shall never forget it. It was really stirring.

I could be taking some wonderful pictures but somehow I don't. I[t] simply doesn't seem appropriate to be snapping a camera when things like this are going on.

I was glad to see Courtney and Patton get their fourth stars.[i] Our fickle public has forgotten that only recently they were trying to hound George out of the service.

Our reorganization in the Pacific has so far made no difference in my immediate chain of command. I still operate under Admiral Nimitz. However, I had a pleasant exchange of radiograms with General MacArthur, each of us having given birth to a copious litter of adjectives.

My social news here may be briefly summarized as "No women, no liquor."

All my love,
Bolivar

Saturday, April 28

Last night began with a romantically beautiful moonrise but there the romance ended. Jap hecklers were around in the air all night. At midnight they buzzed over our CP at very low altitude and bombed the airfield. Later at about 3:00 they did it again. AAA was spectacular but inaccurate. Searchlight work was poor. Night fighters got 2 Jap planes.

Looked over road net to the north and dropped in on III Phibcorps & 6th Mardiv CP.

4:00 PM—Conferred DSM cluster at a small ceremony to Hodge for his Leyte campaign prowess.

After moonrise heavy air attacks began again. Post and I moved our bunks into the dugout. During the afternoon and night the shore-based

---

i   General Courtney H. Hodges and General George S. Patton Jr., commanding respectively First Army and Third Army in Europe.

fighters got 35 planes and the shore & ship AAA an equal number (counting 22 suicide planes). The local carrier based planes also got 35. Yesterday 1 ammunition ship was sunk and another and a destroyer hit. A hospital ship is also reported as struck.

Sunday, April 29

During the morning I went via XXIV Corps Hq to the 27th Div to assure Griner that his being taken out of the line and moved north as the island garrison was no indication that I was not completely satisfied with his Div's performance. He was obviously relieved.

I spent the afternoon visiting the wounded in the 69th Fld. Hospl.[i] Saw a man's brains through a hole in his temple. The doctors said he had an even chance of recovery.

Monday, April 30

More air raids after moonrise last night. The Yonton airfield was shelled from near Naha. One plane destroyed and several badly damaged.

In the morning went aboard the *Eldorado* to see Adm Turner. Had lunch there. Adm Oldendorf was there and brought a letter from Adm Nimitz saying the 24 Okinawan pine trees I had sent him at Guam had arrived in good condition.

Bruce took over from the 96th Div. A Regt of the 1st Mardiv moved into the line relieving the 27th Div. Small counterattacks in the center from 1 Co. to 1 Bn.

At 4:00 PM attended at XXIV Corps Hq the wedding of the Jap captured Capt and the Okinawa girl. Chaplain read civil service. Interpreted. Lost ring made from quarter. Bride delayed ceremony to fix her obi. MP present with shotgun. 1st Sgt said "Bring 'em in" and "Take 'em home." Groom made speech. Photographers present. (I explained to press people the propaganda purpose of the ceremony.) Accordion and tarre added color.

Tuesday, May 1

Accompanied Bruce to two front line Bn Ops. Got splendid view of fighting on the front of the 77th Div.

---

i   A reference to the 69th Field Hospital.

Had 2-hour press conference at 3:00 PM. Some of the correspondents sought to make a scandal out of the "Hollywood wedding" yesterday. I explained its purpose to get information out of him and let Japs know they would be well-treated if they surrendered. Most of them accepted it but a few will want to raise controversial bad feeling for sensational purposes.

Wednesday, May 2

After breakfast visited Arnold in Hospl. Had his appendix out last night. Doing well. I wrote Marg, his wife.

Adm Oldendorf & Adm Deyo[i] arrived at 10:00 AM. I met them at the dock, had them to lunch, showed them the Jap buzz bomb and sent them off to see Hodge & Bradley about naval gunfire support.

I then visited the 1st Mardiv CP. They had great assurance and expected to make large gains at once.

Thursday, May 3

It was apparent to me that the 77th Div and the 1st Mardiv entered the line expecting to show their superiority over their predecessors by a rapid breakthrough of the enemy's position. They were promptly stopped and learned some valuable lessons today. From now on they will be more valuable as all-around fighters.

Spent the morning at the 31st Fld Hospl (Col Rogers Comdg)[ii] and visited the 77th and 1st Mardiv CPs in the afternoon. Del Valle was feeling a little off his feed with a cold.

Buckner letter to Adele Buckner:
May 3, 1945
Dearest:

This morning I spent visiting the wounded in hospitals and this afternoon went up to two of the divisions in line, one army and one marine. Our surgeons are doing wonders. I talked to several men that had been shot in the brain several days ago and they are getting well.

---

i   Rear Admiral Morton L. Deyo, commanding the bombardment fleet supporting Tenth Army.

ii   A reference to the 31st Field Hospital.

There are almost no infected wounds and the blood donations save hundreds who would otherwise die of shock or bleeding. On the whole, the wounded are cheerful and optimistic. It is remarkable how badly a man can be shot up and still recover.

The news that Hitler and Mussolini are both dead is most cheering.[i] Two serious post-war problems are solved and a good precedence set for disposing of some of their ilk.

We continue to move slowly but are killing Japs steadily. We have already killed 30,000 Japs that we know of. This is more than the total killed on Iwo Jima and our losses have been less than half those suffered in taking that island although I consider the Jap defenses here far more formidable than those on Iwo Jima. When we finally break through the percentage of Jap losses to ours will greatly increase, in all probability.

For two nights we have had no air attacks due to rain but tonight it is clear so we can expect a recurrence of moonlight raids. However the moon rises later every night so we will probably not be visited before midnight. I usually sleep in a hole during raids. Eddie and I have a good one near at hand and now manage to sleep through all the noise so as to give the raiders no satisfaction over keeping us awake.

The thunder of artillery continues all day and all night. After dark the sky over the enemy is constantly illuminated by parachute flares and the constant flash of the big guns and shell explosions keeps flickering like distant lightning. This drives the enemy into the ground and gives him very little rest.

Archie Arnold had his appendix out a couple of days ago but is coming along finely and expects to be back commanding his division in a few days. I wrote to Marg and assured her that he was doing well but that the offspring was no credit to him.

Our tanks have been invaluable in reducing Jap pillboxes and fortified caves. They fire into the entrances while the infantry closes with explosive charges or else use incendiaries. The flame-thrower tanks have long range and have been very effective. The main problem is to find a place where

---

i   Benito Mussolini of Italy was executed on April 29, 1945. Adolf Hitler, the leader
     of Nazi Germany, killed himself in Berlin on April 30, 1945.

we can cover and neutralize all the numerous caves that bring crossfire on our infantry in a particular place. We look for soft spots, take them and then surround the stronger hills and reduce them after our frontline has passed them. Often Japs will bob up out of concealed tunnels with machine guns and mortars a mile behind our lines at night. They also slip in after dark with explosives and try to blow up tanks artillery and command posts. We have been very successful in stopping infiltration but it keeps us constantly on guard. Japanese infiltration tactics defeated the British on the Malay Peninsula where the Japs had fewer troops than they had. The Singapore Garrison that surrendered exceeded their captors in numbers.[i]

I feel well satisfied with my troops and confident of the outcome but I must avoid a spectacular hurry in order to save lives.

While the European war seems only about over it will be six to nine months after its close before we can profit here by the transfer of troops to this theater. Meanwhile we will continue to press our enemies and have them in good position for the kill.

Devotedly,

Bolivar

Ushijima's army launched a counteroffensive on the night of May 4. The complicated plan involved attacks across the front, accompanied by amphibious raids and kamikaze attacks into the American rear. It achieved some initial success, but ultimately failed while costing Ushijima 5,000 irreplaceable infantrymen. After two days, all penetrations had been wiped out and the Americans returned to the offensive.

Friday, May 4

Last night heavy air attacks struck Yonton field and the fleet. 8 men were killed in a Hospl. Our CP and the field were shelled again. In the south the Japs tried to envelop both our flanks in barges and penetrate the center at the same time during the night that the air attacks came (about midnight). Each attacking force was a Bn. Naval gunfire sank the eastern Bn, the center was stopped but the western group got ashore

---

i   Singapore surrendered on February 15, 1942, after a 70-day campaign in Malaya and Singapore Island. It was the largest surrender in British military history.

opposite the 1st Mardiv. About 200 in one group were killed but part of another group got inland with about 80 Jap infiltrators that are still at large.

After breakfast I had a staff meeting and gave out decisions regarding the capture of neighboring islands for radar stations to control planes. Adm Turner is impatient about this, so the 2d Mardiv will have to be used if speed is important.

Spent the day at Ie Shima. Thomas (Iscom) recovering from pneumonia. Interviewed his staff to see how I could help their project. They predict readiness of field for fighter group May 12. Adm Spruance sent staff officers to find out date.

Our land-based planes shot down 45 Jap planes today. I sent congratulatory message to Mulcahy—my third.

Saturday, May 5

Met Adm Spruance and Adm Hill at dock and took them to XXIV Corps CP. After reviewing situation, sent them on a tour of the Div CPs and Shenubaru. They left via my CP in the afternoon.

After lunch conferred with G-3 section and gave decisions upon which to issue Army order for attacking with both corps.

Daugherty came ashore from Adm Turner to discuss securing radar picket islands. Turner seems less in a rush now that I have pointed out the necessity for bringing up the 2d Mardiv if speed is essential. Later and more complete information, including a captured enemy order indicates that the counterattack was by the entire 24th Jap Div. It continued sporadically today in our center. Over 3,000 Japs were killed yesterday last night and today.

Sunday, May 6

More air attacks last night but no great damage.

Called at CPs of XXIV Corps, 1st Mardiv, 77th Div and 7th Div. Also watched fighting from 1st Mardiv O.P. Saw Arnold in Hospl. Not much gain today but resistance seems slightly weaker.

Conferred with Geiger regarding details of his going into the line as a corps.

Turner has new ideas on radio picket islands—the third change in three days.

Adm Spruance wants 1st priority given to getting fighters to operate from here. This I have ordered.

During the night the cases of about 8 of our 5-in naval star shells fell in our CP. One near the corner of Raney's tent went 7 feet into the ground. We were not bothered by enemy shells.

Monday, May 7

Conferred with Adms Turner and Hill (the latter will soon succeed Turner) on the *Eldorado* regarding radar islands. Decided to take small ones with local troops. To get a reinforced Regt. of the 2d Mardiv, now on Saipan, to take those with slightly larger garrisons and to take Kume with local troops 30 days after resistance here was over.

Later a message from Cincpoa arrived for 3d July 15.[i] 2d Mardiv was recommended for this and a RCT of the 3d Mardiv to substitute for the 2d in taking radar islands. (This letter was disapproved. 3d Mardiv held for another operation.)

On May 8, good news arrived from Europe. But ominously, significant rain started. Fifteen inches of rain drenched Okinawa between May 7 and May 31, with ten inches falling between May 21 and 31.

Tuesday, May 8

Official word came of Germany's complete surrender. At noon every gun of our land and ship support batteries fired one round at the enemy. We then tuned into the Jap radio frequency and announced in Japanese that the volley was in celebration of the victory. Tomorrow we are dropping an extra of our Jap newspaper with elaboration of this news.

Heavy rain bogged down our tanks and slowed our advance.

Visited III Phibcorps CP but got stuck in the mud trying to visit the 6th Mardiv.

Buckner letter to Adele Buckner:[ii]
May 7, 1945
Cutie:

Tonight it is raining so we will probably be free from the air attacks that come on every clear moonlit night. A couple of nights ago, a bomb

---

i   This directive set the landings for Phase IIId on July 15, 1945.
ii This letter was begun on May 7 and finished May 8.

hit the dugout housing the wounded awaiting air evacuation and killed a dozen or more. Ordinary bombing is directed at the shipping and airfields but we have to take cover from the falling projectiles from our anti-aircraft guns. Several days ago one man in our Hq was killed and another shot through the leg by falling .50 cal. bullets.

The Japs tried a counter offensive several days ago, but we stopped it easily and with great loss to the enemy. We have killed over 33,000 so far.

Now that the northern part of the island has been mopped up, I have made a re-grouping of my divisions that should give impetus to our attack. However, we have to be somewhat deliberate in attacking stone hills honeycombed with connecting galleries and bristling with machine guns.

Our civil government now cares for about 130,000 Okinawan civilians. Although most of their homes and villages have been destroyed, their crops overrun and their young men killed, they seem stoical, docile and actually cheerful. One of our interpreters, an Okinawan from Honolulu, told me that he had talked informally with hundreds of them and that they had said that they were happy that we were here to drive out the Japs who treated them brutally and confiscated ⅔ of all their crops, forced them to labor hard without compensation [and] look down upon them as degenerates. They trust us and feel that we will relieve them from their long period of suffering. Most of our civilians are old men, women and children. Men of military age have been drafted and taken away where they either fight or work in labor battalions. Some of them fight very well if thoroughly indoctrinated by the Japs concerning our cruelty and torture of prisoners. All are surprised at the good treatment they are receiving.

We are collecting them from tunnels, caves and dugouts where they have been hiding in the hills and putting them into the concentration camps wherever shelter can be found. We found 300 in one cave that had a spring in it. Their pigs, chickens, goats and lice were all living with them. Many were wounded. They are dirty but remarkably free from disease except for scabies (mange) resulting from dirt. Most of them were fairly well provided with food or foraged in nearby fields of cabbage, radishes, barley, potatoes and soybeans.

We have organized these camps, using natives as foremen and, with the captured Jap rice and fish, have made them self supporting. They harvest crops under supervision[,] build shelters, thresh and grind grain, make fishing nets and boats[,] keep their premises and themselves clean.

They get regular medical service and are kept busy. They seem cheerful, trusting and apparently without resentment over their losses. However, there is no telling what an oriental is thinking about. When we moved the peaceful old men out of one district we ceased to be bothered by sniping there.

Our best civil government men are practical man-handlers who would make good 1st sergeants or Alaskan chiefs of police like Bob Huttle of Anchorage. The academic experts, lecturers on "Oriental peoples and their Psychology" and Bell for Adono[i] apostles of democracy are worse than useless.

We are replacing the old Jap currency with invasion money in which we are paid. I pay 3 yen for a haircut, the equivalent of $0.30. I am enclosing bills of 50 sen in old Jap currency and 1 yen in our new military currency. 1 of our yen is equal to $0.10 U.S. Currency. The Japs $0.50 equals 5 military sen in value.

May 8

We had a peaceful rainy night and during breakfast secured official news of Germany's surrender. This will give us needed troops and supplies but not for months.

I am enclosing a copy of the Sunday paper that we publish for the Japs in their end of the island and distribute by plane. One Jap officer said that he surrendered as a result of information he had gotten from reading the last edition. The Japs had told him that five of our divisions had just been destroyed by victorious Japanese forces in the Philippines.

Devotedly,

Bolivar

Wednesday, May 9

Spent day driving in jeep to extreme north end of island. Saw plane picked up by station 180 miles away and followed to 134 mi when I left.

Heavy rains bogged down tanks and prevented substantial gains.

Thursday, May 10

V. Adm. Wilkinson came ashore for a visit with some of his staff. V. Adm. McMorris arrived by air and went out to see Adms. Spruance & Turner.

---

i   This is a reference to the popular novel and film *A Bell for Adano*.

Hodge came to my CP regarding slow progress. Thought army attack tomorrow should be postponed until more ground was gained. I told him to gain the ground today. I visited Geiger and told him the same.

At 2:00 PM I held a press conference regarding tomorrow's attack. Told them not to expect anything spectacular but expressed confidence in a steady and successful advance. No heckling today. My great display of patience with hecklers at the last meeting had a good effect.

On May 11 Tenth Army launched a general offensive across its entire front, with the objective of capturing Shuri.

Friday, May 11

Attack started at 7:00 AM. Progress all along the line. Visited both corps CP's and put a little pressure on corps Comdrs. Pocket on right of 77th Div cleaned out. Has held us up some time.

Adm McMorris came ashore and discussed future plans. Nothing definite yet since Joint Chiefs of Staff have handed down no decisions. With MacArthur in command of troops Krueger's army will have the edge on us in important assignments.

Considerable Jap air activity today principally against carriers and picket boats. Over 150 Jap planes reported shot down.

Yesterday [ ] encountered a Jap fighter at 38,000 ft. His guns froze but he brought down the plane by ramming its tail three times with his propeller and cutting it off.

Saturday, May 12

Adm McMorris left early in the morning for Guam and I spent the day visiting both corps CP, all four Div CP's and three forward OP's giving me a view of the entire front. Progress being made on both flanks but not much in the middle. This was expected. Right of 6th Mardiv reached edge of northern part of Naha and left of 96th Div got started well up the N.W. slope of the "Conical Hill."

Sunday, May 13

After breakfast went to III Phibcorps and 96th Div CPs and then joined Col May[i] in 383d Inf OP overlooking attack on "Conical Hill." His handling of the Regt. was a beautiful piece of troop leading. I could

---

i   Colonel Edwin T. May, commanding the 383rd Infantry Regiment.

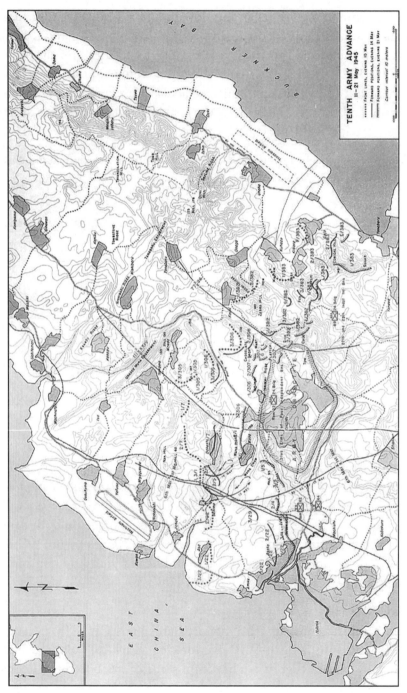

Tenth Army's offensive against Shuri, May 11–21, 1945. *U.S. Army*

watch the Bn & Co movements easily from the OP and even see Japs, effect of fire, etc. I was there over four hours. May should be promoted to BG.[i]

Buckner letter to Adele Buckner:
May 13, 1945
Dearest:

Cowart's combination of overseas service, combat service and practicing paternity service has given him a number of "points" entitling him to go home and he expects to go in the morning so I am entrusting this letter to him for delivery, hoping that he will not become absent minded in his enthusiasm over returning to his family and forget to give it to you.

Today I spent five hours in a forward observation post watching a regiment take a hill, all in plain view. It was a most inspiring sight. Yesterday I visited both corps and four front line command posts and three observation points overlooking the entire battle front. By gaining intimate familiarity with the problems of front line troops and of the terrain features I find it much easier to direct the battle than I could possibly do otherwise.

We are making slow but steady progress and killing lots of Japs. It is tough going and will continue to be for some time, but I feel that we have control of the situation and are ready for any counter-attack. We repulsed the last large one with heavy losses to the enemy and light losses to our men.

The Japs are fighting desperately and are pouring in their air power as fast as they can bring it down. While our shipping is not unscathed, our unloading of equipment and supplies continues to progress smoothly and the drain on Japanese planes has been very heavy. Their pilots show the results of short and hasty training.

Okinawa is barely recognizable with its new network of coral surfaced four-lane roads and its airfields and base facilities. It is remarkable what has been done in so short a time.

Naturally I am eager to get this island completely cleaned up so as to move on to other battlefields, but it can't be hurried without heavy

---

i   "BG" is shorthand for the rank of brigadier general.

losses. With General MacArthur now taking over the army forces it is difficult to predict my future assignments since he has his own group of generals that he that he has been working with and my chances can scarcely be as good as those of Krueger and Eichelberger as the result. However, there appears to be plenty of fighting in prospect to satisfy the most ravenous appetite.

We now have about 130,000 Okinawans to care for and have killed between 30,000 and 40,000 Japs. It is hard to count the latter since many are killed by blowing in the opening of underground fortifications.

The Kodachrome films arrived today and I am most grateful for them. I hope to get some interesting shots if I find time.

If Cowart speaks with an Okinawan accent give him a drink of bourbon and you will no longer need an interpreter. I wish I could be with him and will be so in spirit.

My love and my longing thoughts are yours.

Bolivar

Monday, May 14

Went to forward OP in 6th Mardiv with Sheppard. Two adjoining Regts each apparently waiting for the other to move forward. Told Sheppard to keep them going. Retd. via III Phibcorps.

After lunch had G-3 conference and gave out decisions on Iceberg 3-E.[i]

Dougherty came in with message of impatience from Adm Turner Re: unloading. I conferred with G-4 and later had Wallace in. He felt somewhat harassed and I don't blame him since priorities are constantly changing and requirements mounting without his being given more means of speeding things up.

On our left, Col May advanced his Regt along the coastal flat 2,400 yds and took the Yonabaru air strip. The Japs still hold the fair side of "Conical Hill."

---

i   Phase IIIe was a new creation, calling for the seizure of Iheya Shima by a reinforced regiment from the 2nd Marine Division. Iheya would then be developed as a radar station.

Tuesday, May 15

Visited both Corps CPs in the morning. Very little gains during the day due to rain which impeded tanks and a Bn counter-attack against the 6th Mardiv.

Had conference with G-3 section and approved plan for Phase 3e.

Wednesday, May 16

Considerable air bombing this morning at about 3:00 AM. Yonton & Purple Beach areas struck by bombs: A few killed & 1 plane burned.

Adm. Spruance came ashore. Also 2d Mardiv staff and 3E Iscom & staff arrived to discuss plans.

Adm Hill came ashore. He takes over from Turner tomorrow but the Tenth Army will be directly under Adm Spruance.

Had a G-4 conference regarding an army service area. Deferred decision pending further information from Iscom.

Visited XXIV Corps CP.

During the bombing this morning a 3-in shell fragment from an AA shell went through my tent near the foot of my bed.

Jap guerillas starting a terroristic campaign in the north. Okinawan local headmen beheaded and about 50 women and children murdered by them. This calls for more aggressive patrolling by the 27th Div.

Thursday, May 17

Adm. Turner turned over today to Adm. Hill & I now report directly to Adm Spruance. Hill is in charge of the combined air forces ship and shore based, if I interpret the obscure directive properly. I also control all unloading.

Turner, who has just been nominated as a full admiral (4-star) came ashore and I took him on a tour of the island. He said he had recommended to Adm. Nimitz that I be given command of the troops making the initial landing in Japan proper.

Friday, May 18

Turned down my staff's recommendation to establish an army service area by using service troops now assigned to Iscom. Too complicated and productive of dispute.

Visited III Phibcorps where I also saw Hodge and and then went to all four front-line Div CPs. Also went to a 1st Mardiv OP. Not much progress today but some movement almost everywhere and a good many Japs killed. A great deal of hand-to-hand fighting.

After dark Yonton airfield was bombed by 2 planes with incendiaries, destroying 1 plane, injuring 16 others and setting off a napalm mixing point with a tremendously spectacular explosion. There was no AA firing due to the restrictions of a "control green" alert, in spite of AA requests for permission to fire. Will investigate.

(The explosion subsequently turned out to be a naval bomber with 2 ½ tons of bombs. Only two men wounded. Investigation showed green control due to returning day cap planes. The night cap splashed the Jap who set off the explosion.)

Saturday, May 19

No material change in situation.

Visited new CP & gave instructions regarding new mess Bldg.

Went to see Mulcahy regarding air control. Later saw Iscom.

Sunday, May 20

At noon made a broadcast dedicating the new "Radio Okinawa" station. Knowing that the enemy would listen and translate what I said, a good deal of it was directed at them in a round-about way.

Visited 6th & 1st Mardiv and 96th Div CPs. An air of optimism exists in the front-line Divs who seem to feel a slight weakening in the Japs before them, in spite of the fact that the most savage of hand-to-hand fighting is going on all along the line. Some progress made today, most of it by the 1st Mardiv.

Maj. Gen. Casey Engrs,[i] from Gen MacArthur's command came up to explore air base possibilities to support future operations against Japan by his forces.

He brought an oral message to me from Gen MacArthur which, if quoted correctly by him was anything but complimentary. In effect, he said "Keep your chin up and don't be discouraged even though it may

---

i   Major General Hugh J. Casey, chief of engineers for U.S. Army Pacific.

seem hard, because if you keep on pushing you will be surprised to find that the enemy forces will suddenly break and it will be all over"—a somewhat belittling message if correctly delivered, which I doubt.

Monday, May 21

Last night about 9:30 a well prepared Bn. counterattack against the 6th Mardiv was driven back. About 300 Japs killed & a barge sunk.

Visited both corps and all four Div CPs and went to forward Ops of all but the 1st Mardiv. Got a good view of the left from "Conical Hill." Our front line troops are showing a gradually increasing feeling of optimism, particularly in the 96th Div. Jap resistance on our left appears to be less determined but they still seem strong opposite our right. The 6th Mardiv is less optimistic and its progress a trifle slower than I had hoped. It now looks as though an envelopment of the enemy's left will bring fruitful results.

A captured Jap document shows concern over our methods of reducing their defenses.

On the night of May 21, Ushijima decided to evacuate Shuri and continue the battle from new positions in southern Okinawa. While a line of outposts kept Buckner's forces in check, the rest of Ushijima's troops withdrew southward during the next week. The outpost forces then followed over the succeeding two days.

Tuesday, May 22

I wasted today getting caught up on paperwork. It rained most of the day and made tank operations impossible. Nevertheless, the 6th Mardiv made substantial gains on the right and one Regt of the 7th Div established left flank guard in the foothills southeast of Yonabaru against light resistance and very little artillery fire. This paves the way for an envelopment of the Shuri position from the east.

Had Gen Casey and some of his group in for old fashioned cocktails before supper. We used Okinawan raspberries for cherries & Adm Halsey's liquor.

Turned down a G-1-G-2 recommendation to offer a truce to the Japs while we took civilians into our lines.—Let the Japs feed them as long as possible. They would let us have the useless ones to feed while they kept all capable of work for strengthening their defenses.

Buckner letter to Adele Buckner:
May 22, 1945
Darling:

We are having a deluge of rain today, which is hard on our attack since it bogs down our tanks in the sticky clay and without them it is suicidal for our troops to rush the pill-boxes and cave openings that bristle with machine guns. A constant dribble is coming into my tent through a hole made by a shell fragment a couple of nights ago which does not improve my attitude toward the individual who did it.

Yesterday I spent inspecting the front and looking over the Jap positions in front of all of our divisions on this line. The defenses are still formidable but an increasing air of optimism is evident among our men all along the line. Jap casualties are mounting, their weapons are being knocked out and no replacements are in sight, yet the enemy can see our ships discharging thousands of tons of cargo every day before their very eyes. Jap air attacks continue almost daily but they are gradually weakening and the quality of their pilots is deteriorating. We had hoped that one of the results of our campaign here would be to make a deep cut into Japanese airpower and we seem to be succeeding. Two days after I sent the enclosed message to Mulcahy his boys shot down 45 planes. The outstanding performance among his pilots was when one of them was in a dogfight with a Jap at 28,000 feet and his machine guns jammed. Being unable to shoot he cut the Jap's rudder off with his propeller causing the enemy plane to crash. Our pilot then landed safely with a bent propeller and a plane full of holes.

To give you an idea of the ferocity of the hand to hand fighting on the ground, one hill changed hands nine times before we finally secured it. A wounded officer who could not be brought out when the Japs drove our men out of their position lay in a pile of corpses and played possum twice while the enemy were going through his pockets. When we retook the hill he felt much better.

On another occasion three of our men were driven into a cave by machine gun fire and found the cave to be part of a gallery filled with Japs. They kept quiet for three days while the hill was in Jap hands. A Jap water detail brought them water in the dark which they accepted without expressing gratitude in English. When we recaptured the hill they

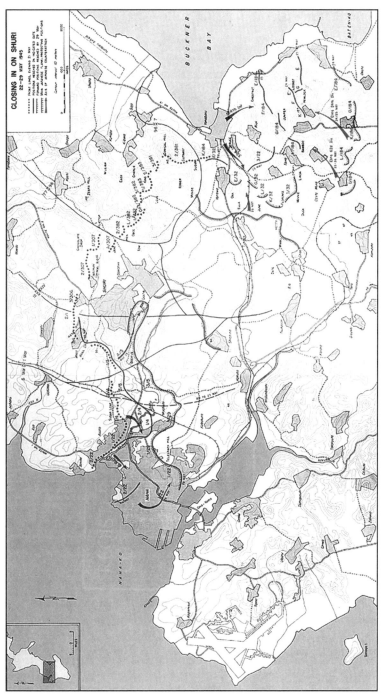

Forcing the Japanese to retreat, May 22–29, 1945. *U.S. Army*

had some interesting tales to tell after a three-day period of considerable nervousness.

It is grand to think of your seeing Claiborne. I sent him a check for $100.00 saying that I hoped he would enjoy spending it on entertaining foolishness.

Naha is a deserted ruin and of no value except as a port. Most of it is burned out and we now have heights controlling it but can't occupy it because the Japs have hills on the other side. Shuri Castle and the neighboring heights are the key to the present enemy line. When we break this, things should move more rapidly. The Japs are defending this with desperation. Today a captured document indicated that they were greatly worried over our methods of warfare and were somewhat at a loss in attempting to stop our slow but steady mopping up of their powerful cave defenses. Our system is working well and our losses in proportion to Japs killed are far less than at Iwo Jima although the Jap defenses are much stronger. We have killed about 50,000 and probably have in the neighborhood of 30,000 still to improve.

If you do go to West Point, give my best to my many friends there. It will be a real treat for you to see them. It would be great to have Buckey join you. I have received no word from him.

The rain has suddenly let up and the air raid siren is sounding, so Mulcahy will have a chance to shoot down some more planes. I shall have a look.

Devotedly,
Bolivar

Wednesday, May 23

Saw a demonstration in the morning of the new recoilless weapons. They look good due to lightness. Directed that they be given to 77th Div for trial against Japs.

Last night at 4:00 AM an attack of about 250 Japs against the 96th Div was exterminated. It was apparently part of a Bn attack.

Adms. Wright and Connolly come after lunch to discuss future operations.

Squeaky Anderson also called during the afternoon and we had a good Alaskan discussion. Steady rain all afternoon.—Bad on tank action.

Small counter-attacks took place pretty much all across the front—possibly in response to our order for a general counter-attack that didn't reach units in time. The 7th Div got past Yonabaru and is turning west. Heavy rain has stopped our tanks and is impeding supply just at a time when rapid progress by the 7th Div is most desirable.

Thursday, May 24

7th Div made about 1,000 yds in enveloping movement. I visited 7th & 6th Marine Divs.

Clear weather and bright moonlight brought heavy air attacks on all 3 fields. At about 9:30 PM five twin-engined bombers, each with 14 men armed with incendiary grenades tried to land on Yonton field. Four were shot down, two in flames which I saw. The fifth made a belly landing on the field and the men set fire to 2 600-drum gasoline dumps and destroyed 8 planes, mostly transports. About 8 of the Japs were shot. They had maps and photographs of the field with arrows and circle marking points to be attacked. Ie Shima and Kadena fields were bombed without serious effect. About 25 75 Jap planes were shot down, 23 of them by A.A. Some bombs dropped in the naval area of Ie Shima killing 30 and wounding 30.

A bridge was established by the 6th Mardiv into Naha and tanks gotten across but the mud prevents their effective use there or elsewhere.

(Two days later 70 Japs were buried from the five planes that attacked Yonton. All 14 from the one that landed were eventually killed. One wounded Jap played possum and threw a grenade, killing one man and maiming two.)

Friday, May 25

On the way to Yonton Field this morning, saw a mongoose cross the road. Yesterday I saw a flock of 25 white herons feeding. No dogs and only 3 cats seen on the island. 2 of the latter were bob-tailed.

Wild white lilies are in bloom, also some very pretty red gladioli. It appears that this place would blossom like Hawaii if flowers were planted but the Okinawans can't spare the land. They can scarcely live off of 2 acres per family if they use only the land for flower gardens. They eat bread and die and seem to have no pleasures other than building tombs.

Deluges of rain came down all day, completely immobilizing all tanks. Despite this, the 7th Div made several hundred yards to the south. Japs are appearing in the open more often, which keeps up the killing rate despite slow progress.

Saturday, May 26
Rain continued all day with a short break in the afternoon marked by an air raid on our shipping. 1 ship reported hit by 2 suicide planes.

The 7th Div made slight progress,

Adm Halsey and some of his staff came ashore in the afternoon to ask what I thought about withdrawing the fast carriers from protecting Okinawa and giving them an offensive mission. I told him that Mr Scipio Africanus had acquired an enviable reputation by displaying similar sentiments.[i]

Had supper with John DeWitt in an embellished Okinawan house with 3 Navy nurses and danced after supper to the accompaniment of Radio Tokyo and artillery fire.

Sunday, May 27
Still bogged down in the mud with no advance, tanks unable to move and supply difficult. About 6" of rain in 48 hrs.

Post and I had dinner with Mulcahy followed by a poor 16mm movie that was stopped in the middle by a considerable air raid.

Monday, May 28
Still wet and sprinkling all day. Heavy air attacks continue, nevertheless. Stubborn resistance against all advances except on the extreme flanks where some progress was made.

I sloshed my way in a jeep to the 27th Div CP. Griner is moving northward and combing the island for Japs. Thinks he has over 100 to 10 heavy machine guns cornered in the mountains. He says the Okinawan civilians are stealing our food and giving it to the Japs.

Suiciders hit 3 ships in Nagakusuku Won. None sunk.

---

i   This is an endorsement of aggression, citing the offensive campaign against Hannibal's Carthage by Scipio Africanus during the Punic Wars.

Buckner letter to Adele Buckner:
May 28, 1945
Darling,

We continue to be deluged with rain, about seven inches having come down during the past four days. This came at an unfortunate time, since I had caught the Japs napping and shoved a division past their right flank. The mud slowed down the movement of our heavy weapons to such an extent that I was unable to take advantage of the initial success thus giving the enemy a chance to man previously constructed but, at the time, unoccupied defensive positions. However, the move has considerably extended the Jap line, thus weakening it for his depleted force. The Jap garrison appears to have considerably exceeded our initial estimate, but we have killed over 55,000 and we will still have the privilege of exterminating a lot more.

While our progress is still slow the Jap casualties continue to be high. Bradley, who commands the 96th Division, was on a particularly slippery range of clay hills when the heaviest of the rains struck him. In his daily report of movement he reported: "Considerable movement by my front lines. Those on forward slopes slid forward and those on reverse slopes slid back."

Jap air attacks continue with great desperation. In fact, one is going on now against our shipping which is unloading. The Jap planes are coming in under the clouds at a very low level. Occasionally they get a ship this way. Night attacks are usually directed at our airfields and come practically every night when it isn't raining. Last night they bombed through the overcast with minor damage but our night fighters went up and got several of the attackers. In all, this campaign has cost Japan about 4,000 planes.

The roar of the anti-aircraft from the shore is increasing and 5-in shells are beginning to whistle uncomfortably near to the top of my tent, so I shall repair to my fox-hole until the shooting subsides.

Out of my hole again. Too cloudy to see the shooting but the raid sounded like a heavy one, the second this morning. Reports will soon come in. Both sides of the island were attacked at once this time and we were in the crossfire of the anti-aircraft, thus making fox-holes popular. One shell hit just outside of my CP but did nothing other than to blow up a lot of mud and cause a certain amount of merriment among those who watched the others trying to dodge it after it had already landed.

Since you mentioned the probability of going East but gave no schedule, I assume that you will pass through Louisville one way or the other and am therefore addressing my letter to you there. If it catches you there be sure to give my love to the whole household.

Hasta La Vista,

Bolivar

Tuesday, May 29

Strong enemy resistance still confronts the 77th & 96th Divs and the right of the 7th. However, the 7th has now advanced 3,000 yds south of and 2,000 yds to the west of Yonabaru. The Naha and Shuri fronts have apparently been deserted permitting the 6th & 1st Mardivs to advance from 1,000 to 1,800 yds giving most of Naha to the 6th and Shuri Castle to the 1st with almost no opposition.

I ordered a rapid drive to the southeast by the III Phibcorps, changing the corps boundary so as to pinch out the 77th Div. The XXIV Corps was ordered to drive west with the 7th Div and meet the III Phibcorps, thus cutting off the Japs still holding the line. The 7th also to be prepared to make a turn later to the south so as to outflank the next fortified line to the south if the enemy gets back to it.

It looks as though the envelopment of the 7th had forced a withdrawal but the Japs made the decision to withdraw after it was too late. Developments will show.

Wednesday, May 30

At 9:00 AM, I went to the 7th Div cemetery and made a Memorial Day address to the assembled Army chaplains, after which they dispersed to hold services at their respective Div cemeteries.

Some progress along the line, with evident enemy weakening. If our estimates of enemy casualties are approximately correct, the Japs will be unable to reorganize another line. I have directed unremitting pressure. Supply and evacuation are our main problems. I am a little disappointed in the progress of the 6th Mardiv on our right. The 7th on the left has done remarkably well. We have had about a foot of rain in one week. Some troops have been taken from airfield construction and put on roads. I shall probably be taken to task for this by higher HQ., but it is the right thing to do.

On May 31 troops of the 1st Marine Division captured Shuri Castle. "Ushijima missed the boat on his withdrawal from the Shuri line," Buckner told his staff on the same day. "It's all over now but cleaning up pockets of resistance. This doesn't mean there won't be stiff fighting but the Japs won't be able to organize another line."

Thursday, May 31

The entire enemy line appears to be crumbling. The two enveloping prongs were directed to join south of the Shuri position, the XXIV Corps to drive southeast to the coast and prevent the enemy from retiring to the [ ] Peninsula[i] and the III Phibcorps to secure the port and airfield of Naha. Supplies being pressed southward by water to new beaches.

Iheya landing was to have been made but Adm Hill notified us it had been postponed due to local conditions.

Friday, June 1

Bad roads prevented my going to the front. Progress continues against weak resistance.

Iheya attack force anchored off Hagushi beaches awaiting orders.

Saturday, June 2

7th Div still advancing, with 96th pinching out 77th.

1st Mardiv seems stuck for no apparent reason. Told Geiger to start them moving (through his CofS whom I found at his CP in his absence).

Iheya attack scheduled for 10:30 tomorrow.

Buckner letter to Adele Buckner:
June 2, 1945
Darling:

The rain is still checking our pursuit and slowing down our drive for the kill. But for the deluge, I feel that the enemy would by this time

---

i   A reference to the Chinen Peninsula.

have been destroyed. As it is, he will have a little time to reorganize but he is leaving his own tanks and artillery stuck in the mud as he retires, and will never regain his former resisting power. We are pressing him as relentless as possible and are supplying our troops near the shores by water and those in the center by air.

The Japs felt that the desperate air attacks aimed at our ships would starve out our expedition but we are still well supplied and the Jap air power is being steadily beaten down.

I am delighted to hear that Courtney Hodges is coming over.[i] However, I hope that too many of the senior officers from Europe don't supersede us here in our commands. We hope to be permitted to finish what we started on a shoe string.

When Admiral Nimitz was here he gave me a quart of rare old liquor which I told him I would open on the day when organized resistance in Okinawa was declared over. I am getting thirsty: Over 60,000 Japs have now been purified.

Not knowing your schedule, I am sending this letter to San Francisco. I wish I could join you in the treat of seeing Claiborne.

Devotedly,
Bolivar

Ushijima consolidated his defenders, now numbering only about 30,000, in southern Okinawa for a last stand. Tenth Army advanced south, but found mud and geography slowed progress. Logistical issues also held up the troops, especially the 1st Marine Division.

Sunday, June 3

Went to church. Flowers in Arty shells.

Talked to Geiger after breakfast and told him to get the 1st Mardiv off its tail. Told him I was dissatisfied with its progress. Sent O.P. Smith down to investigate.

7th Div cut through to southern coast and started with 1 Regt out the Chinen Peninsula. Arnold had delivered to me a bottle of sea water

---

i   General Hodges and Headquarters First Army would oversee troops transferred from Europe to participate in the invasion of the Japanese home islands.

and beach sand and a picture of two soldiers bathing their feet in the southern shore.

Joe Stilwell[i] arrived by air from Manila unannounced at 3:00 PM. With him were Maj Gen's Heilman & Donovan and Brig Gen Burgin.[ii]

[ ]Regt 2d Mardiv[iii] landed on Iheya without opposition. No Japs found. Radio station captured intact.

Monday, June 4

6th Mardiv made amphibious landing just south of Naha, met little resistance and advanced about 1,000 yds.

Regt from 2d Mardiv reported that landing yesterday on Iheya was successful. No Jap troops found there. Radio station undamaged.

Stilwell's party went to visit XXIV Corps, 96th Div & 7th Div CPs and spent the night presumably with the 7th.

7th Div moving southwest & 96th south against light resistance. Corps boundary changed to give XXIV practically all the enemy position due to slow progress of III Phibcorps. 1st Mardiv moving slowly but is still so far behind that the 96th Div right flank has to be protected by troops that could be used profitably elsewhere.

Supplies now landed at Yonabaru.

Heavy rain today. Typhoon reported passing east of us.

Tuesday, June 5

Rr Adm Cotter,[iv] in Chg. Yds & Docks for Adm Nimitz arrived to examine into airfield and base construction by CB's.

Stilwell's party came back and looked the island over from cub planes. ~~Went too low to the Jap lines and got shot at by AAA~~.

Hodge called up and said that Col May, 383d Inf. had been killed near Ewa. I regarded him as the best Regtl. Comdr in the Tenth Army

---

i   General Joseph W. Stilwell, chief of Army Ground Forces.

ii Brigadier General Frank A. Heileman, assistant chief of staff for U.S. Army Forces Western Pacific; General Donovan of OSS; Brigadier General Henry T. Burgin, commanding Pacific Area Base Command.

iii A reference to the 8th Marine Regiment, part of the 2nd Marine Division.

iv Rear Admiral Carl H. Cotter, U.S. Navy.

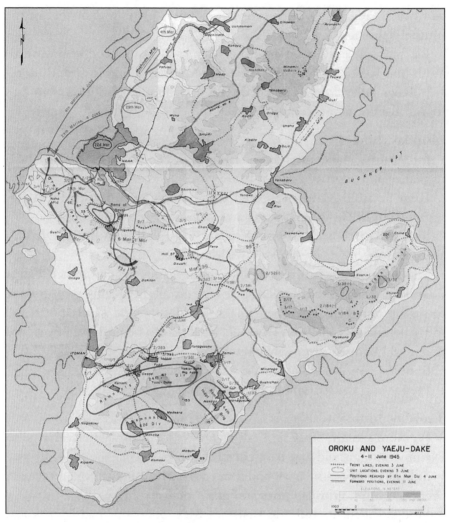

Securing the Oroku Peninsula and confronting Ushijima's final line, June 4–11, 1945.
U.S. Army

and outstanding Gen. Officer material. Had just recommended his promotion.

1st Mardiv still training behind the 96th Div.

Wednesday, June 6

By using a jeep, a command car and three tractors I finally mudded my way via the III Phibcorps & 1st Mardiv to the 7th Mar. Regt CP. My object was to go to Iwa and look over conditions so as to see whether there was any excuse for the 1st Mardiv's being behind the 96th Div. At the 7th CP I met B.G. Jones[i] Asst Div Comdr, 1st Mardiv, who had just heard that the Div had caught up, so I returned to my CP after telling them the purpose of my trip.

Stilwell party visited 77th & 96th Div CPs.

A new Jap defensive line being developed behind the escarpment in the south of the island. 6th Mardiv made a little progress. Taking the rest of Naha airfield and putting a ponton [pontoon] bridge across the inlet.

Thursday, June 7

Stilwell party left for Manila. At press conference, Stilwell said press had underpublicized and failed to appreciate this campaign either in hardships overcome ferocity of fighting or colorful events.

Flew over southern part of island in a cub with Bentley. Followed front line and reconnoitered plateau positions defended by enemy. A tough nut to crack. Stone cliffs full of caves except a difficult approach from the southeast and a somewhat easier one on the west.

1st Mardiv broke through to west coast. Tails up again. Geiger also feels better. After riding both somewhat I gave them a little praise today.

Friday, June 8

Again landing postponed until tomorrow. Gen Hunt USMC[ii] in for lunch today on return from Iheya landing. Returns to his ship today.

Wallace came in feeling downhearted and "sniped at." I was rather severe with him over laxity in permitting unnecessary burning of native houses. I shall have to let him stew a couple of days before giving him any encouragement. He is too sensitive and is inclined to feel that he is persecuted. However, he has ability.

Directive came directing future activities of Tenth Army over which I have every reason to be jubilant.[iii]

---

i   Brigadier General Louis R. Jones, the 1st Marine Division's assistant division commander.

ii Brigadier General LeRoy P. Hunt, the 2nd Marine Division's assistant division commander.

iii This order cancelled all other unexecuted phases of Operation *Iceberg* and directed Buckner to finish the fighting on Okinawa.

Saturday, June 9

Aguni landing reported without resistance. 1 Jap jumped off cliff.

Visited III Phibcorps and 1st & 6th Mardiv. CP's. All commanders in high spirits.

6th Mardiv has now surrounded an estimated 1,500 Jap naval personnel. 50 committed suicide last night. Their commander, a naval captain is reported to have been among them. 1st Mardiv now up against main position in the south. About 15,000 troops estimated to be there.

Last night Jap planes tried to drop artillery fuzes to them by parachute. Most of them fell in the water and 1 'chute within our lines.

Will drop offer of surrender to Japs tomorrow with little hope of results but largely at the behest of psychological warfare "experts."

On June 10, Buckner addressed a letter to Ushijima proposing surrender negotiations and had it dropped behind Japanese lines. The Japanese made no reply; Ushijima did not see it until June 17, and then laughed in response.

Sunday, June 10

Attended morning services. Chap. Hillyer had a photographer there and photographed me as "Exhibit A." When the first services ended the group for second services were there and he wanted me to pose for a picture with the second group. I declined saying that I regarded the services as being devoted to the Lord rather than to the photographer.

Adm Hill dropped in. Wants to speed up radio fighter control stations—(so do we)

Monday, June 11

Adm Byrd[i] arriving by plane to see Adm Hill. Sending him a small can of pemmican in a large basket with the compliments of the Tenth Army.

Mulcahy came to say good-bye. He is being replaced by Maj Gen Wood.[ii]

96th Div got 1 Bn up to the rim of the escarpment. Right of 1st Mardiv made a little progress. 7th Div took "Hill 95" with 60 caves in it.

---

i   Admiral Richard E. Byrd, on a special mission to assess base areas in the Pacific.
ii General Mulcahy was replaced due to ill health.

Tuesday, June 12

Adm Byrd came ashore and, after a very pleasant talk, I sent him on an island tour.

Schick brought in a clipping from the *N.Y. Herald* by David Lawrence apparently instigated by Mr Bigger [i] here saying that the Okinawa campaign was a monumental fiasco of incompetent bungling and demanding that I be investigated for not using the Marines for an amphibious envelopment. He also announced friction between Army and Marines here. Evidently he is seeking to raise a newspaper controversy. The enemy should be pleased by his services for them.

The 6th Mardiv expects to clean up their area tomorrow. The 1st Mardiv has at last advanced to the main enemy position. The 7th Div is meeting many counter-attacks near Hill 95 on the left and, along with the 96th on its right have a foothold on the escarpment.

Wednesday, June 13

Heavy fighting continues without much gain except on the left of the 7th Div. About 1,000 Japs killed. Dropped 45 plane-loads of napalm on reported location of enemy army CP.

Went to visit Adm Hill and Adm Byrd on the former's flagship.

6th Mardiv subdued all organized resistance on Oroku Peninsula. About 3,500 Japs killed in all on their position, mostly Navy personnel. Over 50 surrendered, including a couple of officers, one accompanied by his wife. A number blew themselves up with grenades.

Thursday, June 14

Spent day visiting Bn OP's in the 96th & 7th Divs. Got a good look at the hostile position. On way back stopped at the two Div OP's. Arnold and Bradley in high spirits, having each gotten a Bn and a number of tanks on top of the plateau, and well into the enemy position.

The 383d Inf had its new Col badly wounded and his successor had just arrived when I was at the OP. Last night a Bn advanced into a mine

---

i   A reference to reporter Homer Bigart, who wrote articles critical of Buckner's conduct of the campaign.

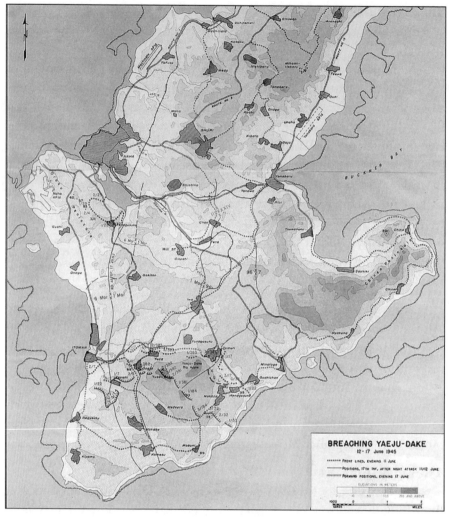

Cracking the Japanese final position, June 12–17, 1945. *U.S. Army*

field, lost 3 Co commanders and a Bn staff officer and fell back. They are cleaning out the mine field today.

This is Adele's birthday.

Buckner letter to Adele Buckner:
June 14, 1945
Happy Birthday—

A radiogram and orchids would be my wish for you but battlefield conditions scarcely permit. I hope I won't have to <u>send</u> you anything next time.

I spent the day at the front looking over the enemy position which showed signs of weakening. But for the rain when we broke the Shuri position which bogged down our heavy weapons in the pursuit, the Japs would never have reached their present stronghold on a plateau almost surrounded by cliffs. However, we pressed today's attack from a quarter that seemed to surprise the enemy and got two battalions and some tanks on top of the plateau. If we can hold on tonight we can probably break this position tomorrow or next day and the Japs will be forced to a final ridge at the southern tip of the island and soon destroyed. They are likely at any time to try a last desperate counter-attack which I would welcome as a quick way of ending the campaign. It has been a tough one but we still have a record of ten Japs killed for every one of ours and have broken the strongest defenses yet seen in the Pacific.

We have splendid relations here between the Army, Navy and Marine components of my command in spite of unpatriotic attempts on the part of certain publicity agents at home who are trying to stir up a controversy between the Army and Marines. I saw an article by David Lawrence saying that I had made a monumental fiasco of the whole campaign by not doing it the "Marine way". By the same mail I got a letter from the Army-Navy Staff College saying that their studies of the campaign indicated that it had been handled beautifully. Take your choice. Incidentally, the count of Jap dead today reached a total of over 75,000 killed since we landed.

We are now attacking Japan every day from our fields here and have already developed our island into a powerful offensive base. When we clean up the Japs here General MacArthur will probably take over our command and I hope he will point us toward Tokyo. It would be great to fight our way all the way through Japan and the Kurils and return via the Aleutians.

May our next flag raising be in Anchorage. All my love,
Bolivar

On June 15 Buckner told his staff "We have passed the speculative phase of the campaign and are down to the final kill."

Friday, June 15

Investigated burning of some shacks by Engrs in Machinato. Found it justifiable.

Had press conference at 4:00 PM outlining whole campaign, Stressed teamwork rather than spectacular events but gave credit to May and 383d Inf for taking "Conical Hill" which made envelopment of Shuri position possible but dwelt on the importance of pressure by other units.

Saturday, June 16

XXIV Corps has half of the plateau. Japs are beginning to blow themselves up or cut their own throats. A dozen or so did today. Large attempts at infiltration. 6th Mardiv and 8th Mar. Regt from 2d Mardiv to go in line on the right tomorrow. Looks as though the enemy were at the end of his rope so far as organized defense is concerned as soon as we get the rest of the plateau.

Moved to new C.P. this evening after supper.

Buckner letter to William Claiborne Buckner:
June 16, 1945
Dear Claiborne:

Forty-one years ago today I entered the East sally-port, drew in my chin, alternately dropped and picked up my suitcase, was vociferously informed of my shortcomings in posture, urged to move with great alacrity and initiated into the lowest form of military servitude as a lowly beast. A year later I discovered by experience that the easiest way in the world of losing a Christmas leave or any other privilege dependent upon the fewness of demerits was to drop into the usual period of exalted relaxation during my yearling summer. Watch your demerits the first month and you will find it pays good dividends.

I have just made a personal reconnaissance of the enemy's present position. It is a strong one surrounded by coral rock cliffs on most of the front and heavily fortified by tunnels, caves and concealed rock gun and machine gun emplacements. But for the torrential rain following our envelopment of the Shuri position, we would never have gotten to his present position but I don't think he can stand our pounding much longer and, unless something unexpected happens, I believe we should be able to destroy the last organized remnants of the Japanese 32nd Army within a week. It has been a tough fight, but our men have fought superbly and killed Japs at a rate of twelve of them to one of ours which is remarkable considering the formidable character of their defense. Already we have developed our air base here to the point where we attack Japan everyday with part of my tactical air force while the rest stands guard over our installations here, shoots down Japanese air raids and helps the ground troops by strafing, bombing and rocket attacks. After nearly three months of continuous fighting, our units will require a period of rest and rehabilitation but I hope for nothing more glorious than to be with the spearhead of the final assault on Tokyo. That being over, I shall then be content to return to Alaska and get caught up on shooting Kodiak bears and other small game that doesn't shoot back.

I feel sure that you have enjoyed your furlough and met some interesting people. Louisville is a most hospitable city and I have many friends there.

I hope that by the time you get this our flag will wave over all of Okinawa.

Affectionately,

Father.

Sunday, June 17

Inspected naval base developments on east coast.

No progress by our XXIV Corps and stiffer resistance as result of Jap's 32d Div[i] remnants reinforcing line there. About 700 yds progress in center of III Phibcorps zone.

---

i   This is a mix-up in unit designations between the Japanese 62nd Division and Thirty-Second Army.

CHAPTER 6

"You're Going Home"

Simon Bolivar Buckner Jr. awoke on the morning of June 18, 1945, and took his usual breakfast. After looking at some papers, about 8:30 AM he bid farewell to General Post and departed for the front, accompanied by several staff officers. He wore his usual uniform and pistol in shoulder holster, while his helmet and jeep displayed the three stars of his rank. He traveled southward toward the front lines near Naha.[107]

In late morning, Buckner arrived at the sector of the 8th Marines, a detached regiment of the 2nd Marine Division seeing its first action on Okinawa. That morning, the 8th had attacked southward from Mezado against Japanese defenses on Ibaru Ridge. The regiment's 2nd Battalion was in the lead, with the 3rd Battalion in support and 1st Battalion in reserve.[108]

The 8th's commander, Colonel Clarence R. Wallace, had established an observation post on a hill near Mezado, and General Buckner headed there. Behind the hill he found some of the regiment's 1st Battalion, and took time to shake hands and interact with the newly-arrived Marines. "These exchanges meant a great deal to the Marines he encountered, and they gathered around him in small groups," recalled Captain J. Fred Haley, commanding Company A. "The presence of the 10th Army commander, a three-star general, on the frontlines gave a tremendous boost to morale."[109]

Buckner discussed tactics with the Marine officers, expressing concern about Okinawan civilians caught up in the fighting. He noticed the body of Lieutenant David Schneider, a famous athlete at the University of Iowa, who had been killed a short while ago commanding a platoon. After expressing a desire to write to Schneider's family, Buckner knelt down and wiped mud off his face. "It was obvious that he was stirred by seeing Schneider's body," recalled Haley.

The Tenth Army commander then walked up the hill, where he met with Wallace and Major William Chamberlin, the regimental G-3. Most everyone else stayed behind under cover, but the three men stood close to some coral boulders on the crest—easy cover if needed. They watched the fighting for some time as Wallace's Marines continued their attack across the valley and into the fire of Japanese machine guns and light artillery. Troops below radioed that the stars on Buckner's helmet were visible, and he exchanged it for a plain helmet. Shortly afterward, a photographer took a picture of the group.

After about an hour atop the hill, Buckner decided he had seen enough. "Things are going so well here," he said, "I think I'll move on to another unit." Just after that comment, a Japanese 47mm shell struck the boulder next to him, knocking the officers down. Wallace and Chamberlin were shaken but unharmed. Buckner was more seriously hurt, as a piece of coral had embedded in his chest. He began gasping for air, and asked if everyone else was OK.[110]

Marines quickly carried him to the hill's back slope and put him on a stretcher. A group gathered as word spread. The 1st Battalion's surgeon, U.S. Navy Lieutenant Tom Sullivan, soon joined and gave him plasma as staff officers radioed for medical evacuation. Buckner kept trying to speak, but could not. He reached out his right hand for assistance in standing. Private Harry Sarkisian grabbed it with both hands and leaned over the struggling man. "You're going home, General," he told Buckner. "You are homeward bound." Sarkisian repeated these words as Simon Bolivar Buckner Jr. gasped his last breaths.

"Those present were in a state of shock," recalled Captain Haley. "It was so totally unexpected, we were stunned." One of Buckner's aides recited Psalm 23. Sarkisian held Buckner's hand for a long moment, then released it as Sullivan closed Buckner's eyes. Soon an ambulance arrived and carried the body to the rear, where Buckner was officially pronounced dead at a nearby aid station.

The next morning, Lieutenant General Simon Bolivar Buckner Jr. received a military funeral in a 7th Infantry Division military cemetery on Okinawa. As flags flapped in the breeze, he was laid to rest among his soldiers. Fittingly, he lay among representatives of units who had fought in the Aleutians.

That evening, General Post wrote to Adele and related what he knew about what had happened:

June 19, 1945
My dear Adele:

This is hard for me but I know you want it. I shall give you the circumstances regarding Bolivar's death as clearly as I can. I refrained until I heard the radio announcement from San Francisco.

Yesterday morning about 8:30 AM he left me at my command post, saying he was going down toward the front to see how 'his'" boys were doing. It was routine for him to do this—every day that office duties permitted he was down encouraging and inspiring his subordinates. He was particularly anxious to get down yesterday as he was enthusiastic about the prospects of decisive gains.

At 1:30 PM I received a phone call from the front informing me that Bolivar had been wounded—<u>they</u> were afraid rather badly. The informer was rather confused as to the extent of the injury but felt it was bad and that I should know.

Immediately—I started for the location I had instructed them to bring him [to]. Shortly before arriving at my destination, I met General Geiger, who informed me Bolivar had died. I reached him about an hour and a half after he had been wounded—saw him and issued instructions regarding disposition of his body. He was wounded at 1:15 PM, June 18. Eastern date.

His aide, Major Hubbard, was with him when he was hit and I am now able to give you a clear, accurate picture of exactly what happened. After leaving me at 8:30 AM he went down through Naha—stopped at one of the division headquarters—then preceded to a Battalion observation post where he believed he would be able to follow closely the progress of an attack. Before reaching the OP a marine Lieutenant Colonel told him the place he intended going was too dangerous and advised against it. Bolivar told the officer that if his men were there he too would go for he wanted to see first hand what they were up against.

He reached a good vantage point a few hundred yards behind the fight. There before him was the whole panoply of war. He enjoyed witnessing the successful operation for about an hour. He was watching through a narrow (about a foot wide) opening between two rather large rocks. Suddenly, without any warning whatever an artillery shell burst right in front of the opening. A large fragment hit him in the chest—right center. He died almost immediately. A medical officer was nearby and within a minute after the explosion first aid was administered. But Bolivar was beyond human help. The doctor believes he died immediately after being hit.

I saw him an hour and a half later—Had his magnificent body moved from the ambulance to a tent where I had him uncovered so that I could see for the last time the man whom I had worshipped for so many years. You may be pleased to know that he looked marvelous—He had been hit by only one fragment—in the chest. His face looked completely natural, as though in peaceful sleep, with the suggestion of a smile on his face.

Bolivar's funeral services were thoroughly planned and smoothly executed. He was buried in the 7th Division (Archie Arnold) cemetery. I made that decision for I felt that would be his wish. The service was simple and brief—All of his many friends and admirers were present. He was buried at 9:00 AM June 19 with simple rites of a soldier fallen in battle. I had colored movies taken for mailing to you. It may take some time for them to reach you because of censorship restrictions.

I represented the family at the funeral and in that capacity received the flag that covered his casket. I shall send it to you along with his three star General's Flag.

There are many personal effects. I shall not try to sort them out—only discarding those articles that obviously you would not care to have. There is a diary that I know is particularly valuable. He kept careful notes on all happenings. I believe he intended at some future date to write of his experiences and associations. There are many little things—clothing, books, and the like—that I am sure you would not want.

It is hard for me, Adele, to express my grief. As you know I've been intimately associated with him for about eight years. I have often felt that except for you I knew him better than anyone in the world. The country has lost a great man—the Army a superb leader—and I, the friendship of a man whom I regarded as perfect in every respect. My deepest sympathy to you for I know of the great loss you have suffered.

I shall write Claiborne. Bolivar talked at great lengths of him—as he did all of you—but Claib being a Plebe caused him to discuss his activities quite often. He had great faith in that young man and felt confident that he would one day be a great soldier. I feel I should write him.

It is my sincere hope that you will find readjustment not too difficult. Because of your many interests in life, I know you will be so occupied as to ease your mental burden. I know Virginia is most anxious to be of assistance.

My love and sympathy—
Eddie

A nearly identical letter went to Claiborne at West Point.[111]

Meanwhile, there was a battle to fight. On the afternoon of June 18, Post notified Major Generals Geiger of III Amphibious Corps, Hodge of XXIV Corps, and Island Command's Fred Wallace about Buckner's death. The three met and confirmed that Geiger would succeed Buckner. On June 19 Geiger announced his promotion to lieutenant general and accession to command of Tenth Army, the first (and only) U.S. Marine, and aviator of any service, to ever command an American field army.[112]

Tenth Army continued its southward advance with a new aggression, fueled by rage over Buckner's death. In the 8th Marines, what Captain Haley termed a "slowly rising anger" spurred the regiment to become "an avenging avalanche sweeping all before it, a whirlwind finish, which brought us to the beach at the southern tip of Okinawa." During the 72 hours which followed Buckner's death, over 7,000 Japanese were killed as the Americans slashed forward against diminishing resistance.[113]

U.S. Army Chief of Staff General George Marshall assigned General Joseph W. Stilwell as the new permanent commander of Tenth Army. On June 22 Geiger declared Okinawa secure and hosted a ceremonial flag raising. The next morning, Stilwell arrived on Okinawa and assumed command as Geiger returned to his corps.[114]

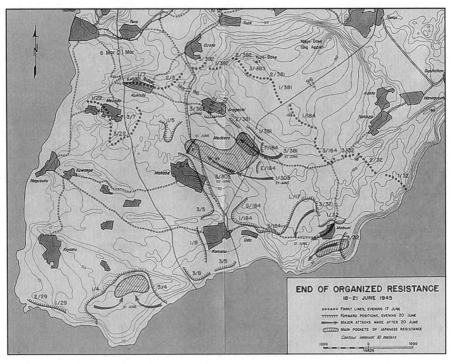

The end in southern Okinawa. Buckner was killed near Mezado in the upper left. *U.S. Army*

On Okinawa's southeast coast, General Ushijima and his staff sheltered in a seaside cave. Many of his staff cheered Buckner's death, but Ushijima was more philosophical. He knew the same fate awaited him, as surrender was unthinkable for an Imperial Japanese Army general officer. As American troops drew near, on the evening of June 21 he had a farewell banquet with his staff. In the predawn hours of June 22, Ushijima, his chief of staff, and several staff officers committed suicide.[115]

Despite Geiger's assertion that the island was secure, fighting lasted another week as Stilwell directed a systematic advance northward. In the last days of June 1945, Tenth Army killed 8,975 Japanese and captured over 2,900 prisoners. Thousands of dazed civilians were coaxed from caves. On July 2, 1945, major combat operations on Okinawa ended and Operation *Iceberg* was terminated. It had been 91 days since Buckner led his forces ashore at Hagushi.[116]

The invasion of Okinawa was the bloodiest engagement seen in the Pacific War, and ranks as the largest sea-air-land battle of all time. In three months, Tenth Army lost 7,374 killed, 31,807 wounded, and 239 missing; Navy losses offshore added another 4,907 killed and 4,824 wounded, for a total of 49,151. The invasion fleet lost 36 ships sunk and 368 damaged over the same period. There were also more than 26,000 non-battle casualties, mostly accidental and psychological, for a grand total of over 75,000 American casualties. Japanese losses totaled over 110,000 military personnel killed and over 7,000 taken prisoner, plus over 7,000 planes and 16 ships destroyed. Of Okinawa's population, over 82,000 died in the battle to all causes, including suicide.[117]

For both sides, the obvious next steps beyond Okinawa would be an invasion of the Japanese home islands of Kyushu and Honshu. On June 18, 1945, the day General Buckner died, U.S. senior leaders met in Washington to discuss prospects for the invasion, codenamed Operation *Downfall*. The bloodletting on Okinawa made a deep impression, and helped influence the decision to drop atomic bombs on Hiroshima on August 6 and Nagasaki on August 9. Japan signaled her surrender on August 15, 1945. Thus, Okinawa became the last major battle of the Pacific War and of the preatomic era.[118]

★ ★ ★

For the Buckner family, victory on Okinawa was bittersweet. Adele was visiting relatives in Louisville when she received the official news that her husband had been killed. Claiborne and his siblings heard through the media. "My mother was in good hands," remembered Claiborne, who was consoled by senior officers at West Point. He buried himself into life at the Academy. "It was war," he reasoned, "and combat deaths were continuing."[119]

General Buckner's death inspired many tributes and expressions of condolence. Adele heard from virtually all of the Army's senior officers. Other less official persons also reached out: "We are so grieved over General Buckner's death, and wish to express to you and your family our deepest sympathy," wrote Mary Moore of Western Kentucky University. "The nation has lost a great leader—one who made all feel he was their friend, as we do." That theme also showed in newspaper tributes. "Gen. Buckner was one of the most popular and efficient officers ever to serve at Fort McClellan," mused the *Anniston Star,* "and although he was stationed here for just a year, he made many staunch and lasting friendships in the civilian community."[120]

Adele tried to make the best of it. "Thank you for your very sweet message to me in my great loss," she wrote on August 1 to a cousin in northern Kentucky. "I know Bolivar's courageous spirit lives on in the hearts of the men he led. But for me and my children and the hearts of those who loved him, this tragedy of his untimely passing is immeasurable."[121]

As next of kin, she received the awards her husband earned on Okinawa. The Army awarded him the Distinguished Service Cross for his "outstanding leadership, tactical genius, and personal courage" at the front, during the overall battle but specifically on June 18. The Navy's Distinguished Service Medal cited General Buckner's "exceptional ability in planning for the campaign and supervis[ing] the equipping of troops and their rigid training in preparation there for. He quickly established his lines of power of all units of all branches of the armed services under his command. His well-planned maneuver and masterful handling of troops were an inspiration to our fighting forces."[122]

Japan signed its formal surrender in Tokyo Bay on September 2, 1945. General MacArthur presided over the ceremony, with Nimitz, Stilwell, and Geiger present among the American dignitaries. "The issues, involving divergent ideals and ideologies, have been determined on the battlefields and hence are not for our discussion or debate," said MacArthur, who expressed the wish that "a better world shall emerge out of the blood and carnage of the past."[123]

★ ★ ★

Simon Bolivar Buckner Jr. was the most senior American officer killed by enemy fire in both World War II and the entirety of the 20th century. As with all American overseas deaths 1941–1945, the next of kin received a one-time choice: leave their servicemember buried in an overseas cemetery, or have the United States government return them for interment at a place of the family's choosing. Adele Buckner chose to bring her husband home to the family plot in Frankfort. He would lay alongside his parents.[124]

On a cloudy and cool February 9, 1949, Simon Bolivar Buckner Jr. was laid to rest for the final time. Lieutenant General Leonard T. Gerow, the former Fifteenth Army commander, escorted the remains to the graveside. In addition to the family, mourners included General Omar Bradley, the U.S. Army chief of staff; Generals Hodge, Bruce, Hodges, Shepherd, and Oliver Smith; Admiral Kinkaid; and dozens of family friends and lesser-ranking comrades. (The local newspaper called it "Frankfort's greatest assembly of high ranking officers.") Some attendees noted the Buckner plot's proximity to the grave of Daniel Boone and the magnificent view of Frankfort and the Kentucky River below.[125]

The ceremony was "as simple as that of a private," according to a press report. Chaplain C. R. Stinnette, who had conducted the Okinawa service in 1945, presided. The Buckner family laid a lily wreath, which Adele felt was "an exquisite tribute." As the salute volleys crashed and echoed off the Kentucky hills, Simon Bolivar Buckner Jr. had indeed come home.[126]

It provided an important closure. "The strain and fatigue is gradually slipping away," Adele wrote a few days later. Adele never remarried, and lived until just after her 95th birthday in 1988. She lies next to her husband under a stone that notes "The spirit of adventure never left her."[127]

In tribute, many U.S. military installations named a road, building, or other feature for Buckner. West Point's summer camp became Camp Buckner, and Nakagusuku Wan became known as Buckner Bay. A transport ship USNS *Simon B. Buckner* served from 1946 to 1970, including in the Korean and Vietnam Wars.

In 1954, Congress posthumously gave Buckner a fourth star and the rank of General. His gravestone was not updated, and to this day shows three stars of a Lieutenant General.[128] The inscription reads:

COMMANDING GENERAL OF 10TH U.S. ARMY
HE WAS KILLED BY ENEMY ARTILLERY FIRE
ON OKINAWA, JUNE 18, 1945
LEADING HIS TROOPS TO FINAL VICTORY

CHAPTER 7

Simon Bolivar Buckner Jr.: Assessment of an Army Commander

In light of the information presented in General Buckner's diaries and letters, it is now possible to provide a fuller, more detailed assessment of General Buckner's tenure in command of Tenth Army. General Buckner commanded Tenth Army for 11 months, from July 5, 1944, until his death on June 18, 1945. He led it in only one battle, but spent much of his tenure preparing it for action and helping determine where it would fight.

Most analyses of General Buckner as Tenth Army's commander focus on his battle command on Okinawa. However, it is worth considering the multiple roles of a U.S. field army commander in World War II, especially in the Pacific. The 1942 Field Service Regulations outlined an army commander's job as follows:

> The army commander plans and puts into execution the operations necessary to carry out most suitably and decisively the mission assigned the army. During the planning phase the army commander should keep the major subordinate commanders advised of the contemplated operations so that these commanders may prepare their plans, make recommendations, execute required troop movements, and reconnaissances, and effect deception and surprise measures. In his planning the army commander must project himself well into the future; his plans must cover considerable periods of operations; and while one operation, which may extend over many days or weeks, is progressing, he must be planning the next. The plans of the army commander must be flexible so that full exploitation of favorable situations can be effected, and unfavorable situations, should they occur, can be rectified.[129]

This definition should be kept in mind when evaluating any U.S. army commander in World War II.

Tenth Army was the last U.S. field army to enter battle in World War II. General Buckner created the staff from a nucleus of his Alaska headquarters and personnel from the United States. He needed to coordinate and coalesce his staff, subordinate commanders, and units into an effective team around a shared plan for Operation *Iceberg*, the invasion of Okinawa. This task would have been challenging if all the units had been in Hawaii with Buckner's headquarters; as it was, almost all of Tenth Army's assigned fighting units were thousands of miles from Hawaii, either in training in the Solomon Islands or in combat in the Philippines. Much the same dispersion applied to the Tenth Army's supporting air and naval forces. The distances, plus the potential of inter-service misunderstandings, made planning and preparation fraught with pitfalls. That all these elements came together at the right place and time, under a good plan, to make a successful landing and campaign was quite an achievement.

Buckner's personal leadership in this process should not be overlooked. He refused to allow interservice rivalries to impede Tenth Army's functioning as a cohesive unit, and used personal visits to build and sustain bonds around a shared concept of operations. "The battle of Okinawa represented joint service cooperation at its finest," opined a Marine officer and historian. "This was General Buckner's greatest achievement, and General Geiger continued the sense of teamwork after Buckner's death. Okinawa remains a model of interservice cooperation to succeeding generations of military professionals." Indeed, the battle is notable for the number of times artillery and aircraft of each service supported troops of the other. In at least one case, Army troops loaned supplies to Marines because their logistics had not kept up. In this way, all of Buckner's troops leveraged Army and Marine strengths to help ensure victory. "The Tenth Army, in my opinion, did a magnificent job and made a major contribution toward winning the war," said Oliver P. Smith, Buckner's Marine deputy chief of staff, in 1946.[130]

In addition to the challenges of creating an organization essentially from scratch, Buckner needed to navigate the political waters of the

Pacific Ocean Areas. Tenth Army fell administratively under Richardson and later MacArthur, both of whom Buckner had served with before, but Buckner knew that operationally his fate would be determined by Nimitz and his subordinates. General Buckner needed to be a good field commander and take care of his U.S. Army troops while reassuring his U.S. Navy and U.S. Marine colleagues he could work with all services. His diaries and letters record how Buckner successfully cultivated those relationships by means professional and social. Ironically, this conduct later opened him to charges from MacArthur's staff about currying too much favor with Nimitz and his staff.

Buckner led Tenth Army into Operation *Iceberg*, which entailed the seizure of Okinawa and surrounding islands. The overall plan, and its estimate of 60,000 defenders, must always be kept in mind when considering Buckner's thoughts and decisions during the battle. *Iceberg* envisioned a three-phase operation. Phase I involved landing at Hagushi on Okinawa's west coast and capturing the southern part of the island. Phase II would then follow with the conquest of northern Okinawa. Phase III envisioned capturing at least one island, and possibly more islands further north, to use as airbases and radar stations, and would start immediately after Okinawa's capture. Virtually all of this needed to be done with troops on hand.[131]

Tenth Army also fought under conditions unique in the Pacific and only replicated once in Europe. Buckner was senior ground commander for Operation *Iceberg*. Unlike his counterparts in Sixth and Eighth Armies, who could largely focus on fighting and defer other tasks to higher headquarters or the Philippine government, Buckner as Tenth Army commander had to run civil government and base development (Island Command) while fighting an active campaign. Also, a significant part of his subordinate units were not U.S. Army troops—they were U.S. Marines in III Amphibious Corps. Balancing and integrating the two services with their different doctrines, standards, and outlooks was a difficult task, and one that had not always been done successfully in previous years.

Of the U.S. field armies employed in World War II, only two—Fifth Army in Italy and Tenth Army on Okinawa—contained a significant proportion of non-U.S. Army troops. Fifth Army, as senior American field headquarters in Italy, also had expanded civil government and rear-area responsibilities relative to the field armies in France. General Buckner thus faced a more complex task than most of his peers.

The nature of Tenth Army's opponents should also be kept in mind. Ushijima, alongside Yamashita Tomoyuki and Homma Masaharu, was one of the best Japanese field army commanders the United States faced in the Pacific. Ushijima was a smart soldier who led a large and motivated force in a skillful defense, and had Buckner's respect.

A close reading of his diary shows that these tactical and administrative concerns weighed on General Buckner throughout the battle on Okinawa. With all this in mind, the reasoning behind his command decisions becomes clearer.

General Buckner made two critical decisions that shaped the fighting on Okinawa. The first was on April 3 when he authorized Geiger to advance his corps into northern Okinawa and commence Phase II. This bold decision, 48 hours after landing and before the main body of Japanese resistance had been encountered, demonstrated Buckner's aggressiveness and flexibility. He effectively reversed the plan after landing and sought to capitalize on the momentum generated from lighter-than-expected Japanese resistance to Tenth Army's advance. Geiger's victory in northern Okinawa sped up the campaign and made the III Amphibious Corps fully available for commitment against the strong Japanese defenses in the south.

The second, and far more controversial, decision came in late April, after the capture of Ie Shima and northern Okinawa, when both the 77th Infantry Division and Geiger's corps were free for redeployment. Buckner chose to forgo proposals for an enveloping landing behind the Shuri Line at Minatoga, instead sending the three divisions to relieve tired elements of the XXIV Corps in front of Shuri. This decision generated much heated discussion at the time among the officers involved and in the press; on the day Buckner died, Nimitz was defending him to reporters.

The XXIV Corps was severely battered after three solid weeks of fighting, with many units suffering significant losses in men and equipment. "All three Army divisions, the 7th, 27th, and 96th were all at a low state of combat efficiency due to losses and fatigue," recalled a staff officer. "In order to maintain the pressure on the Japs it was felt that it was better to relieve these divisions as far as possible." Minatoga's terrain was also a factor in the decision. The beaches were treacherous and later proved difficult to land supplies at, which would have been a serious problem in an invasion. Inland stood formidable heights which would aid the defenders. After the battle, it emerged that Ushijima had expected a landing there and planned an aggressive reception.[132]

Eddie Post, Tenth Army's chief of staff, recalled that "General Buckner wanted very much to make the landings on the southern shore" at Minatoga. "He studied the matter thoroughly, discussed it at length with Admiral Turner, and the commanders involved. It was only after he had weighed all factors that he dismissed the plan as being too hazardous ... Admiral Turner stood ready to back any decision of General Buckner's which he considered his forces could support. He considered General Buckner's decision correct and sound."[133]

Particularly revealing is Buckner's comment that the Minatoga landing would be "Another Anzio, but worse." This was a reference to the Italian Campaign, which in late 1943 had bogged down among German mountain defenses near Cassino south of Rome. On January 22, 1944, the U.S. VI Corps landed at Anzio in an effort to flank the defenders and force a German retreat. Instead, the Anglo-American force was trapped and fought off several German attempts to drive it into the sea, requiring heavy reinforcements to do so. Meanwhile, the Fifth Army and British Eighth Army repeatedly failed to break through at Cassino, resulting in a bloody stalemate. Only in late May, four months after the Anzio landing and with extensive reinforcements, did the Allies advance past Cassino and link up with the Anzio forces. "Anzio became the epic stand on a lonely beachhead," wrote the official Army historian of the campaign. "But the dogged courage of the men on that isolated front could not dispel the general disappointment—the amphibious operation had not led to the quick capture of Rome. Furthermore, the expedition had approached disaster, averted only by the grim determination of the troops to hold."[134]

Buckner did not want to divide his combat power between an isolated beachhead and the main front, with neither force being strong enough to win and both taking significant casualties. Plus, his intelligence officers indicated there were less defenders in and around Shuri than in fact there were. The Japanese were also suffering nearly 15 men killed for every American, a rate much higher than during recent battles at Iwo Jima or in the Philippines. It appeared that breaking the Shuri Line would effectively end the battle, and victory was close. In addition, the requirements of Phase III—estimated at one or more divisions—were never far from Buckner's mind.[135]

In the end, based on what he knew and when he knew it, plus taking into account the requirements of Phase III, Buckner's decision to forego a landing at Minatoga is defensible. He did not rule out all amphibious envelopments, as the 6th Marine Division's successful assault on the Oroku Peninsula near Naha bore out.

These debates also obscure an important point: Tenth Army under General Buckner had essentially won its battle when he died on June 18. Buckner had successfully built an army, melded its disparate elements into a fighting force over great distance and time, and led it to the cusp of victory. The wisdom of his appointment is clear—in fact, his experience in Alaska offered superb preparation for what Buckner needed to do as Tenth Army commander.

Among the officers who led the nine numbered U.S. field armies in battle during World War II, General Buckner often ranks among the most obscure and least appreciated. In reality, he made important contributions to the Pacific War's conduct and outcome. His performance as Tenth Army commander must rank higher than it has before.

Endnotes

1   Unless otherwise indicated, all biographical information on the Buckner family and Simon Bolivar Buckner Sr. is taken from Arndt Mathias Stickles, *Simon Bolivar Buckner: Borderland Knight* (Chapel Hill: UNC Press, 1940), passim.

2   For more on the Kentucky Campaign and the Bluegrass in the war, see Christopher L. Kolakowski, *The Civil War at Perryville: Battling for the Bluegrass* (Charleston SC: The History Press, 2009), passim.

3   For more on these actions, see Christopher L. Kolakowski, *The Stones River and Tullahoma Campaigns: This Army Does Not Retreat* (Charleston SC: The History Press, 2011), passim; and Robert M. Dunkerly, *To the Bitter End* (El Dorado Hills CA: SavasBeatie, 2015), passim.

4   *New York Times,* September 4, 1896; see also Lillian B. Miller et al., *"If Elected": Unsuccessful Candidates for the Presidency* (Washington D.C.: Smithsonian, 1972), pp. 278–280; 289–290. Palmer at 78 and Buckner at 73 are the oldest combined ticket in U.S. presidential election history. Joseph Biden has since equaled Palmer's record as the oldest nominee for president.

5   Stickles, pp. 405–409; David G. Wittels, "Simon Bolivar Buckner," in Walter Millis, ed. *These are the Generals* (New York: Knopf, 1943), pp. 70–83. The quote comes from page 80.

6   See a memoir by "A Classmate," in the 2008 *Register of Graduates and Former Cadets.* Here after cited as Classmate. George Patton took a similar route, spending a year at VMI before going to West Point in 1904.

7   Stickles, pp. 420–421. This request was not a surprise to Roosevelt. A letter from Roosevelt to Delia in the Library of Congress dated February 14, 1903, includes a handwritten note that asks: "When am I to appoint your boy? This year?"

8   This profile of West Point is drawn from several sources, most notably William Manchester, *American Caesar* (Boston: Little, Brown, 1978), pp. 48–51; Barbara Tuchman, *Stilwell and the American Experience in China 1911–45* (New York: Macmillan, 1972), pp. 13–15; and Carlo d'Este, *Patton: A Genius For War* (New York: HarperCollins 1995), pp. 70–81. See also the *Register of Graduates for the U.S. Military Academy* for the years 1900–1909.

9   Martin Blumenson, *The Patton Papers Vol I* (New York: Da Capo, 1998), pp. 87–117; d'Este, p. 71–74.

10 *Howitzer*, 1908; Classmate.
11 Buckner Sr. to Buckner Jr., March 18, 1905, typescript provided to author by William C. Buckner.
12 Buckner Sr. to Buckner Jr., February 11, 1906, and November 26, 1906, typescripts provided to author by William C. Buckner. Simon Bolivar Buckner Sr. was 81 when his son entered West Point.
13 Classmate. This event usually took place in June, but occurred several months early because the Army faced a shortage of junior officers.
14 Classmate.
15 *Confederate Veteran* Volume XVII, pp. 64, 83.
16 Buckner Sr. to Buckner Jr., August 1 and 22, 1910, and October 26, 1910, typescripts provided to author by William C. Buckner. The book was self-published by William C. Buckner in 2019 as *Tales of the Philippines*. An example of Buckner Sr.'s encouragement is the letter of August 1, 1910:

> By the time this letter reaches you, the novelty of your surroundings will have worn off and you will be prepared to settle down to occupations and to a course of preparation for future usefulness to your country.
>
> You have now laid a good and solid foundation for a useful life; but you have yet to rear the superstructure. If this should prove insubstantial even the foundation will crumble and leave only a shapeless ruin behind.
>
> It may be that in the future you will be called to the discharge of duties important, not only to your own welfare and reputation, but also to that of your country. In this heyday of your youth you should collect and carefully prepare all materials necessary to rear a comely superstructure on the good foundation that you have laid. Profound study, not only of your special profession, but of that larger field of history and literature which will prepare for the duties of life, are essential to your future success.
>
> When Napoleon was a young officer of engineers, his constant application to study enabled him to grow a store of knowledge which fitted him for the discharge of the important functions which devolved upon in after life. But for this assiduity in early life he could never have attained the eminent positions to which he was called.
>
> We are all too apt to defer to a subsequent day what it would be better to perform in the present.
>
> Let me suggest that for a month, you keep an accurate account of how every hour is employed. You will be surprised, at the end of the month to find how many hours have been lost, never to be regained.
>
> The profound interest we both feel in your future success, has induced me to offer these suggestions to you.

17 Buckner Jr. to Delia C. Buckner, February 14, 1911, typescript provided the author by William C. Buckner.

18 Buckner Jr. to Delia C. Buckner, April 7, 1913, typescript provided the author by William C. Buckner.

19 Buckner Jr. to Delia C. Buckner, July 11, 1913, typescript provided to the author by William C. Buckner.

20 Ibid.

21 Stickles, pp. 423–424.

22 Military History of Simon B. Buckner Jr., U.S. Army, 1956. Copy in author's collection. Hereafter cited as Service Summary.

23 See Louisa Frick letter of October 7, 1916, in the collections of the Filson Historical Society. A slightly different version is in *Tales of the Philippines,* pp. 173–174.

24 *Tales of the Philippines,* p. 174–175.

25 Ibid., Wittels, p. 81.

26 Delia Buckner letter, December 12, 1918, in the collections of the Filson Historical Society.

27 Data on these classes is from the 2008 *Register of Graduates and Former Cadets.*

28 Manchester, pp. 116–127; Steven L. Ossad, *Omar Nelson Bradley: America's GI General* (Columbia MO: University of Missouri Press, 2017), pp. 55–60.

29 Manchester, pp. 116–127.

30 Wittels, p. 74.

31 Wittels, p. 74–76.

32 Data on these classes is from the 2008 *Register of Graduates and Former Cadets.*

33 Service Summary. See also Roger Willock, *Unaccustomed to Fear: A Biography of the Late General Roy S. Geiger* (Quantico VA: USMC Association, 1968), pp. 131–135. Also attending Leavenworth in Buckner's student year were future generals Willis Crittenberger, Jacob Devers, Benjamin Foulois, Courtney Hodges, Alexander Patch, and William Simpson of the Army; and Thomas Holcomb, future Commandant of the Marine Corps from 1936 to 1943.

34 Martin Blumenson, ed., *The Patton Papers Vol I,* pp. 869–870.

35 Stickles, p. 424.

36 Lewis Sorley, *Thunderbolt: General Creighton Abrams and the Army of His Times* (Bloomington IN: IU Press, 2008), pp. 22–23. See also the 2008 *Register of Graduates and Former Cadets.*

37 Benjamin O. Davis Jr., *Benjamin O. Davis Jr.: American* (Washington D.C.: Smithsonian Press, 1991), p. 27.

38 Ibid., p. 24–31.

39 William Westmoreland, *A Soldier Reports* (New York: Dell, 1980), pp. 11–12; Davis, pp. 37–38. See also the 2008 *Register of Graduates and Former Cadets.*

40 Davis, pp. 37–38. The camp was renamed Camp Buckner after World War II.

41 Ibid.

42 Westmoreland, p. 12.

43 The 2008 *Register of Graduates and Former Cadets.*

44 This and the preceding paragraph are taken from William C. Buckner, "The Buckner Mint Julep Ceremony," located on the family website at http://www.thebucknerhome.com/julep/index.html.

45 Ossad, p. 74.

46 Service Summary.

47 Ibid., see also Gordon A. Blaker, *Iron Knights: The U.S. 66th Armored Regiment in WWII* (Mechanicsburg PA: Stackpole, 1999), pp. 41–45.

48 Ibid.

49 *The Evening Times* (Sayre, PA), July 2, 1938.

50 Service Summary; 2008 *Register of Graduates and Former Cadets*; Stetson Conn, Rose C. Engelman, and Byron Fairchild, *Guarding the United States and its Outposts* (Washington D.C.: U.S. Army, 1961), pp. 230–231.

51 This profile of Alaska is from Conn et al., pp. 225–229; Wittels, pp. 82–83; and Brian Garfield, *The Thousand Mile War: World War II in Alaska and the Aleutians* (Fairbanks: University of Alaska Press, 1995), pp. 58–59. In 1940 Fairbanks and Anchorage each numbered just over 3,000 residents; Juneau, 5,000; and Seward, just under 1,000.

52 Ibid.

53 Garfield, pp. 59–60.

54 Ibid., Wittels, p. 81; 2008 *Register of Graduates and Former Cadets*.

55 Conn et al., pp. 225–228.

56 Conn et al., pp. 225.

57 Garfield, pp. 71–72; Conn et al., p. 228. The recurring low has been compared to a smaller version of Jupiter's famous Red Spot.

58 Conn et al., pp. 232–240.

59 Wittels, pp. 71–72; Garfield, p. 64.

60 Garfield, pp. 64–65. Fort Richardson was named for Brigadier General Wilds P. Richardson, who had done much to map and develop Alaska before World War I. Richardson Highway between Valdez and Fairbanks was also named for the general.

61 Wittels, p. 79.

62 Conn et al., pp. 232–238; Garfield, pp. 69–71.

63 Garfield, p. 71. Some of the nautical charts for the region were from the 19th century.

64 Garfield, pp. 68–69.

65 Ibid.

66 Conn et al., pp. 246–247.

67 Garfield, pp. 57–77; Conn et al., pp. 232–238. Much of this infrastructure is still in use.

68 Benjamin B. Talley and Virginia Talley, "Building Alaska's Defenses in World War II," in Fern Chandonnet, ed. *Alaska at War, 1941–1945: The Forgotten War Remembered* (Anchorage: Alaska at War Committee, 1995), pp. 59–61. The *Alaska*

at War book is a collection of papers presented at a conference commemorating the 50th Anniversary of World War II; it is hereafter cited as *AAW* on first reference and then by paper author name on all subsequent references.

69 Garfield, pp. 62–66, 76; Conn et al., pp. 247–249. The first elements came by sea, while others flew up the new Northwest Staging Route.

70 For information on this, see Christopher L. Kolakowski, *Last Stand on Bataan: The Defense of the Philippines, December 1941–May 1942* (Jefferson NC: McFarland, 2016), pp. 3–15.

71 Conn et al., pp. 230–252; Service Summary.

72 Kolakowski, *Last Stand On Bataan*, p. 13; Garfield, p. 76.

73 David A. Hales, "World War II in Alaska: A View from the Diaries of Ernest Gruening," in AAW, pp. 197–199.

74 Garfield, pp. 81–83.

75 Ibid., see also "Alaskan Air Defense and the Japanese Invasion of the Aleutians," Army Air Forces Historical Study No. 4 (March 1944), pp. 82, 105. Hereafter cited as 11AF.

76 Garfield, p. 82.

77 Ibid., pp. 82–83. See also Buck Delkettie, "An Alaska Scout Remembers," AAW, pp. 43–47.

78 Garfield, pp. 82–83; Conn et al., pp. 115–149; see also Ronald K. Inouye, "For Immediate Sale: Tokyo Bathhouse—How World War II Affected Alaska's Japanese Civilians," AAW, pp. 259–263; and Sylvia K. Kobayashi, "I Remember What I want To Forget," AAW, pp. 285–288.

79 Kolakowski, *Last Stand on Bataan*, passim; see also Christopher L. Kolakowski, *Nations in the Balance: The India-Burma Campaigns, December 1943–August 1944* (Oxford: Casemate 2022), pp. 1–4.

80 For more on the Doolittle Raid, see James M. Scott, *Target Tokyo* (New York: Norton, 2015), passim. Doolittle earned the Medal of Honor for his leadership of the raid, while all raiders received the Distinguished Flying Cross.

81 Hisashi Takahashi, "The Aleutians Campaign in Alaska as Seen from the Strategic Perspective," AAW, p. 36.

82 Jonathan Parshall and Anthony Tully, *Shattered Sword: The Untold Story of the Battle of Midway* (Potomac Books 2010), pp. 42–48.

83 William S Hanable, "Theobald Revisited," AAW, pp. 75–80.

84 Ibid.

85 Ibid., see also Garfield, pp. 18–26.

86 Conn et al., pp. 261–263. One Zero fighter was lost to ground fire on June 4, 1942, and crashed relatively intact on Akutan Island east of Dutch Harbor. It was recovered a month later and transported to the United States, where it was restored to flying status and tested. The lessons from the "Akutan Zero" influenced U.S. training and aviation doctrine for the rest of the war.

87 Conn et al., pp. 263–265.

88 Conn et al., pp. 270–276.

89 Garfield, pp. 150–151.

90 Conn et al., pp. 268–270; see also Tatiana Kosheleva, "The Construction and Use of the Fairbanks-Krasnoiarsk Air Route, 1942–1945," AAW, p. 327–332; Alexander B. Dolitsky, "Asia-Siberia Lend-Lease to Russia," AAW, pp. 333–340; and David S. Raisman, "The Alaska-Siberia Friendship Route," AAW, pp. 341–344.

91 Norman Bush, "The ALCAN Saga," AAW, pp. 179–184.

92 Charles Hendricks, "Race Relations and the Contributions of Minority Troops in Alaska: A Challenge to the Status Quo?" AAW, pp. 277–283.

93 Ibid., p. 278.

94 Garfield, pp. 155–163.

95 Wittels, p. 77; see also a "1943 Guide to Mount McKinley Army Recreation Camp," in the Edwin C. Purucker Papers, Wisconsin Veterans Museum Archives.

96 Text provided to the author by Bill Buckner.

97 Hanable, pp. 79–80.

98 Garfield, pp. 239–242.

99 Garfield, pp. 219–234.

100 Conn et al., pp. 279–285; Service Summary.

101 Garfield, pp. 295–307, has the best explanation of the circumstances that led to Brown's relief.

102 Garfield, pp. 307–338; Conn et al., pp. 283–295.

103 Garfield, pp. 357–372.

104 Conn et al., pp. 295–298.

105 Buckner's message is in *The Battle of the Aleutians: A Graphic History 1942–1943,* copy in the author's collection. This book was produced by Buckner's headquarters in October 1943 as a short overview of what had been accomplished since the bombing of Dutch Harbor.

106 Conn et al., pp. 298–300.

107 Eddie Post correspondence, Eisenhower Presidential Library.

108 Richard W. Johnston, *Follow Me! The History of the Second Marine Division in World War II* (New York: Random House 1948), pp. 270–272. See also the official histories of the battle of Okinawa—Roy E. Appleman, et al., *Okinawa: The Last Battle* (Washington D.C.: U.S. Army, 1948); and Charles S. Nichols, Jr., and Henry I. Shaw, Jr., *Okinawa: Victory in the Pacific* (Washington D.C,. U.S. Marine Corps, 1955), passim.

109 Unless otherwise cited, this section is based on J. Fred Haney, "The Death of Gen Simon Bolivar Buckner," in *Marine Corps Gazette,* November 1982, pp. 100–106.

110 Johnston, pp. 270–271.

111 Eddie Post correspondence, Eisenhower Presidential Library.

112 Stephen R. Taaffe, *Commanding the Pacific: Marine Corps Generals in World War II* (Annapolis, MD: Naval Institute Press, 2021), p. 172; Willock, p. 302. Wallace asserted he should assume command as the senior officer on the island. Geiger,

backed by Hodge, cited amphibious doctrine favoring combatant generals in command succession; he also noted Buckner's preference for Geiger to succeed him. Wallace gave way at that point.

113 Appleman et al., pp. 463–465; Haney, p. 106.

114 Taaffe, pp. 172–173; Willock, pp. 302–303. For more on Stilwell's selection, see Tuchman, pp. 518–520. Stilwell's background and activities earlier in World War II are discussed in Kolakowski, *Nations In the Balance*. The relevant messages are in the MacArthur Memorial Archives, Record Group 4.

115 Accounts of this are in Appleman, et al., pp. 470–471.

116 Ibid., pp. 471–474.

117 Ibid., see also Nichols and Shaw, p. 260.

118 The best discussion of this process is in George Feifer, *Tennozan: The Battle of Okinawa and the Atomic Bomb* (New York: Ticknor & Fields, 1992), pp. 566–584.

119 William C. Buckner, correspondence with the author, January 2, 2023. Bill graduated in 1948, the third generation of Buckner West Point alumni.

120 Mary Moore correspondence, Western Kentucky University Special Collections; *Anniston Star*, June 19, 1945.

121 Adele Buckner correspondence, Filson Historical Society.

122 Headquarters, U.S. Army Forces-Middle Pacific, General Orders No. 5 (1945); Commander in Chief: Serial 5497 (July 6, 1945). The full citations are available at https://valor.militarytimes.com/hero/6042.

123 Douglas MacArthur, *Reminiscences* (New York: Fawcett, 1965), pp. 314–315; Tuchman, pp. 522–523; Willock, p. 306.

124 *The Kentucky Advocate*, February 6, 1949; *Washington Evening Star*, February 7, 1949. The next time enemy action would kill such a senior officer would be Lieutenant General Timothy J. Maude's death in the Pentagon on September 11, 2001. Maude was from neighboring Indiana.

125 *The Kentucky Advocate*, February 6, 1949; *Washington Evening Star*, February 10, 1949.

126 *The Kentucky Advocate*, February 6, 1949; *Washington Evening Star*, February 10, 1949; Adele Buckner Correspondence, Filson Historical Society.

127 Adele Buckner Correspondence, Filson Historical Society; several personal visits to the Buckner family plot.

128 Several personal visits to the Buckner family plot.

129 FM 100-15, *Field Service Regulations Larger Units* (Washington D.C.: U.S. Army, 1942), p. 52.

130 Joseph H. Alexander, *The Final Campaign: Marines in the Victory on Okinawa* (Washington D.C.: USMC, 1996), pp. 30–31, 33–34, 51–52; O.P. Smith, letter to Harry Maloney, July 30, 1946, NARA.

131 For full details on the *Iceberg* plan, see the Joint Staff Study, *ICEBERG* Operation, 2 December 1944, in the files at the Joint Forces Staff College. A copy is in the author's possession.

132 This and the preceding paragraph are based on Appleman et al., pp. 258–264. The quote comes from Blakelock memo to John Stevens, February 6, 1946, NARA.

133 Eddie Post, correspondence with John Stevens, June 19, 1946, NARA.

134 There have been many fine histories written about the Anzio-Cassino battles. A good overview is found in the U.S. Army's official histories: Martin Blumenson, *Salerno to Cassino* (Washington D.C.: U.S. Army, 1969), and Ernest F. Fischer, Jr., *Cassino to the Alps* (Washington D.C.: U.S. Army, 1977). The quote comes from Blumenson, p. 453.

135 The casualty rate is in Appleman et al., pp. 473–474, 489.

Bibliography

Primary Sources

Unpublished Primary Sources

Author's Collection
    William C. Buckner Correspondence
    Operation *CAUSEWAY* Staff Study
    Operation *ICEBERG* Staff Study
    Battle of the Aleutians: A Graphic History 1942–43

William C. Buckner Personal Collections

Dwight D. Eisenhower Presidential Library
    Simon Bolivar Buckner Jr. Papers
    Eddie Post Correspondence

Filson Historical Society
    Adele Buckner Correspondence

MacArthur Memorial Archives Collections
    Record Group 4 USAFPAC Records
    Record Group 15 Contributions from the Public

National World War II Museum Archives
    Simon Bolivar Buckner Jr. Papers

U.S. National Archives
    Correspondence, Blakelock, Post, and O.P. Smith
    U.S. Military Academy Annual Reports

Western Kentucky University Special Collections
    Mary Moore Correspondence

Wisconsin Veterans Museum Archives
    Edwin C. Purucker Papers

Books

Blumenson, Martin, ed. *The Patton Papers* 2 Vols. New York: Da Capo, 1998.

Buckner, Jr., Simon B. *Tales of the Philippines.* Kansas City, MO: William C. Buckner, 2019.

Davis, Jr., Benjamin O. *Benjamin O. Davis Jr.: American.* Washington D.C.: Smithsonian Press, 1991.

MacArthur, Douglas. *Reminiscences.* New York: Fawcett, 1965.

Millis, Walter, ed. *These Are the Generals.* New York: Knopf, 1943.

U.S. Army. *FM 100-15, Field Service Regulations Larger Units.* Washington D.C.: U.S. Army, 1942.

U.S. Military Academy. *The Howitzer,* 1908.

Westmoreland, William. *A Soldier Reports.* New York: Dell, 1980.

Periodicals and Newspapers

Anniston Star

Confederate Veteran

Evening Times (Sayre, PA)

Kentucky Advocate

Marine Corps Gazette

New York Times

West Point *Register of Graduates & Former Cadets*

Washington Evening Star

Secondary Sources

Books

Alexander, Joseph H. *The Final Campaign: Marines in the Victory on Okinawa.* Washington D.C.: USMC, 1996.

Appleman, Roy E., James M. Burns, Russell A. Gugeler, and John Stevens. *Okinawa: The Last Battle.* Washington D.C.: U.S. Army, 1948.

Barker, A. J. *Okinawa.* New York: Galahad, 1981.

Belote, James, and William Belote. *Typhoon of Steel: The Battle for Okinawa.* New York: Harper & Row, 1970.

Bissinger, Buzz. *The Mosquito Bowl.* New York: HarperCollins, 2022.

Blaker, Gordon A. *Iron Knights: The U.S. 66th Armored Regiment in WWII.* Mechanicsburg PA: Stackpole, 1999.

Blumenson, Martin. *Salerno to Cassino.* Washington D.C.: U.S. Army, 1969.

Butler, Gerald W. *Shemya: America's Cold War Sentinel.* Stroud: Fonthill, 2020.

Cass, Bevan G., ed. *History of the Sixth Marine Division*. Washington D.C.: Infantry Journal Press, 1948.

Chandonnet, Fern, ed. *Alaska at War, 1941–1945: The Forgotten War Remembered*. Anchorage: Alaska at War Committee, 1995.

Conn, Stetson, Rose C. Engelman, and Byron Fairchild. *Guarding the United States and its Outposts*. Washington D.C.: U.S. Army, 1961.

Crowl, Philip A. *The Campaign in the Marianas*. Washington D.C.: U.S. Army, 1960.

d'Este, Carlo. *Patton: A Genius for War*. New York: HarperCollins, 1995.

Dunkerly, Robert M. *To the Bitter End*. El Dorado Hills CA: SavasBeatie, 2015.

Feifer, George. Tennozan: *The Battle of Okinawa and the Atomic Bomb*. New York: Ticknor & Fields, 1992.

Fischer, Jr., Ernest F. *Cassino to the Alps*. Washington D.C.: U.S. Army, 1977.

Garfield, Brian. *The Thousand Mile War: World War II in Alaska and the Aleutians*. Fairbanks: University of Alaska Press, 1995.

Gailey, Harry A. *"Howlin Mad" vs the Army: Conflict in Command Saipan 1944*. Novato, CA: Presidio, 1986.

Hallas, James H. *Killing Ground on Okinawa: The Battle for Sugar Loaf Hill*. London: Praeger, 1996.

Johnston, Richard W. *Follow Me! The History of the Second Marine Division in World War II*. New York: Random House, 1948.

Kolakowski, Christopher L. *The Civil War at Perryville: Battling for the Bluegrass*. Charleston, SC: The History Press, 2009.

―――. *The Stones River and Tullahoma Campaigns: This Army Does Not Retreat*. Charleston, SC: The History Press, 2011.

―――. *Last Stand on Bataan: The Defense of the Philippines, December 1941–May 1942*. Jefferson, NC: McFarland, 2016.

―――. *Nations in the Balance: The India-Burma Campaigns, December 1943–August 1944*. Oxford: Casemate, 2022.

Leckie, Robert. *Okinawa: The Last Battle of World War II*. New York: Viking, 1995.

Love, Edmund G. *The 27th Infantry Division in World War II*. Nashville, TN: The Battery Press, 2001.

Manchester, William. *American Caesar*. Boston: Little, Brown & Company, 1978.

Matloff, Maurice. *Strategic Planning for Coalition Warfare, 1943–44*. Washington D.C.: U.S. Army, 1958.

McMillan, George. *The Old Breed: A History of the First Marine Division in World War II*. Washington D.C.: Infantry Journal Press, 1949.

Miller, Lillian B. ed. *"If Elected": Unsuccessful Candidates for the Presidency*. Washington D.C.: Smithsonian, 1972.

Morison, Samuel E. *Victory in the Pacific 1945*. Boston: Little, Brown & Company, 1990.

Morton, Louis. *Strategy and Command: The First Two Years*. Washington D.C.: U.S. Army, 1961.

Nichols, Jr., Charles S., and Henry I. Shaw, Jr. *Okinawa: Victory in the Pacific*. Washington D.C., U.S. Marine Corps, 1955.

O'Brien, Francis A. *Battling for Saipan*. New York: Ballantine, 2003.

Ossad, Steven L. *Omar Nelson Bradley: America's GI General*. Columbia MO: University of Missouri Press, 2017.

Parshall, Jonathan, and Anthony Tully. *Shattered Sword: The Untold Story of the Battle of Midway*. Washington D.C.: Potomac Books, 2010.

Sarantakes, Nicholas E., ed. *Seven Stars: The Okinawa Battle Diaries of Simon Bolivar Buckner, Jr., and Joseph Stilwell*. College Station, TX: Texas A&M, 2004.

Scott, James M. *Target Tokyo*. New York: Norton, 2015.

Sorley, Lewis. *Thunderbolt: General Creighton Abrams and the Army of His Times*. Bloomington, IN: Indiana University Press, 2008.

Spector, Ronald. *Eagle Against the Sun*. New York: Vintage, 1985.

Stickles, Arndt M. *Simon Bolivar Buckner: Borderland Knight*. Chapel Hill: UNC Press, 1940.

Symonds, Craig L. *Nimitz at War: Command Leadership from Pearl Harbor to Tokyo Bay*. Oxford: Oxford University Press, 2022.

Taaffe, Stephen R. *Marshall and His Generals: U.S. Army Commanders in World War II*. Lawrence, KS: University Press of Kansas, 2011.

———. *Commanding the Pacific: Marine Corps Generals in World War II*. Annapolis, MD: U.S. Naval Institute, 2021.

Toland, John. *The Rising Sun 2 Vols*. New York: Random House, 1970.

Tuchman, Barbara W. *Stilwell and the American Experience in China 1911–45*. New York: Macmillan, 1971.

Wheelan, Joseph. *Bloody Okinawa*. New York: Da Capo, 2020.

Willock, Roger. *Unaccustomed to Fear: A Biography of the Late General Roy S. Geiger*. Quantico, VA: USMC Association, 1968.

Willmott, H. P. *The Second World War in the Far East*. London: Cassell, 2000.

Index

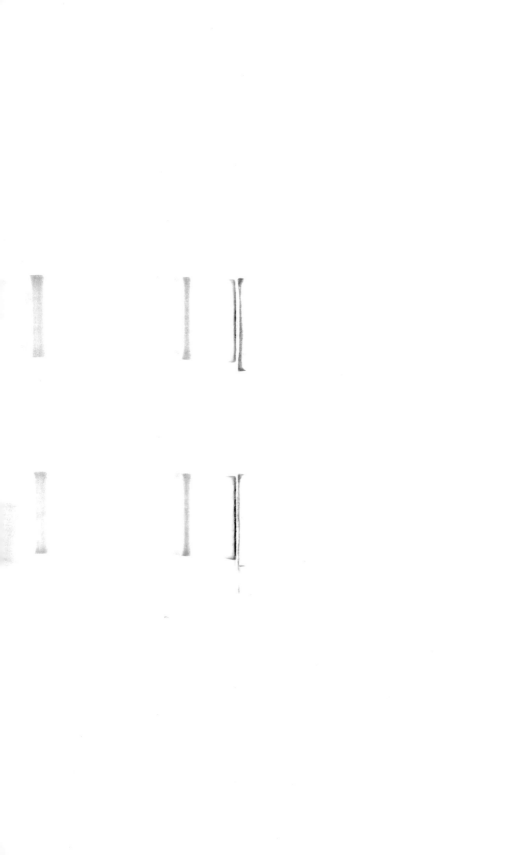